DAILY LIFE IN BIBLE TIMES

DAILY LIFE
IN BIBLE TIMES

by

Albert Edward Bailey

NEW YORK

Charles Scribner's Sons

FOREWORD

The last two decades have seen an unprecedented enlargement of our knowledge of ancient life. Archaeologists, armed with new skills and furnished by more enlightened Eastern governments with greater facilities for research, have been digging in all Bible lands, and have turned up more material than several generations of scholars can fully exploit. All this new data offers a great enrichment to those who can take advantage of it—to the specialists and scholars whose profession is antiquity. Efforts are being made also to popularize this knowledge. Publications like the Bulletins of the American Schools of Archaeology are partly intelligible to the laity, and very stimulating; the *Biblical Archaeologist*, also published by the Schools, is successful in eliminating technical and linguistic apparatus, but is necessarily limited to short monographs. *What Mean These Stones?* by Dr. Millar Burrows is a rewarding account of the aims and general accomplishments of Near East archaeology; and there are other scholarly books that, while difficult reading, are not beyond the average intelligence. Nevertheless there is still room for a book that will help the layman who is interested in the Bible—be he general reader or teacher—to reconstruct imaginatively the life of Bible times in its various epochs.

This book is a teacher's attempt to fill that gap. I have tried to furnish the data necessary to visualization. We live in an eye-minded age; we think in pictures. And unless the reader, and especially the teacher of the Bible, can supply the units of experience, either first- or second-hand, out of which pictures are made, his imagination suffers a blackout; he fails in realization and consequently in that emotionalizing of his subject which is necessary to bring the dead past to life. Perhaps the organized descriptions, narratives and simple dramatizations here attempted will help.

My debt to others is gratefully acknowledged and in the bibliographical references is more exactly documented.

The reader will of course understand that the Imaginative Reconstructions given in several chapters are not accounts of any one's actual experiences. They endeavor to paint the times more vividly than can be done in ordinary exposition. The data given in them, however, can be trusted as essentially correct.

Scripture citations are from Smith and Goodspeed: *The Bible: An American Translation*, by courtesy of the publisher, the University of Chicago Press.

Special thanks are due to Dr. William A. Irwin of the University of Chicago Divinity School, and to Dr. Leroy A. Campbell of Hiram College, Ohio, for reading the manuscript and making valuable suggestions; likewise to my wife and my daughter Lois, whose constructive criticisms have helped to smooth the reader's path.

A. E. BAILEY

Worcester, Massachusetts

CONTENTS

ILLUSTRATIONS

Illustrations

DAILY LIFE IN BIBLE TIMES

CHAPTER I

THE UNFATHOMABLE PIT OF BEGINNINGS

IF BIBLE times begin with the first verse in Genesis, "In the beginning," we must go back a long way!

In the seventeenth century of our era an Irishman named Usher figured from the Bible data that Father Adam was created 4004 B.C. Some one promptly put that date in the King James version of Genesis, where it still is. In those days no one knew anything about pre-history. But in the nineteenth century the archeologists began to turn the searchlight upon the caves of France and Spain, then in the twentieth century upon the caves of Palestine, with the result that the bottom has dropped out of the Usher chronology and we begin to peer into what is really a bottomless pit. As our faint ray searches the sides of the pit we can see deeper and deeper levels of humanity, until at last— darkness. Adam is now regarded as a late intruder (Fig. 1).

THE OLD STONE AGE, 1,500,000–10,000 B.C.

The earliest traces of man yet found in Palestine are a few surface flints belonging to the Early period of the Old Stone Age. Their date corresponds with the Second Interglacial period, say 750,000 to 200,000 years ago. Increasing cold during the period of the Worm glacier in Europe sent Palestine man into caves, where the earliest deposits date from 200,000 to 150,000 B.C. With the coming of the Middle period of the Old Stone Age, remains of man himself appear. The oldest citizens of Palestine are four residents of Jebel Qafze south of Nazareth. M. Neuville dug into their resting-place in 1934 after they had slumbered peacefully for at least 150,000 years. A decade earlier, Mr. Turville-Petre had found part of a skull in a cave of the Wady (valley) Amud that runs towards the sea of Galilee on the northwest. It belonged to a lady cousin of the four Nazarenes. Beginning in 1932 an expedition led by Miss Dorothy Garrod unearthed eighteen additional skeletons of the same type as these earlier ones, in the caves of the Wady Mughara on the western skirts of Mt. Carmel. They were embedded in earth that had solidified to stone and had to be chipped out most carefully. Miss Garrod has named these people *Paleanthropus Palestinus* (Fig. 2). They are similar in skeletal type to the Neanderthal man of Europe, though there are variations in the direction of *Homo Sapiens*. One interesting detail was found: the hip joint of one of them had been shivered. When a cast was taken of the hole in the femur and pelvis, it formed the shape of a four-sided spear head. This is the earliest war wound known to surgeons.[1]

These people apparently lived not in isolation but in communities in or near caves. The caves chosen were in the sides of low hills that bound the maritime plain, easily accessible and near to water and to hunting grounds. In the case of the largest of the caves, the rambling chambers were probably dissolved out by the waters of a spring (Fig. 3). In this epoch the community lived on the little terrace at the mouth of the cave, taking refuge within it only in emergencies. As yet there was little fear of marauding men: animals were their only foes. But at a later period when the spring dried up through slackening of the rainfall, and the climate became colder, the family moved inside the cave. Here they lived for countless generations; the ashes of their fires, their discarded tools and the bones of the animals they ate, mingled with the wind-blown dust to make a slowly rising floor. The excavators in one cave had to cut through more than sixty feet of debris, of which about twenty-five feet belonged to this particular culture.[2] The heterogeneous remains of this level show the various types of stone implements that characterize the Mousterian culture. But most interesting of all, they tell us with what kinds of animals they had to deal. Surely if the men had efficient weapons

[1] *Palestine Exploration Quarterly,* Apr. 1938, p. 76–7.
[2] *Ibid.,* Jan. 1935, p. 6.

FIG. 1. PRE-HISTORY IN PALESTINE.

Read from the bottom upwards

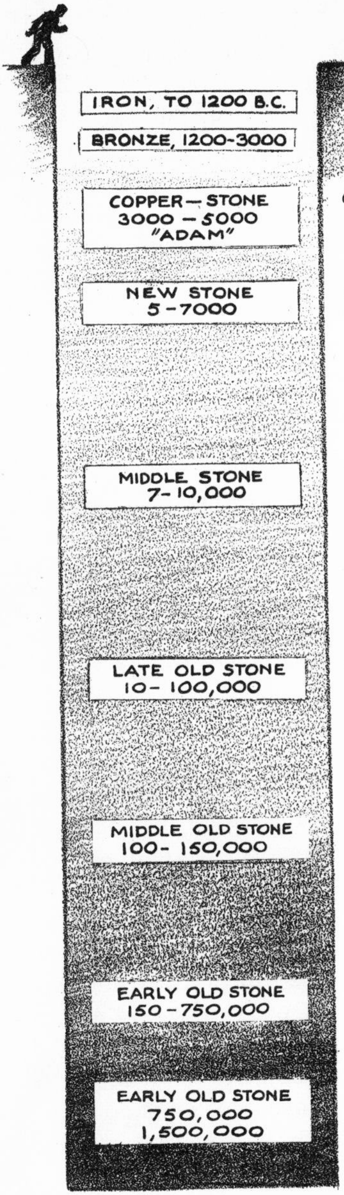

IRON, TO 1200 B.C.

BRONZE, 1200-3000

COPPER—STONE
3000 — 5000
"ADAM"

NEW STONE
5 -7000

MIDDLE STONE
7- 10,000

LATE OLD STONE
10- 100,000

MIDDLE OLD STONE
100- 150,000

EARLY OLD STONE
150 -750,000

EARLY OLD STONE
750,000
1,500,000

6. "Ghassulian" culture. Extensive irrigation of plains and river valleys; greatly enlarged food supply. Hand-made pottery; wheel pottery, painted. Art of building well developed. Frescoes.

5. Only a few remains, found mostly at Jericho. Agriculture and cattle-breeding. Oldest built houses. Cultic statues. Megolithic monuments.

4. "Natufian" culture, named from deposits found in 1930 by M. Neuville in the Wady Natuf, western Judea. Also, 59 skeletons of the "Mediterranean" race (of *homo sapiens*) found by Miss Garrod in 1932-4 on Mt. Carmel. Settled communities living in caves. Cultivation of cereals; domestication of animals. Art used with "sympathetic magic."

3. *"Homo sapiens"* arrives in Palestine. Culture, contemporary with the Aurignacian of Europe. Evidences of hunting, fishing, weaving of nets and mats. Earliest art: statuettes and reliefs in stone, bone and ivory. Dead interred with tools and weapons.

2. Neanderthal man with "Mousterian" culture, found in three places: (a) Fragment of skull found by Mr. Turville-Petre in 1925 in the Wady Amud, Galilee; (b) 18 skeletons found by Miss Garrod in 1932 in caves on Mt. Carmel; (c) 4 skeletons found by M. Neuville in 1934 at Jebel Qafze, near Nazareth. Named *Palæanthropus Palestinus.*

1. Contemporary with the 2nd and 3rd interglacial periods of Europe, and the Chellean and Acheulean cultures: earliest surface artifacts and cave deposits of human origin.

Contemporary with the 1st interglacial period and the Pre-Chellean culture of Europe.
No remains yet found in the Near East.

they needed not to starve. Herds of elephants, wild asses, oxen, deer and gazelle roamed the plains, the larger animals probably having migrated hither from India. In addition, the cavemen would often encounter certain species of pig and fox, now extinct; the single-toothed hartebeest, large river turtles, long-legged pheasants and other smaller game. But crocodiles crouched in the near-by rivers; the wolf, Mediterranean bear, panther and wild boar lay in wait for the unwary, while the great bustard kept watch for the carcasses of man and beast. Life hung on the throw of a stone or the stroke of a club.

Exciting though life was, it was enclosed in the simple circle of birth, killing for food, being killed, burial. Did such a life include any of the experiences that are so meaningful for us? Were there any hopes to transfigure the tragedy of existence? We have only one hint: when bodies were not devoured by animals but were buried in the floor of the caves, they were placed on their side with the knees bent up against their chest in embryonic position—as if they expected some day to be born again out of Mother Earth. Thus it was with ten skeletons from the cave of Et-Tabun. The germs of art may also be traced back into the obscurity of these caves: the excavators found the skull of a little child to which still adhered a head-dress of shells. Love of beauty not only existed but was able, so they thought, to bridge the gulf of death. So slight and yet so unmistakable is the hint that to this extent at least these primitives laid hold on things of the spirit.

The late period of the Old Stone Age lasted from about 100,000 to 10,000 years ago. In this epoch new human elements appeared. Just as the men of the earlier culture had undoubtedly moved into Palestine from somewhere else, probably central Asia, so they in turn were dispossessed by a superior race known as *homo sapiens*. This intrusion occurred perhaps 50,000 B.C.; and the new *homo sapiens* showed his sapience by wiping out old *Paleanthropus* and taking possession of his caves and hunting grounds. The newcomers showed every evidence of superiority in brain capacity, skill, resourcefulness and survival power, for this

FIG. 2. SKELETON OF *PALEANTHROPUS PALESTINUS*.

From the "Valley of the Kids" (Mugharet es-Skhul), Mt. Carmel. The covering stone
has been chipped away, showing the embryonic position of the body.

race has never ceased to exist. In Palestine it has left a continuous record of its occupation, though succeeding tribes of the same
or different stock swept in and mingled with the first-comers.
Then the climate of Palestine changed; it became drier and
colder. The old pachyderms died off or ran away and a host of
new animals invaded the land to serve *homo sapiens* as food or as
enemy. At this level the caves yield the bones of the modern wolf,
badger, martin, hare, wildcat, tree squirrel, hedgehog, pig, spotted

hyena, the large ox and the true horse. These men have left
· evidences of hunting, fishing, the weaving of nets and mats. Art
has developed: they carved reliefs in stone, bone, ivory; they
made statuettes of nude women, no doubt for use with magical
fertility rites. They interred their dead with flint tools, weapons,
and ornaments of shells, teeth, and bone—clear indication of
developing belief about the after-life.

MIDDLE STONE AGE, 10,000–7,000 B.C.

As the centuries slip by, the Old Stone Age (Paleolithic) gives
place to the Middle Stone Age (Mesolithic), and a new variety of
homo sapiens presents himself in Palestine. He is classified as
"Mediterranean" and his advanced stage of culture has been
named by the Palestine archeologists "Natufian," because it was
first clearly identified at diggings in the Wady en-Natuf, northwestern Judea. Owing to the abundance of their relics it is easy
to construct the daily life of these Natufians. We know, for
example, that by 10,000 B.C. they had ceased to live in caves and
were constructing villages—an innovation ascribed in the Bible
to Cain (Gen. 4:17). The caves under the village now served as
cemeteries or as storage pits. Since men were still hunters they
left us beautifully worked arrow and spear heads, and stone axes.
They became so successful in their hunting that according to the
Bible one of them, Nimrod, attracted the favorable attention of
Yahweh (Gen. 10:8, 9). They improved also the art of fishing;
they made harpoons out of bone with barbs on the side. Towards
the end of this era man learned how to domesticate animals, first a
large dog, later sheep and goats. Genesis 4:2 says that Abel was
the first shepherd, and he had a fixed home. Nomadism came
when the shepherd left his own pastures for grazing far away,
and lived in tents when he needed shelter. The first nomadic tent
dweller, according to Genesis 4:20, was Jabal, sixth generation
after Cain.

Agriculture first appears in this Natufian culture. Not only did
men grow a primitive hard wheat that antedates our extant

FIG. 3. CAVES IN THE WADY EL-MUGHARA, MT. CARMEL.

Entrances to several caves are visible. In front of the largest is the pile of debris left by the excavations of 1934.

varieties, but they left us samples of the sickles they used in harvesting it. These consist of finely serrated blades of flint, accurately set side by side in the groove of a bone haft. We find also numberless mortars and pestles of basalt in which the grain was pounded into flour. According to Genesis 2 : 15 the art of husbandry antedates all others, for Adam was a tiller of the ground in Eden before Eve was created, and still pursued that occupation, as Cain did, after the expulsion. But archaeology says that hunting came first and herding next, with farming a late third. By the time the Hebrews came on the scene, the era of the preagricultural hunter had dropped out of memory.

When the climate of Palestine grew colder, clothing became a necessity. Naturally none of the textiles of the Natufians has survived, but the tools with which they dressed the skins of animals, obviously with intent to wear them, are found in abundance: the flint scrapers, blades, lunates and rubbers with which to shape the pelts; the bone borers, awls from the antler of a deer, bone points and pins made from the small ankle bones of gazelles, used evidently to fasten the skins together. This process of adapting animal pelts for clothing was so wonderful that its invention is ascribed by the Hebrews to Yahweh himself (Gen. 3 :21) ; though evidently Eve had already thought up the use of leaves for clothing (Gen. 3 :7).

These Natufian men in Palestine give proof of a love of beauty and the impulse to create it. While as yet in Bible lands we have not found anything so remarkable as the bisons of Altamira or the mastodons, the stags and the huntsmen of the caves in central France and eastern Spain, still Mount Carmel has yielded something comparable. On the end of a piece of long bone, probably used as a sickle haft, some one carved a young deer, his legs running lengthwise of the bone and his body forming the end. Such a carving on such a tool could hardly have the magic significance usually assigned to prehistoric art; it must have been made simply for love of ornament. From the Mount Carmel caves come also a human head carved in calcite, and bone pendants arranged

Fig. 4.   ART OBJECTS.
Deer on sickle haft (*left*) and human head in calcite.

bisymmetrically to form a necklace (Fig. 4). The Natufians seem also to have had some sort of religion. We saw in the mode of burial used by the Mousterian cave dwellers the faint glimmer of religion. With the arrival of *homo sapiens* religion rose to a place of greater importance. But the general nature of it does not change; it is still the cult of the dead. As the centuries go by, more and more attention is paid to burial and to equipment of the dead for the shadowy life to which they have gone. The inference cannot be escaped that the care bestowed was motivated partly by the desire to protect the living against any possible ill-will the dead might cherish. These customs and hopes survived into historic times transformed and moralized.

NEW STONE AGE, 7,000–5,000 B.C.

Of this age very few remains have been found to date, and
those chiefly at Jericho. We know that the people were engaged
in agriculture and cattle-breeding, and lived in the oldest permanent houses yet discovered. Their art achievement now adds to
the small figurines of their predecessors some full-sized statues
of "divine triads," which had some unknown cultic significance.
This was the age also of the megalithic structures, chiefly in
Transjordan, that have hitherto defied accurate dating.

COPPER-STONE AGE (CHALCOLITHIC), 5,000–3,000 B.C.

We now enter the culture called "Ghassulian," from the village
in the lower Jordan valley where it was first identified. It is the
earliest strictly sedentary culture, made possible by the development of irrigation in plains and river valleys. Many grains, fruits
and vegetables were now cultivated. And as this ancient life
developed towards historic times, many another invention helped
satisfy the wants of man.

Some time before the fourth millennium B.C., man learned to
control fire.

Hebrew tradition tells us of the earliest manufacture of bricks
for houses as against the use of wattle and daub: "In the plain of
Shinar [Babylonia] they said, 'Come, let us make bricks, burning
them well'; so they used bricks for stone and bitumen for mortar"
(Gen. 11:3, 4). We now know that the earliest burnt bricks found
to date come from Ur in the plain of Shinar and that their date is
before 4000 B.C.

Near this same date, the art of reducing copper was discovered
and commerce began with the search for that metal and the
exchange of manufactured objects. This discovery is credited by
the Bible to Tubal-cain, sixth descendant from Cain; and the
fearful havoc wrought by copper weapons against the old wielders
of stone is set forth in the "Song of the Terrible Lamech," probably the oldest fragment in our Bible:

Adah and Zillah, hear my voice,
You wives of Lamech, give ear to my words;
I kill a man for wounding me

. . . .

If Cain is to be avenged seven-fold,
Then Lamech seventy and seven-fold
(Gen. 4:23–24)

It was Lamech's son who is said to have made the discovery of how to smelt metal, but the father put it to its first practical use in fighting. The Hebrew sagaman, singing centuries after the event, credited Tubal-cain with smelting iron also. But that was in error; iron was known to the Egyptians in the early third millennium B.C., was first manufactured by the Hitties in the fourteenth century B.C., and was brought to the Israelites by the Philistines about 1200 B.C.

In this same fourth millennium, some unnamed person daubed clay on a woven wicker vessel, and lo! it would hold water. Some one else found that without the aid of the wicker work he could mold a clay vessel that would hold water just as well. Generations later, some one put the clay jar too near a fire; it turned to red stone and became a hundred times more useful. This hand-made pottery was now painted with polychrome geometric and floral designs.

Around 3400 B.C., some one in Egypt invented the potter's wheel and forthwith put symmetry and beauty into the humblest household utensil. Its use came to Palestine half a millennium later. The Bible takes all these inventions for granted.

So from the darkness and gropings of our bottomless pit we have climbed to the light of day, bringing with us the achievements of the millenniums. How few they are and how slowly on the dial of time they appeared; but how invaluable and fateful nevertheless.

CHAPTER II

IN THE DAYS OF ABRAHAM

WE THINK of Palestine as the Bible land proper, and so it is; but Noah and Abraham take us to an equally important land, Mesopotamia, which is virtually the present kingdom of Irak. In this region civilization began—at least the civilization which most powerfully affected the Hebrews. Out of it into the light of history came the Hebrews themselves and many of the earlier and later tribes who mingled with them. Out of it came the arts and sciences and many of the religious ideas that shaped Hebrew culture. Out of it too came the conquerors who for many generations watered Palestine with human blood; and to it went unwillingly the Hebrew exiles, the flower of the citizenry of Israel and Judah, to lose themselves in the life that throbbed with such vitality in the lands of the Two Rivers.

The earliest seat of civilization in this valley was Babylonia, the flat, hot, alluvial plain that begins where the grass lands of upper Mesopotamia leave off and extends to the Persian gulf. By the time men occupied this valley, the Tigris and Euphrates had built out their deltas to a few miles southeast of where Abraham's old city of Ur now stands excavated. Not that this land was all solid and arable; there were large lakes, numerous patches of marsh and a good many desert spots left by the shifting courses of the rivers. But by and large it was a goodly land, a haven for the pursued and the hungry (Fig. 5).

While we know that this was Abraham's early home, we are not so certain about his date. For the last fifty years scholars have synchronized him with Hammurabi of Babylon, but unfortunately they have not yet succeeded in anchoring Hammurabi to a calendar. Formerly they dated him c. 2350 B.C. but on receiving new light they gradually brought him down to 1792–1750 B.C.[1] Abraham must probably follow suit. We have to admit at the outset, however, that outside of the Bible we have no indication that Abraham was an historical character. He may be the personification of a tribe or clan, and in part he certainly is an idealized figure created by the prophetic writers of Israel from the ninth to the fifth centuries B.C. If Abraham was an historical person he was only one member of a numerous family known to scholars as the "Habiru," a name regarded as the equivalent of our "Hebrews." About them we are gradually learning a good deal. On the tablets they first appear earlier than 2000 B.C. in southern Mesopotamia. They had been driven in by necessity from the Arabian desert or drawn in by hope of gain. While their families in their black tents hovered about the skirts of the alluvium, the men picked up whatever jobs they could get tending cattle for the town-dwellers, working as roustabouts on river boats, doing odd jobs of the unskilled sort, hiring out as soldiers in the Sumerian army, or even signing up as slaves to some wealthy family for the sake of securing a living.[2] They were a tough lot, their name being synonymous with brigand, rascal, cut-throat. As soon as any of them became absorbed in the towns they served, others pressed in to do the rough jobs and keep up the evil reputation of their predecessors.

After the defeat of the Sumerians by Hammurabi in the eighteenth century B.C., the Habiru are no more mentioned in southern Mesopotamia, whereas mention of them begins to appear at Mari on the middle Euphrates and in northern Mesopotamia not far from Haran. The names of Haran, Abraham's second home, and of Nahor, home of Rebekah, are specifically mentioned in the Mari archives. This migration of the Habiru is without doubt the one of which the clan of Terah and Abraham formed a part.

[1] W. F. Albright: *Bul. Amer. Schools of Oriental Research,* 77:25 ff; 79:36.
[2] So in a tablet from Nuzu. *Bibl. Archaeologist* III, 1, p. 12.

It may have begun before Hammurabi's conquest, perhaps as early as 1850 B.C.

Whatever evidence may yet be adduced for or against the historicity of Abraham, there is no doubt that the Bible stories contain a genuine reflection of the culture of ancient Mesopotamia, which was the matrix in which grew many elements of Hebrew civilization. This culture is therefore worth describing as an essential part of the daily life of Bible times. While, for the sake of vividness, we shall speak of Abraham and the other patriarchs as persons, let it be understood that the names stand for the Semitic people of the cultural epoch 1800–1700 B.C. in Mesopotamia and 1700–1600 B.C. in Palestine.

UR, CITY OF ABRAHAM

The Bible is quite explicit in saying that Abraham's first home was Ur (Gen. 11:28, 31; 15:7) although this statement discounts the readings in the Septuagint version, "the country of Ur." Like all Mesopotamian cities Ur was built chiefly of sun-dried mud brick. When the brick crumbles through age or war or the winter rains, the house owner levels off the debris and builds another house on top. Thus the site rises. By Abraham's time Ur had risen twenty feet above the river and had spread enormously until its area including suburbs was four square miles of closely packed houses holding a population of probably half a million. Seen from the river the mound was rather imposing. It was protected from the river by sloping ramparts of brick; on the level top rose the house walls in a continuous line, their flat roofs edged with battlements from which the inhabitants could repel attack. With the river on one side and a large navigable canal on the other, the city might reckon itself well defended. For exits and entrances there were sloping covered runways that led down from the houses to the river, each connecting with a ferry; and on the east an arched-over road issued from the shadow of a lofty tower, crossed the canal on a wooden bridge and halted in the garden suburbs. The

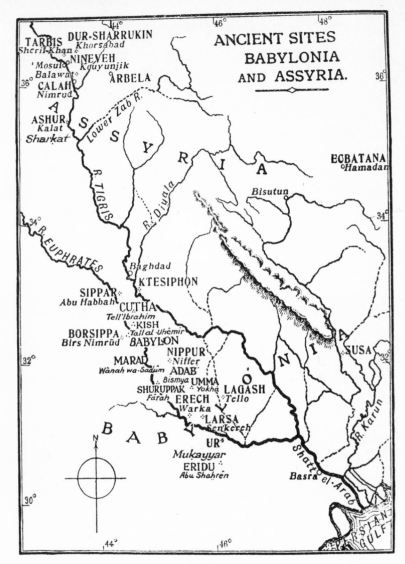

FIG. 5.

The group of names in the south-central portion (Babylonia) represent the Sumerian, Babylonian and Chaldean occupations. The northern group is exclusively Assyrian. Ecbatana in the north-east is Persian.

buildings were plain rectilinear masses huddled close together and connected by a labyrinth of narrow lanes (Fig. 6).

HOUSES

Since Abraham's father Terah was probably in the livestock business, as Abraham himself was later (Gen. 12:16; 13:2, 5-7; 24:10) he had a prosperous merchant's home. Terah would enter his house from the street by way of a wooden door, the valves of which turned on pivots set into socket-stones. Once through the door, he had to go down steps or an incline to reach the house floor, for, since everybody threw rubbish into the streets, the street level had a way of growing up on the house wall. Once inside, Terah found himself in a little lobby with facilities for washing hands or feet. Beyond this was a central paved court, around which a dozen or so rooms were disposed in two stories. Immediately to the right, Terah would find stairs to the second story, and behind the stairs, a lavatory with drain of terra cotta. Next came the kitchen with its fireplace and mill stones. Other doors led to guest rooms, servants' rooms, and the like. The second-floor rooms were the living quarters of the family. They were made accessible by a wooden gallery that ran around on four sides, were supported on posts and protected from rain and sun by the house roof that projected inward toward the court. With rugs, hangings, mattresses and cushions, such a house though built of mud brick was very comfortable and attractive. This is all made clear by Fig. 7.

Somewhere on the ground floor was also a chapel. At one end of this room on a slightly raised platform, an altar was built against the wall; in the same wall was a niche for the reception of images either of gods or of ancestors; and under the floor a vaulted brick tomb in which each member of the family was buried in due course beneath an inverted clay coffin. In smaller houses without a chapel the family dead were buried under one of the regular rooms. In this way the dead person continued to be a member of the family and to live in his old home; only now he was more than an ancestor. He became a god to whom reverence

Fɪɢ. 6.   MODERN NINEVEH FROM THE AIR (1000 FEET).

Removing the mosque (center) and the khan (lower left), the remaining formless mass represents fairly well the small mud brick houses of ancient Ur and all other Mesopotamian towns. The height of the mound is not adequately shown.

was due and offerings must be made.[3] In Gen. 31:19, 34–35, the word "teraphim" (translated "household gods") is used for such beings, while in verses 30 and 32 another word is used (translated "gods"). This would suggest an amalgamation of the two ideas of ancestor and divinity.

[3] See T. J. Meek: *Hebrew Origins,* pp. 80–84. Also Deut. 26:14; 1 Sam. 28:13; Is. 8:19; Amos 6:10; Jer. 34:5; 2 Chron. 16:14; 21:19; Ps. 106:28.

WRITING

The art of writing as developed in the Sumerian cities was destined to spread all over Bible lands. It became the instrument of all business and ultimately the language of government also. That is why the official correspondence between the kings of Canaanite Palestine cities and the Pharaohs of Egypt in the fourteenth century B.C. (the Tell el-Amarna tablets) was written not in hieroglyphic, the language of the overlord, but in cuneiform, the language of the subjugated people. It will be interesting to examine this art.

While we cannot say that the people of Ur were mostly literate, there were many who could write. That is because the law required a written document for every business transaction. "Stenographers" and accountants were in great demand and their training required as much time and skill as the mastery of English demands today. All writing was done on clay with a three-cornered stick. This character is called "cuneiform" (from the Latin *cuneus*, a wedge) because all the marks left by the stylus in the clay are wedge-shaped. Whether or not the Sumerians invented it, they certainly brought it to Mesopotamia where it underwent the usual evolution from picture-writing to syllabic. How modern men learned to decipher it has often been told, but nowhere so fully and attractively as in Dr. Chiera's book, *They Wrote on Clay*.

Let us visit a professional scribe and see the writing process. Nahor, we may imagine, who was left behind to handle the Ur branch of the livestock business when Terah and Abraham moved their main office to Haran (implied in Gen. 11:27–31), is about to send up river a string of a thousand donkeys purchased from a Hebrew tribesman who has just arrived from Arabia.[4] He goes at once to the place where letter-writers have their stand, namely,

---

[4] All the stories in Genesis state that the livestock of the patriarchs included camels, and that long-distance travel was accomplished by means of them. We must now regard this as an anachronism. See Chap. VII.

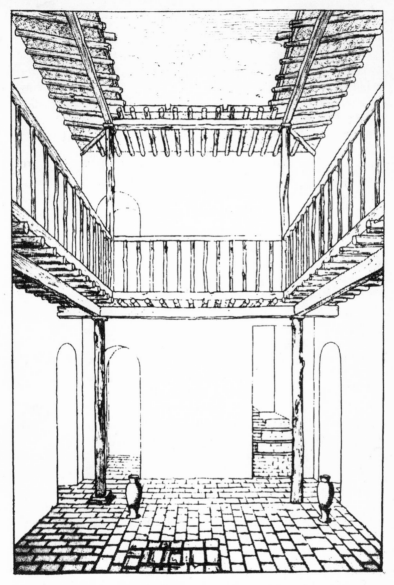

FIG. 7.   RESTORATION OF A HOUSE INTERIOR
OF THE TIME OF ABRAHAM.

Rooms as many as fourteen were arranged in two stories about an open court. Walls
were of brick, unbroken by windows; galleries, roof beams and supports were of wood.

near the gate of the city. He picks out a scribe who has a reputation for neatness and accuracy and tells him the nature of the document to be written. The scribe takes from his bucket a lump of clay of the probable size required. Either he or a special manufacturer has worked this clay into condition, clay of a certain quality, washed clean of impurities, kneaded to the right consistency, and shaped to the form of a small shredded wheat biscuit. Holding the clay in his left palm, the scribe presses his three-cornered stylus into the soft surface, turning the stick rapidly from horizontal to vertical or diagonal until both sides of the tablet are nearly covered. Now Nahor must affix his signature. Accordingly he reaches inside the neck-band of his tunic, gets hold of a string, and finally draws up on the end of it a small cylinder of agate, about an inch high and three-eighths of an inch in diameter. The cylinder is covered with figures cut into the stone (intaglio). Rolling this cylinder along the bottom of the tablet where there is a clear space, he leaves on the clay a rectangular relief of the design. It is not Nahor's name but a device he has adopted to serve as his signature, and all his business agents recognize it. Moreover, the scribe certifies by the addition of cuneiform characters that this is the signature of Nahor of Ur. Witnesses will also affix their seals if witnesses are required. The scribe now takes another lump of clay, flattens it to the thickness of a pie crust and wraps it tightly around the letter, taking care to remove all excess clay and smooth over the joints so that the new enlarged tablet looks just like the inner one. This is literally the envelope for the letter. The original document cannot now be tampered with. On this envelope the scribe will write the name and address of the recipient, just as we do on our envelopes; or if required, he will write an exact duplicate of the inner document, on which the signer and witnesses will affix their identical seals. Any attempt to change the figures or the wording on this outer copy can readily be detected by breaking open the envelope and reading the original (Fig. 8). Strangely enough the envelope did not adhere.

There are obvious disadvantages to this system of writing.

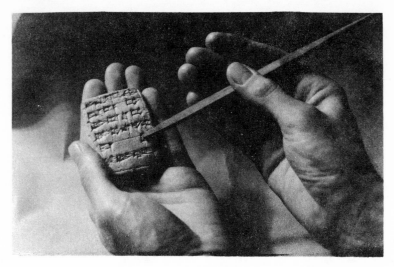

FIG. 8. TABLET WITH CUNEIFORM CHARACTERS
AND SEAL IMPRESSION.

The wedge shape of the marks left by the stylus is evident, as well as the neatness of
their arrangement.

Where correspondence is voluminous, the documents would be
tremendously heavy. Imagine the number of trucks the post office
department would require to deliver one day's mail in London or
New York; and imagine the space necessary for one of our giant
life insurance companies to file all its scores of millions of documents. Yet the system has the advantage of permanence. While a
few hundred years hence most of the modern books in our libraries
will be yellow dust, every cuneiform document that accident has
not broken—receipts, contracts, vouchers, the minute details of
business and of household life—is still readable.

Of no ancient nation on earth do we know as many intimate
details as of the peoples of the Two Rivers.

Schools

Not everybody in Ur was educated, but if any parent had the
ambition to get his son into a white-collar job—and there were a

good many such—the only entrance was through a school. The
boy must learn to write and cipher at least. What the Sumerian
boys learned about arithmetic and geometry is of interest to us
because we are their heirs in some important particulars. They
were taught to count in 60's and multiples of 60, and in 10's. If
the scribe were asked, for example, to write 84, he would put it
down 60 + 20 + 4. If he had to write 4235, he would write
1 *sar* (3600) + 1 *ner* (600) + 30 + 5. Out of this predilection
for 60's we get our tables of time and degrees. Out of the 10 idea
we get our decimal system. The Frenchman will no doubt see here
the origin of his word for seventy "soixant-dix" (60 + 10). The
British Museum has tablets giving tables of multiplication, division, square and cube roots, and geometrical progressions.

Astronomy, especially in its primitive form of astrology, was
cultivated from earliest times. Abraham knew the five planets—
Mercury, Venus, Mars, Jupiter, and Saturn—the signs of the
zodiac and the phases of the moon. The earliest year was lunar;
priests announced the new moon every month, and at the end of
the year intercalated the right number of days to make the total
correspond with the solar year. It was from the Babylonians of the
first dynasty that the Hebrews adopted their Biblical calendar.

BUSINESS

Though Ur lay in the midst of an agricultural country, it was
far too large to have served merely as a local market center. We
know that its interests were world-wide. Situated on both a navigable river and a navigable canal, it could send its ships well up
towards Armenia on the north and down the Persian Gulf to the
south as far as the captain's courage would permit. Caravan trails
also led through Ur from the four quarters of the earth. Commerce
was therefore a means of livelihood for many thousands, and the
manufacture of raw materials into all kinds of usable goods gave a
livelihood to more thousands. The god Nannar was the greatest
business man of Ur Boats came up-river and down-river and from
across the sea bringing whatever the god might require for his

pleasure or profit—usable timber of which the river lands had none, diorite for statues, alabaster for decorations in relief, copper for all kinds of objects, gold and silver and ivory. All this the temple slaves brought up the long ramps from the river and stored away in the chambers around the courts and corridors. In this area also manufacturing went on, and from it were sold or exported the articles needed by the cities and the farms of the god's domain. The temple was a hive of industry.

There were many private business houses also that had world-wide connections, not only foreign customers but branch offices. We have, for example, a host of business tablets written in the purest Assyrian and belonging to the Assyrian colony in the city of Caesarea in Asia Minor, 2000 B.C., which acted as agent for merchants all over the known world.

Carrying on business in distant places was an intricate matter. The merchant had to have agents whom he could trust. Transport by land or water must be dependable; that involved policing of important routes and an understanding with foreign rulers through whose territory his goods passed. That "understanding" was usually a money payment; but sometimes a foreign rascal had to hear the tread of Babylonian soldiers before his understanding became acute. Then postal arrangements as well as transport were necessary. Within the limits of any Sumerian state there were by Abraham's time regular lines of couriers who carried official dispatches, with posting stations at fixed intervals, and the merchants maintained a similar service.

Then the matter of payments had to be settled. Money payments for goods were out of the question; there was no coin till the eighth century B.C. Trade balances could hardly be settled by the transportation of commodities. So the merchants agreed upon a "commodity dollar," using as the unit of value that by which men have to live—barley. A bale of cloth or a piece of lapis lazuli was reckoned as worth so many bushels of barley. For local transactions, barter exchanges could be easily arranged; but barley was the fixed unit of the merchant even after silver and gold entered largely as elements of trade. A man's weekly wage, for example, might be worth two bushels of barley; but if he preferred to be paid in silver, the barley-value of silver had to be reckoned, and the paymaster would weigh out on a pair of scales two barley-bushels' worth of silver. So Abraham paid Ephron the Hittite for the cave in Hebron; "Four hundred shekels of silver of commercial standard,"—not coin, but weighed metal (Gen. 23 : 16). But when silver became common, the transport of large quantities of it to pay balances was risky. These brainy Sumerians therefore invented letters of credit, bills of exchange, cheques, all written of course on clay tablets and carried by the agent or supercargo in charge of the consignment of goods, or by regular post.

Sumerian Law

When Hammurabi, king of Babylon, defeated Rim-Sin, king of Larsa, and took over his dependent Sumerian cities, including Ur, in order to unify his peoples of north and south he caused a new compilation of laws to be made. He would naturally make as few changes as possible, for he must avoid upsetting the people he was trying to amalgamate; but there were probably Semitic additions. That Sumero-Babylonian law code we have practically intact (Fig. 9). The eight-foot stela on which it was engraved was set up in the court of the temple of Marduk at Babylon where any person could consult it to see what were his rights under the law.

The code is interesting for the light it sheds upon the everyday life of Babylonia in the age of Abraham, and for the parallels it offers to Hebrew law. The 282 laws define the responsibilities and privileges of the different classes of society and present a series of cases beginning "If a man . . ."

The following selection from this code is found in G. A. Barton: *Archaeology* and the Bible, chap. XIII :

Sec. 1. If a man brings an accusation against a man that he hath laid a death spell upon him, and has not proved it, the accuser shall be put to death (*cf*. Ex. 22 : 18; Deut. 18 : 10–12).

Fig. 9.   STELA OF HAMMURABI
(LOUVRE).

Of black basalt about 8 ft. high. Found
at Susa in 1901. At the top, Hammurabi
who makes the "prayer gesture," receives
the approval of the sun-god Shamash. On
the rest of the stela are engraved the
laws of the empire.

Sec. 3. If in a case a man has borne false witness, or accused a man without proving it, if that case is a capital case, that man shall be put to death (*cf.* Deut. 19:16–19).

Sec. 8. If a man has stolen ox, or sheep, or ass, or pig, or a boat, either from a god or a palace, he shall pay thirtyfold. If he is a poor man he shall restore tenfold. If the thief has nothing to pay he shall be put to death (*cf.* Ex. 22:1–4).

Sec. 14. If a man steals the son of a man who is a minor, he shall be put to death (*cf.* Ex. 21:16).

Sec. 117. If a man is subjected to an attachment for debt and sells his wife, son, or daughter, or they are given over to service, for three years they shall work in the house of their purchaser or temporary master; in the fourth year they shall be set free (*cf.* Ex. 21:2–11).

Sec. 206. If a man strikes a man in a quarrel and wounds him, he shall swear, "I did not strike him with intent," and he shall pay for the physician (*cf.* Ex. 21:18–19).

Sec. 215. If a physician operates upon a man for a severe wound with a bronze lancet and saves the man's life, or if he operates for cataract with a bronze lancet and saves the man's eye, he shall receive 10 shekels of silver. Sec. 218. If the man's eye is destroyed, they shall cut off his hand.

Sec. 250. If an ox when passing along the street gores a man and causes his death, there is no penalty in that case. Sec. 251. If the ox of a man has the habit of goring and they have informed him of his fault and his horns he has not protected nor kept his ox in, and that ox gores a man and causes his death, the owner of the ox shall pay ½ mana of money (*cf.* Ex. 21:28–29).

INDUSTRIES

As a boy, Abraham no doubt looked in at the various booths in the bazaar with a boy's curiosity about the way things are made. All the processes were carried on in plain sight in little boxlike rooms, open their entire width and height on the street. Let us take a walk with him along the bazaar street, for what we shall see is characteristic of all cities in the Near East from Abraham's day to the present.

First is a seal-maker. He squats cross-legged on a counter flush with the street. His raw materials are quartz, jasper, carnelian, lapis lazuli, agate, obsidian—in fact, any hard stone he can buy; and then for cheaper seals, he has limestone or gypsum. Just now a caravan man is trying to sell him a piece of jade that he brought from Tabriz; the man who sold it to him said he got it in Samarcand from a man who came from China (using modern names). The haggling has been going on for half an hour; but they have

Fig. 10   CYLINDER SEAL AND IMPRESSION.

At the right, the stone cylinder with the design engraved *intaglio*. A hole pierces the axis and by a string the owner hangs it around his neck. At the left, the impression made by the seal when rolled on clay. In this case the relief has been half repeated.

reached an agreement, and the dealer is weighing out some silver in payment. In the meantime we look at the sealmaker's tools. They are of bronze, hardened and brought to a sharp edge or point. Chief among them are the V-shaped graver and the drill. The latter is rotated by a bow. Even so it is difficult to imagine how such tiny figures as the craftsman engraves on the curved surface of the cylinder can be so lifelike, have so much detail of feature and costume, and be so graceful (Fig. 10).

Seals are often mentioned in the Bible (Gen. 38:18; 1 Kgs. 21:8; Jer. 32:44; Rev. 5:1). Their use in Palestine was derived from both Mesopotamia and Egypt. One poetical passage (Job 38:12–14) is worth noting. The rising sun is said to make visible from the darkness the contours and colors of the land, its mountains, gorges, farms, vineyards—as a seal brings out its design on a bit of clay.

Next door is a cabinetmaker. He has an extensive establishment with several helpers and can handle almost any job that involves both construction and decoration. Just now he is engaged on a hope-chest for the daughter of the king of Ur. The structural parts of the box are of cedar of Lebanon, but the decorations on the surface consist of small rectangular plaques. The main design is cut from the solid central column of a large conch-shell. In color these pieces are like ivory. Sometimes the master cuts them into figures in silhouette and then expresses their inner details by engraved lines. Then he sets these figures against a background of lapis lazuli mosaic. Sometimes he carves the figures in low relief, or even engraves upon the surface of the rectilinear plaque some attractive subject, and fills the channels with red or black paste. This type of ornamentation is destined to become fashionable throughout the Eastern world for many centuries. We shall find it in the Canaanite palace of Megiddo and in Ahab's palace in Samaria.

Farther along the street are the metal workers and jewelers. Their art is ancient and many of the patterns now in use have come down through more than a thousand years. On the gold-smiths' shelves are lovely ribbed cups, beakers with long snouts, and cult objects partly of gold and partly of lapis lazuli. One of them is a bull's head made of thin sheet-gold hammered over a wooden form; strangely enough it has a beard of lapis lazuli, no doubt in deference to some ancient myth in which he figured. Other workers are making lyres with large sounding-boards, decorated with the shell and mosaic plaques described above. It is hard to leave this fascinating shop.

Of course the humbler crafts are going full blast. But since they all survive practically without change into Israelitish times, description will be deferred to Chapter IX.

DRESS

Do we know how Abraham and Sarah dressed while they **were** citizens of Ur? In certain **essential** particulars, yes. Our sources of knowledge are first, the representations of people we find on monuments, reliefs, seals and plaques; second, the testimony of graves. The latter of course tell us little because after 4000 years all that is perishable has perished. Only a fine powder is left of what was once their thicker fabrics. The thin fabric of a woman's skirt and undergarments has wholly evaporated, but of the jacket we find the buttons, made of shell or stone, the ornaments of all shorts and the bronze or silver pins with which the garments were held, arranged in rows or patterns which show clearly that they served to hold the garments in place. Sarah, for example, wore a simple undergarment that went under her right shoulder and was gathered up over her left shoulder with a pin of bronze or silver about nine inches long. This gathering made a kind of sleeve. The tunic was held about the waist with a girdle, woven or twisted. Sarah's jacket would be brightly colored, most likely red. It had tight sleeves coming to the wrist. At the cuff there was a row of ornaments of shell or beads; the waistline was set off with a belt-like row of ornaments—carnelian, gold, lapis, whatever Abraham could afford to give her. A row of stone buttons ran down the front.

Sarah wore her hair long and held it up with bronze pins; for dress occasion she wore a sort of high Spanish comb. Jewelry, of course—earrings, necklaces and ornaments of gold or semi-precious stones attached to the hair in various places—and ribbons, no doubt, which in royal tombs are represented by long streamers of gold. When she went out she wore a head cloth or veil probably no thicker than was necessary and as thin as permissible.

Make-up? Certainly. Her compact consisted of a couple of scallop shells from the Persian gulf—one to hold the cosmetics and one for a cover. Her colors, whether paint or powder we do not know, would be green and black anyway, and in addition a little white, red, yellow and blue for extra touches as occasion required. Just where she applied the colors we do not know. At her girdle she carried a small conical copper box with leather cover that held her toilet kit : tweezers, ear-pick, stiletto, and a round-ended paint stick. More than likely at home she kept a bronze razor, and used cuttlefish bone as a depilatory. When she was ready for the parade she must have been a beauty. Though she may have discarded a good deal of this town make-up when her husband became a nomad, she kept it by her for occasion. According to the story in Genesis 12 : 12–16, when she went back to civilization for a time in Egypt even the Pharaoh couldn't resist her!

Abraham as town-dweller wore a short tunic open at the neck and fastened with a row of buttons down the front. This was held in place at the waist with a belt often ornamented with shell rings. From it was suspended his knife or dagger, a whetstone, his cylinder seal—though this might be worn around the neck, or held by the shoulder pin—and a little case of toilet instruments like Sarah's except that there was no paint stick. Over this tunic Abraham threw his mantle arranged like Sarah's, and on his head, which was shaved, he wore a cloth as a protection from the sun, and a fillet or coil (such as the modern Arab wears) to keep it on. If he went to a party, he would wear a wig. His chief ornament was a single earring—never a pair. At home he was sure to have a pair of bronze razors also.

Costumes worn by kings, high officials, priests and priestesses were on ceremonial occasions very elaborate, involving much gold, silver and a mixture of the two called electrum.

RELIGION

We must pay some attention to the religion of Ur, for Abraham could overlook religion no more than he could fail to eat. Religion with its countless gods was everywhere.

The chief temple belonged to the moon god Nannar. It occupied a great quadrangle 1200 by 600 feet, and was made conspicuous from afar by its Ziggurat or terraced tower of solid brick covering a rectangle 195 by 130 feet. It rose in four stories to the height of 92 feet, the sides sloping somewhat inward. Each story was sheathed in glazed brick of a different bright color—

Fig. 11.   THE ZIGGURAT OF UR.

A restoration based upon extant remains. The ascent was made by three stairways on the front that gave access to the lowest terrace but were focussed upon the second. Thence through a lofty gate the priests mounted to the shrine on the third terrace. Other stairways made inter-terrace circulation easy.

white, black, red. Stairs led from the ground to the top, whereon stood the shrine of the Moon God in brilliant blue symbolizing the heavens. The whole was a reminiscence of the mountain shrines in which the Sumerians worshipped their god before they descended to the plains. It was in effect an artificial mountain with gardens. This temple was old in Abraham's day and must have been one of the most familiar sights of his boyhood. So well was it built that it stood practically intact for sixteen hundred years. Only the abandonment of the city ruined it (Fig. 11). It was just such a ruined tower that gave rise to the story of the Tower of Babel (Gen. 11:1-9).

Within the sacred enclosure also were a citadel well stocked with arms, half a dozen other shrines for the gods and goddesses who served Nannar, and a palace for the high priestess of the Moon God's wife, who was usually if not always the daughter of the reigning king. Then there were storehouses for the food which the gods and the priests consumed, kitchens where the food was prepared and a long court surrounded by chambers where worshippers brought their gifts and paid their taxes. Into it as a sort of caravanserai came a constant procession of donkeys loaded with produce; men and women with gifts of a thousand kinds; the tenants of the wide-flung farms owned by the god, bringing rent and taxes in the form of barley, cheese, milk, sheep and cattle; merchants with their tithes of gold, silver, copper, linen and wool. Into this center of activity came goods from farther afield, for the god was a trader as well as a divinity and landlord. Boats came up-river and down-river and from across the sea, bringing whatever the god might require for his pleasure or profit—usable timber, of which the river lands had none, diorite for statues, alabaster for decorations in relief, copper for all kinds of objects, gold and silver and ivory. All this the temple slaves brought up the long ramps from the river and stored away in the chambers around the courts and corridors. The temple was in very fact the chief institution in Ur.

In this imposing temple on state occasions Abraham would attend the elaborate ceremonies in which litanies and antiphons were used, accompanied by drums and flutes; and at the New Year festival he would see the greatest ceremonial of all at which a passion play was enacted, showing the death, the resurrection and the triumph of the god Nannar.

But this state religion did not enter very deeply into the average citizen's life. Far more influential with Abraham were the less important gods whose worship was not maintained by the state. Their chapels were found at the intersection of all the important streets of Ur. Abraham would stop on his way to business to pay respect to some small divinity who he felt was especially close to him, or to ask protection as he undertook some new and risky venture. The shrine entrance would be flanked by reliefs in terra cotta of a good demon who could avert the evil eye—half bull and half man, holding a spear. In the lobby would be a little cup-board containing clay models of carts or even of clubs that men carry on a journey, votive offerings left by those who desired to benefit by the god's intervention or thank offerings left by return-ing travellers. Advancing to the court Abraham would find always an image of the god or goddess and a table where he could leave his gift. A priest was usually in attendance. Such a chapel —there were hundreds of them in Ur—always was meant for the ordinary citizen. Seldom would he have need to call the attention of the great state gods to himself, but these little departmental deities fitted into his need for health and wealth and safety.

But most powerful of all in their personal appeal were Abra-ham's own ancestors who were buried beneath the floor of his father's house. (See section on Religion, Chapter III)

It is apparent, therefore, that although the Bible is silent about nearly all the details of life in these far-off times, we need not be ignorant about them. Though we may see in the lofty character of Abraham and in the incidents of his wanderings the idealiza-tion of much later prophetic writers, we are also compelled to recognize behind the written narrative the unwritten traditions of generations of sagamen based on solid fact. Certainly the life of the people of Ur in Abraham's day lies open before us. It is the key to an understanding of city life throughout Bible times.

CHAPTER III

BEING A PATRIARCH

HEBREW HISTORY entered the age of the Patriarchs when Abraham left Haran for Canaan; when he renounced civilization and became a nomad. Assuming that the story in Gen. 12–13 represents a tribal migration, Abraham's progress southward may be equated with the Habiru raids in that direction mentioned in the archives of Mari [1] and the push still further south may be associated with the Hurrian migration that penetrated Palestine so completely from 1900–1700 B.C. that Egyptian records of the XVIII Dynasty call Palestine the "land of the Hurrians." We shall continue to speak of Abraham as a person and to use Biblical references freely, because whatever the epoch, nomad life remains the same, practically changeless from age to age. [2]

THE NEW HOME

Abraham entered Palestine as a peaceful penetrator. His clan was small and his requests for pasturage could not seriously disturb the old inhabitants who were few in number. Nevertheless vested rights had to be respected. Had he gone into the Jordan valley he would have found the land well sprinkled with towns.

---

[1] W. F. Albright: *Bul. Amer. Schools of Oriental Research* 67:28, 30.

[2] In a lecture given in Chicago, Nov. 10, 1939, Dr. Nelson Glueck told of being entertained recently in the tent of an important sheikh in Transjordan. The *pièce de résistance* of the banquet was a kid that had been boiled in its mother's milk. The sheikh of course never had heard that boiling a kid in its mother's milk was part of the ritual in Ugarit temples perhaps 3800 years earlier and that such practices were forbidden to Israelites 3100 years ago (Ex. 34:26).

Had he gone westward down the tempting wadies to the maritime plain he would have found not only cities and broad acres of farm land but busy traffic routes where caravans and armies tracked back and forth—and the certainty of paying taxes to local chieftains if not to Egypt. So he chose the open highlands.

Since the high valleys around Shechem were already cultivated by the Shechemites, Abraham moved to Bethel and farther south to the stony pasture-lands of Hebron (Fig. 12). All of central Palestine was sparsely settled. "Ephraim," the country between Shechem and Bethel, was largely forest. The only towns along the watershed besides the two mentioned were Gibeon and Jerusalem, neither of them large. The terraced hills upon which they stood were preempted for olives and grapes. Farther south and west toward Beersheba the land was wide open, sloping gently down toward the arid wastes of the peninsula of Sinai. This was ideal country for a man with flocks. While at times Abraham might have to dispute with other nomads the possession of springs and wells, at least he would avoid the anger of town-dwellers over possible trespass.

Abraham and his descendants were not nomads; they were semi-nomads. They stayed put as long as possible. Abraham's tent was pitched for years under the oaks of Mamre, a mile northwest of Hebron (Gen. 18:1). Also in southwestern Palestine, at Beersheba (Gen. 22:19; 21:25–34) and near Bethel (Gen. 13:3–4). Isaac made Gerar, Beer-lahai-roi and Beersheba his permanent headquarters (Gen. 26:1–6; 25:11; 26:23–25). Jacob lived sometimes near Bethel (Gen. 35:1, 6) but mostly near Hebron (Gen. 35:27). The Golden Rule oath that Abraham made with Abimelech, king of Gerar, to treat the king and his land as kindly as he had himself been treated (Gen. 21:22–31), and that Isaac made later with the same king (Gen. 26:26–33), shows the only possible basis on which town-dwellers and immigrant settlers could get along. This mutual good will and courtesy is further strikingly shown by the story of Abraham's buying the cave of Machpelah (Gen. 23:1–20). If water failed, the tribe had to move; and that always brought up again the problem of adjustment to new localities and personalities. When the patriarchs impinged on the fields or pastures of the older inhabitants, they invariably provoked envy and hostility (Gen. 26:13–22). But the difficulties could usually be settled peaceably.

Food

The true Bedouins live perforce off their animals. Ready-made food is the milk of goats, ewes and camels in that order of preference. These are available wherever and whenever the animals are in good condition. Abraham treated his guests to curds and milk and the flesh of a young bullock (Gen. 18:7–8). The meats, eaten on rare occasions are bullocks, lambs, kids (Gen. 27:8–9) and game (Gen. 25:28). They are boiled or roasted on hot stones, or made into stew. Food is served in the same containers in which it has been cooked. Equally ready-made are certain products of the earth, if one happens to find them. Dates grow, for example, where there are heat and moisture as in the oases; and honey is found in the cracks of the rocks, provided there are flowers. When the patriarchs entered Palestine they could enjoy an ample menu. A certain Egyptian named Sinuhe, who is supposed to have been of the retinue of Pharaoh Sesostris I (1970–38 B.C.) has left his travel-notes in which he describes a residence on the highlands of Palestine. He waxes enthusiastic over the fertility of the land:

"There were figs and grapes and more wine than water. Honey was abundant and [olive] oil was plentiful, and all sorts of fruit hung on the trees. There were wheat and barley." Even the names of places bear witness to the fruitfulness of the land: Carmel, "field of fruit"; Beth-bacherem, "house of vineyards"; Bethphage, "house of figs"; Beth-haggan, "house of gardens"; Engannim, "garden of springs"; Nahal-eschol, "valley of grapes." Most of these names and many others were in existence in patriarchal times. While the usual drink was water, on festival occasions it would be wine (Gen. 27:25).

FIG. 12.   HEBRON.

The appearance of this ancient city has changed little since Abraham's day, though probably the site has shifted here from the hilltops to the left. The houses are wholly of stone with a stone domed roof. The famous pool (2 Sam. 4:12) lies toward the left, the bazaars specializing in the manufacture of glass are in the center, and at the right, marked by two minarets, is the Harem or sacred enclosure that covers the burial-place of Abraham and his family. The present walls of the enclosure were built by Herod the Great; the mosque within was originally a crusader's church of the 11th century. Peek-holes allow visitors to look below the floor into the cave with its Arabic cenotaphs that represent the patriarchs.

We get an interesting side-light on what may be regarded as the "delicacies" of the land in the naive words of Jacob when he recommends a suitable "baksheesh" for his sons to take to the Grand Vizier of Egypt. Some of them, at any rate, are good to eat: "Take some of the country's best in your receptacles, and take it down to the man as a present—a little balm, a little honey, gum, laudanum, pistachio nuts and almonds" (Gen. 43:11).

Of made foods we know that the patriarchs ate bread ("cakes") usually of the unleavened variety (Gen. 19:3; 21:14; 27:17), and that implies farming. The fact that the patriarchs' headquarters were more or less fixed enabled them to raise grain, the first step in the change from nomad to citizen. In his larder Abraham kept flour of at least two kinds ready for quick call, whether he raised the grain or bought it (Gen. 18:6). Isaac definitely cultivated the soil at Gerar and was blessed with a bumper crop (Gen. 26:12). Jacob not only could get bread from his mother's tent, but lentils for his famous red stew—again clearly implying cultivation. When Jacob was stabilized in Haran, he learned how to cultivate wheat (Gen. 30:14); and when he established himself in Canaan, he planted on a scale so large that eleven of his sons had to take a hand in reaping (Gen. 37:7). Evidently his clan had so largely abandoned the nomad's diet of animal products that they thought they could not live without grain (Gen. 42:1-2). Grain was usually pounded with a pestle in a stone mortar (Lev. 2:14), but the patriarchs would probably have a mill made of two circular stones, the upper of which could be rotated by hand on the lower. This produced flour more or less fine (Ex. 29:2, 40; Gen. 18:6). To make unleavened bread the flour was mixed with water and salt in a wooden kneading bowl (Ex. 8:3; 12:34). The dough was made into flat cakes for baking, usually twelve to sixteen inches in diameter and from one-eighth to one-quarter of an inch thick. To bake bread a fire was built on a flat stone. When the stone was thoroughly heated the embers were raked off, the cake laid on and covered with the embers and ashes. To bake the other side the process was repeated

with the cake turned over (Hosea 7:8, "half-baked"). Leavened
bread was made by adding to the dough a lump saved from the

FIG. 13.   ASIATICS ENTERING EGYPT.
A mural painting on the North wall of the main chamber of the tomb of
Khnum-hotep, XII Dynasty.

previous baking (1 Cor. 5:6). Most nomads carry a metal plate
for baking which may be placed directly over a fire built in a
hole in the ground or over a little fireplace at the corner of
the tent.

CLOTHING

The clothing of primitive nomads was made of skins from the
flocks. But Abraham and his early descendants were not primitives; they came from civilized cities and never lost contact with
them. We have already seen what clothes Abraham and Sarah
wore in Ur. Now that they lived more in the open they doubtless adopted, for example, a head-cloth like the "kuffiyeh" still
worn by the shepherds of Palestine. This was kept in place by a
black coil of goat's hair, the "aghal." For the main articles of

men's clothing there were: the woolen or linen tunic reaching from neck to knee or shin and provided with a girdle (as in Ur), and a heavier outer coat of wool, like the "abbayeh" of the modern peasant. Men of leisure used a longer tunic reaching to the ankles and provided with sleeves. Such a tunic or cloak was given to Joseph by his father as a special distinction (Gen. 37:3). The patriarchs also wore sandals (Gen. 14:23). We know less about the clothing of women. Rebekah wore a veil (Gen. 24:65), probably like the women's head-cloth of modern times.

Some costumes of patriarchal times are pictured on the walls of the tomb of Khnum-hotep, a provincial governor under Sesostris II (1906–1887 B.C.) (Fig. 13). The picture shows thirty-seven traders belonging to a Semitic tribe who lived east of Palestine and had come down to Egypt to sell "eye paint," spices and the like. The men have beards and are armed with bows, arrows and metal-tipped spears. Both men and women wear woolen garments, finely patterned and woven in many colors, and sandals of leather. The men have a shirt only, reaching to the knee, though one of them has a coat that hangs from the shoulder. The women wear a single-piece dress that falls from the shoulder to the lower shin; they have long hair but no head-dress except a fillet. Strangely enough, one of the men is carrying a richly wrought lyre (Fig. 13). Female beauty was helped out by jewelry. By the well at Haran, Abraham's slave Eliezar won the heart of Rebekah—and incidentally lodgings for the night—by putting in her nose a gold ring weighing half a shekel, and on her wrists two gold bracelets weighing ten shekels (Gen. 24:22). We have no intimation of their form but many examples of jewelry of the time of the patriarchs have been found, notably W. M. F. Petrie's treasure from Old Gaza (Tell el-Ajjul) (Fig. 14).

DWELLINGS

Nomads must have portable houses. The patriarchs all lived in tents the cloth for which was woven by the women of the household out of the black to reddish-brown hair of the goat. The size of the tent varied with the size of the household, the average being perhaps ten by fifteen feet. The roof was made of strips of cloth sewed tightly together and supported by nine poles arranged in

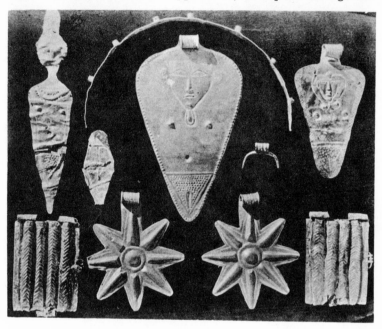

Fig. 14. HYKSOS JEWELRY FROM GAZA.

This gold work, found by Petrie at Old Gaza (Tell el-Ajjul) is unlike anything so far found in Egypt or Mesopotamia. It dates from the period of the Patriarchs. The three upper pieces represent the Syrian Mother-Goddess. The large stars suggest the worship of the planets.

rows of three. The middle three, set lengthwise of the roof, were six or seven feet high; the other rows ran parallel along the front and back edges. When once shrunk, the roof was quite water-tight. It was stretched taut by long ropes and fastened into the ground by wooden pegs (Fig. 15). The making, pitching, and striking of tents was wholly a woman's job, and the women became expert in all of its phases. In the time of the Judges, Jael turned her skill to good account: she killed Sisera as he lay asleep by holding a tent pin in one hand and, with a maul in the other, driving the pin home through his skull! (Jdg. 4:21)

FIG. 15.   A NOMAD'S TENT.
One of a group clustered in a pleasant vale. It is of the normal 9-pole variety with eight guy-ropes.

For protection against wind, rain and intruders, curtains of cloth were hung around the exposed sides of the tent. A cross curtain fixed on the tent poles divided the tent into quarters for the men and the women. Sometimes when the family was wealthy, the women would have separate tents. This would be especially necessary if the sheik had several wives. Jacob was wealthy enough to give a tent each to Leah, the two maids, and Rachel (Gen. 31:33). At the encampment the tents were usually staked out in a circle.

The furnishings of the patriarchs' tents were very simple. Mats of straw or rugs of wool made a floor by day and beds by night. Pots and pans were of wood or metal, for clay is easily broken in transit; the tent lamp, however, was of clay. The half-tanned

FIG. 16.   WATER SKINS.

After being scraped and tanned the goatskin is made up in the natural shape of the animal: legs are quite in evidence and the neck of the goat forms the neck of the bottle, which is sealed by doubling over the leather and winding with string or rag. The water-man slings the skin on his shoulder by a rope, and protects himself from leakage by wearing a piece of leather on his shoulders and back.

skins of goats were made into containers of various kinds—bottles for water (Gen. 21:14) and wine, butter, milk and other liquids (Fig. 16), and bags pursed up at one end to hold the flat loaves of bread. A shepherd's bag for provisions was made from the entire skin of a kid. A whole goatskin, hair on the outside, was slung on a tripod to serve as a butter churn (Fig. 17). Other containers, for clothes (Gen. 27:15, Esau's best clothes), grain (Gen. 42:27), fodder and the like were woven of goats' hair. For seats other than the ground, the camel saddles served, covered with some coarse cloth or a pair of saddlebags (Gen. 31:34). All this scant equipment could be packed up in short order and put on a camel. It represents the minimum human demand worked out by generations of nomads.

WEALTH

What did the patriarchs own in addition to household gear? Naturally the most valuable property would be the livestock that furnished their families with food and drink, shelter and clothing, and that could travel on its own feet. This is stressed in the stories of each of the patriarchs. When Abraham left Haran he took "the property that they had accumulated and the persons that they had acquired" (Gen. 12:5, which is a summary without details); but in Egypt he received from the Pharaoh presents of sheep, cattle, he-asses, she-asses and camels, male and female slaves. By the time he reached the South-country (Gen. 13:2) he was "very rich in cattle, silver and gold." When he and Lot reached Bethel they had so much livestock that they could not find pasture for both groups. When he reached Mamre again (Gen. 14:14) his household slaves numbered three hundred eighteen. In Gerar (Gen. 20:14, 16) King Abimelech gave him sheep, oxen, male and female slaves, and a thousand shekels of silver. Isaac besides inheriting all this property (Gen. 25:5), had a business instinct of his own, "so that the man grew rich, and kept on growing richer and richer until he became very rich indeed; he had flocks of sheep and herds of cattle, and so many

work animals (asses?) that the Philistines vented their spite on
him" (Gen. 26:13–14). When Jacob left Haran, the only property he took aside from wives and children and slaves was live-

FIG. 17.   CHURNING BUTTER.

From the crotch of the stout tripod is slung a horizontal bar which in turn carries and
keeps taut the goatskin container. The squatting woman grasps the skin by a leg and
violently agitates it back and forth.

stock (Gen. 31:18): oxen, asses, flocks (Gen. 32:5) and camels
(Gen. 32:7). How numerous these were can be inferred from
the size of his gift to Esau: 200 she-goats, 20 he-goats, 200 ewes,
20 rams, 30 milch camels with their colts, 40 cows and 10 bulls,
20 she-asses and 10 he-asses (Gen. 32:13–15). We must remember, however, the caution given on page 18.

Aside from slaves and livestock there was nothing a nomad
could own except silver and gold. These metals came into their
possession by gift to insure their good will, and by selling animals

to caravan-men and town-dwellers who needed beasts of burden. Occasions for spending were few: the only recorded ones are Abraham's purchase of a burying place (Gen. 23:16), gifts, jewelry and clothing to a prospective bride and her family (Gen. 24:53) and the purchase of grain in famine times (Gen. 42:2, 25).

SHEPHERDING

Shepherding was a man's job and called for skill and hardihood (Gen. 31:38-40; 33:13-14). Flocks were usually led, but if large they were also driven and kept together by a man and a dog behind (Job 30:1). Various flocks under their separate shepherds often met around a spring (Gen. 29:2-11) and usually at night in natural caves or sheep-folds made by enclosing a space with a four-foot wall for mutual protection against wild beasts and robbers. Watchmen were posted and relieved one another at intervals. Campfires, songs, flute-playing and stories (Jdg. 5:11) helped dispel the loneliness. In the morning the flocks separated, each following the call of its own leader (Jn. 10:1-5). The shepherd's weapons were a club (Ps. 23:4)—an oak stick with a knob on one end the size of one's fist or larger; and a sling woven in leisure moments out of tufts of wool gleaned from the bushes where the sheep have walked. With the sling a shepherd kept his flock from straying: he landed a stone six inches in front of the nose of a sheep which was headed in the wrong direction; with it also he killed preying animals (1 Sam. 17:34-35). Naturally shepherds became expert marksmen (Jdg. 20:16). Then there was the rivalry of hostile herdsmen to contend with, usually violence against violence (Ex. 2:16-17; Gen. 21:25; 26:15-21). A "Good Shepherd" sometimes even gave his life for his sheep (Jn. 10:11) (Fig. 18).

This description of shepherd life holds good from earliest Biblical times till the latest.

Fig. 18.   A BEDOUIN PIPER.

A piper and other shepherds with their flocks at the pools of King Solomon.

SOCIAL ORGANIZATION

The patriarchs are so called not because of their long life but because they were the heads of the social organization called a patriarchy. In this form the father is the legal and religious head of his family or clan; the wife or wives and children are dependent on him, and the reckoning of descent is by the male line. This is in distinction from a matriarchy in which descent is reckoned through the mother, or from any form of citizenship or organization not based on the family.

The father of each family was the autocratic head of his house. He had the power of life and death over his children (Gen. 22:9; Jdg. 11:30-39), and children were bound to obey their parents (Ex. 20:12). The father was also the priest of his family (Ex. 12:21; Job 1:5). Adult sons and their families lived under the patriarch's roof unless for some reason the latter sent them away. On the father's death the oldest son became the new patriarch unless the father appointed another son, as Jacob is said to have done (Gen. 49:8). Thus in the course of a few generations the family became a clan. When the group got unwieldy, as for example when there was not pasturage for all, a separation occurred (Gen. 36:6-8; 38:1), some of the brothers set up patriarchies and clans for themselves; and a tribe resulted, the members being scattered but conscious of their relationship and ready on call to act with the others as a unit in time of need (Gen. 36:9-19).

This description of tribal organization is more or less schematic and ideal. In the Bible it is not clearly indicated just how or when the two sons of the patriarch Joseph, for example, were transformed into the tribes of Ephraim and Manasseh; but reference is constantly made to "elders," who are heads of the constituent families. These heads of the clans were virtually a democracy in which each elder's voice counted in the decisions, the eldest brother preferably being the president of the council, or the sheik, and maintaining authority if he could show sufficient wisdom and personal worth. Sometimes the sheiks were chosen on their worth alone irrespective of their family rank. Witness Moses, Joshua and the various judges who arose when the tribes were becoming stabilized. Since a patriarchy is essentially a nomadic form of organization, settled life in towns breaks it down. The judges were a transitional step from a patriarchy to a monarchy.

Law and order within the tribe and between tribes was maintained by "blood revenge," by which the family of the slain or injured man was bound to seek vengeance on the wrongdoer or his clan. Many instances are given in the Old Testament (e.g., 2 Sam. 14:5-7; 3:27) and the general principle is laid down, "I will hold men accountable for one another's lives; whoever sheds the blood of man, by man shall his blood be shed" (Gen. 9:5b-6a). A man without a tribe—if there were such a one, that is, a stranger or an alien—was in a precarious position (Gen. 4:14) until the growth of social experience led men to regard Jahweh as his special protector (Ex. 22:21; Num. 35:15; Deut. 10:17-19; Ps. 146:9). Then the stranger was given consideration.

MARRIAGE

Fathers bought wives for their sons and sold their daughters in marriage (Gen. 31:14-15). Legally the wife was a chattel, and whatever other status she had was achieved by her personality. At least she was not secluded but went about her duties as a free person. The wife was usually chosen from within the clan or even within the family itself. Abraham's wife Sarah was his half-sister (Gen. 20:11-12); Isaac's wife Rebekah was his cousin's daughter (Gen. 24:15); Jacob married his first cousins Leah and Rachel (Gen. 28:5). We cannot help suspecting that behind Abraham's loyalty to his clan was a disdain of the alien culture of the Canaanites and the ways of settled folk. That is no doubt the chief reason why he would not allow Isaac to marry a Canaanite girl (Gen. 24:3) but kept him a bachelor for forty years (Gen. 25:20); and that same consciousness of superiority set Isaac and Rebekah against Esau's Canaanite wives (Gen. 26:35; 27:46; 28:8).

However that did not always prevent a man's marrying other wives outside the pale, especially if his first wife were barren. When Sarah presented her maid to Abraham (Gen. 16:1-2) she was doing only what was expected of her, not only by custom but by the law of Ur under which she and Abraham had been brought up. Hammurabi's ˙code (146) prescribes that in case of a wife's barrenness the man could either divorce her or he could take another wife of secondary rank, not to be put on an equality with his first wife; or the wife herself might offer a concubine to her husband from among her own slaves. This last alternative was the one Sarah took, as a little later Rachel did with Bilhah (Gen. 30:3). The tablets from Nuzu indicate that a similar arrangement obtained at this period among the Hurrians.[3]

But polygamy brought maladjustments within the family. Sarah became jealous of Hagar and did with Abraham's approval what seems to us to be an inexcusable act: she treated Hagar so cruelly that Hagar ran away (Gen. 16:4-6). Yet here again Abraham and Sarah were acting within their right under Sumero-Babylonian law. Thus Hammurabi's Code (146): "If she has given a maid to her husband and she has borne children and afterwards that maid has made herself equal with her mistress, because she has borne children her mistress shall not sell her for money, she shall reduce her to bondage and count her among the female slaves." In saying "Thy maid is in thy hand; do to her what is good in thine eyes," Abraham reminded Sarah that her word was law to her own slave and that he had no choice in the matter.[4]

Abraham had also another concubine named Keturah (Gen. 25:1) by whom he had six children. From them are said to have

---

[3] See *The Bibl. Archaeologist* III, 1, p. 3.
[4] There are also recently found parallels in Hurrian law. See T. Meek: *Hebrew Origins,* pp. 15 and 75 note; and Gordon: "Biblical Customs and the Nuzu Tablets," *The Bibl. Archaeologist* III, 1, Feb. 1940.

sprung all the tribes of Arabia. Jacob had besides his two chief wives two concubines of undesignated race (Gen. 32:22). Esau married two Hittite girls (Gen. 26:34) and later married his half-cousin, daughter of Ishmael (Gen. 28:9). One of his sons, Eliphaz, married a Hurrian (Horite) girl (Gen. 36:12, 20–22). Joseph had only one wife and she was an Egyptian (Gen. 41:45). Nothing could more clearly indicate the composite nature of the Semitic tribes in Bible times.

It is impossible to say how much of these data relates to actual men and women by these names, and how much represents the Hebrew consciousness of relationship to various Semitic tribes. It really does not much matter; personal history shades off into tribal history, and the sagas tell us at least what was believed and handed down, and what racial strains entered into the composites we call Hebrews and Semites. It was put in the form of the mixed marriages of individuals in a polygamous household.

CHILDREN AND THE LAWS OF INHERITANCE

The purpose of marriage was to have children. The blessing shouted by her relatives after the departing Rebekah was, "May you become a thousand myriads!" (Gen. 24:60). "Give me children or I die," cried Rachel to her husband (Gen. 30:1). Magic and various aphrodisiacs were invoked in case of failure to bear children (Gen. 30:14–18). As a final resort a wife could arrange to bear children by proxy; that is, to give her husband a slave as Rachel did, and then when the birth occurs to hold the mother in her lap and insofar as possible suffer with her (Gen. 30:3). The child is then said to be Rachel's own.[5]

All this mixture of wives and concubines would normally result in confusion and strife over the rights of children were it not that custom and law made everything clear. Abraham and his imme-

[5] For a vivid fictional description of this act, see Thomas Mann: *The Tales of Jacob*, pp. 309–310.

diate descendants acted in accordance with Sumero-Babylonian
and perhaps Hurrian law. By it, all children of whatever wives
are legitimate, and share equally the property. Says the code of
Hammurabi (170): "If a man's wife has borne him sons and
his maidservant has borne him sons, and the father in his lifetime
has said to the sons which the maidservant has borne him 'My
sons,' and has numbered them with the sons of his wife; after the
father has gone to his fate the sons of the wife and the sons of
the maidservant shall share equally in the goods of the father's
house."

If this was so, there had to be some manipulation on Abraham's
part to make Isaac his sole heir (Gen. 25:5). This situation again
is covered by Babylonian law. The Code (171a) permitted a
father during his lifetime to make over anything he chose to any
of his sons, or specifically to will it to him. That property then
became the son's sole share of the estate; the residue went to the
eldest son. This is what Abraham did for the sons of his concubine Keturah (Gen. 25:6)—gave them a gift and sent them
away. He should have provided in this way for Ishmael, and it
took what he believed was a special revelation from his God as
well as strong pressure from Sarah to induce him to cut Ishmael
off without a penny (Gen. 21:9–13). Isaac made his younger son
Jacob his heir by verbal will before his death (Gen. 27:27–29).
What provision he made for Esau is not stated; but before the
death of his father, Esau was a rich man (Gen. 32:6; 33:9),
and after Isaac's death Esau and Jacob had to separate because
their flocks were so great (Gen. 36:6–8). It is legitimate to infer
therefore that Isaac must have made ample provision for his
eldest son.

A childless man could secure a son by adoption. Thus Abraham
took Eliezar of Damascus as slave and ultimate heir (Gen.
15:2–3); but when Ishmael was born the inheritance passed
from Eliezar to him (Gen. 15:4).[6]

[6] So also among the Hurrians of Nuzu. See *Bibl. Archaeologist* III, 1,
pp. 2–3.

RELIGION

We know next to nothing about the religion of the patriarchs. What is given in the stories of Genesis reflects the age in which the stories were written. Nevertheless there seems to be no doubt of the religious primitiveness of the Habiru, confirmed as it is by our present knowledge of the religions of Ur and Haran and by the statement of the "E" document,[7] "In days of old, your fathers lived beyond the River, namely, Terah the father of Abraham and Nahor, and served alien gods" (Josh. 24:2). In fact we learn from some tablets from Ras Shamra on the north Syrian coast that the Aramaic equivalent for the Sumerian name for the moon-god Nannar was Terah! Abraham's father must therefore have been named for this god whose primary seat was Ur and who was the special patron also of Haran. That there was a change is indirectly implied by the absence of moon worship in the religion of the Hebrews, and it is directly expressed in the story of the covenant or contract by which Abraham bound himself to a special divinity in return for certain favors (Gen. 12:1-3; 15:18; 17:1-8).

It seems probable also that the patriarchs brought with them from Mesopotamia their household gods, mentioned above, and that the possession of them lay with the head of the tribe and brought a special degree of protection and prosperity. This is why Laban was so upset when he found that Jacob (Rachel) had stolen his teraphim. It meant that leadership had passed from himself and his sons to the Hebrew Jacob—and that is doubtless the reason why the Bible preserved the incident (Gen. 31:19,

[7] Biblical students have found that underlying the historical books of the Old Testament are certain "documents" or source books. Of these, two at least were based upon earlier oral traditions: "J" written in Judea between 950–850 B.C.; "E," written in Ephraim (the northern kingdom) c. 750 B.C. Two others are in the nature of comments or explanations: "D" which represents comments by an editor (c. 550 B.C.) who followed the point of view of the Book of Deuteronomy; and "P" (about 450 B.C.) who added much material that explained the historic origin of Israelite institutions, particularly the Law and the Priesthood.

26–30). All this is made clear in a tablet from Nuzu describing a contract similar to the one made between Laban and Jacob. The act of adoption conferred on the son the right to inherit not only the property but the household gods.[8]

Later these images were discarded (Gen. 35:1–5). But this abandonment of the teraphim was not permanent. The little gods came back and continued to be used by the Israelites till the time of the Exile. There were teraphim in Micah's sanctuary in the highlands of Ephraim (Jdg. 17:5) : David had a life-sized one in his home (1 Sam. 19:13–16) ; and Hosea says that the teraphim were reckoned part of the legitimate apparatus of religion (Hos. 3:4). In this later time, however, the ancestor idea seems wholly to have evaporated from them and doubtless through Hyksos and Canaanite influence the teraphim became images of "Ishtar" or "Astarte," the mother-goddess of fertility. Little figurines of her are the objects most frequently dug up today in all Palestine sites.

In spite of the magic virtue residing in names in patriarchal times, Abraham's special god had no name. To Laban he was simply the god of Abraham and his ancestors (Gen. 31:51–53) ; to Jacob he was not merely that, but "the Awe of his father Isaac" (Gen. 31:58) and "the god of his father Isaac" (Gen. 46:1. See also 48:15–16). Jacob himself did not know his name when he wrestled with him at the brook Jabbok and could not find out (Gen. 32:29). In speaking to his brothers Joseph called him simply "the god of your father" (Gen. 43:23). To these family names Jacob's own was added at the Burning Bush : it is henceforth "the god of Abraham, Isaac and Jacob" (Ex. 3:6), the patron deity of the Israelite tribes, but nameless still.

YAHWEH

There is considerable doubt about the origin of Yahweh who ultimately became the god of Israel. Some scholars think he was

---

[8] *The Bibl. Archaeologist* III, 1, pp. 5–6.

an original god of the Habiru, as might be implied in Gen. 4:26; some affirm that the name is found in the Hurrian pantheon, whence it must have been borrowed by the Habiru; the Book of Exodus tells us that the tribes under Moses were first introduced to him in the land of Midian (Ex. 3:13-15; 6:3). Whatever his origin, by the time he became the god of the Israelite confederation he was a god of storms and a war god of the most uncompromising kind: jealous, vengeful, a reflection of the fierceness of the conquering Israelites and most fittingly visualized by them in volcanic eruptions and thunder storms.[9] That the patriarchs themselves were not unworthy followers of such a deity can be gathered from the Biblical narratives. Abraham was capable of a good fight (Gen. 14:13-16); Jacob's entry into Canaan was something like an Habiru raid (Gen. 48:22); and two of his sons, Simeon and Levi, were guilty of treachery, murder and spoliation (Gen. 34:24-29). Evidently the partriarchal religion had not developed the type of character the prophetic story-tellers would have us believe. Nevertheless it cannot be denied that out of the religion of Abraham grew finally three grand monotheisms that have had a tremendous influence in shaping the destinies of mankind—Judaism, Christianity and Islam.

[9] Yahweh's physical manifestations:— In the volcano: Gen. 19:23-25; Ex. 19:11-13b. In storm and lightning: Josh. 10:11; Jdg. 5:4-5; 1 Sam. 7:10; 12:18.

His personal qualities:— Jealous and vengeful: Ex. 4:24; 22:22-24; 32:10, 14, 35; Num. 11:33; 14:26-35; 25:1-4, 9; Deut. 29:20-28.

His qualities a reflection of early Hebrew character:— The anger of Moses: Ex. 32:19-21. The fierceness of the Israelites: Num. 21:2-3, 34-35; Josh. 6:20-21; 7:24-26; 10:28-30.

CHAPTER IV

IN THE EGYPT OF JOSEPH AND MOSES

THOUGH EGYPT looms as the sinister background behind many of the Biblical narratives from Abraham to Jesus, she becomes in a special sense a Bible land through her connection with the stories of Joseph and Moses. The Joseph-saga in particular presents a truthful picture of the land and life of that oldest of countries: the lordly river with its rich bottom-lands, kine on the banks and in the marshes, the lush plenty and the store-cities of the good years, the famine when the Nile is low; a civilization based upon despotism and human slavery; arbitrary power that consigns to prison or death, or that 'exalts a slave to great place; its hierarchy of officials—captain of the guard, butler, baker, magicians, wise men, priests; its elaborate court etiquette; abundant wealth—rings, chains of gold, collars of gold, fine linen, chariots, wagons, great houses with hosts of slaves and an underground prison life; elaborate funerals, embalmings, mournings—the most magnificent cult of the dead in history. Not only are these described in the saga but they live for us, every item of them, on the painted and sculptured monuments of Egypt.

The exact date of Joseph's alleged life in Egypt is unimportant, for the forms of life hold steady for two thousand years even though the individuals that Time pours into them were evanescent. We shall assume, however, that Joseph's date was approximately the seventeenth century B.C. during the domination of Egypt by the Hyksos kings from southwestern Asia.

Joseph came to Egypt as a slave. Whoever brought him, whether Ishmaelites (J document) or Midianites (E document), (Gen. 37:28), they were in charge of a trunk-line caravan. They

56

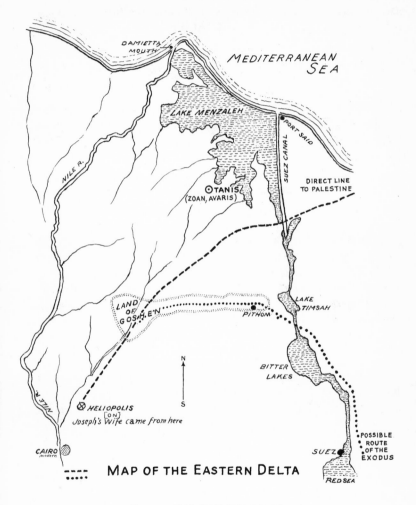

MAP OF THE EASTERN DELTA

FIG. 19.   THE EASTERN DELTA.

would be stopped at the Egyptian border where the route crossed the "bridge"—modern El-Kantara—a narrow neck of land between huge lake Menzaleh on the north and the Bitter lake extensions of the Red sea on the south. At that point was the guardian

FIG. 20.   PLANTING DURING INUNDATION.

fortress Thaku and a garrison whose business it was to repel enemies in time of war and examine passports or the equivalent in time of peace (Fig. 19). Having been admitted, the leader of the caravan made straight for Avaris, the capital city in the northeastern delta where they were sure to find a market for goods and slaves.

FARMERS

On the way, Joseph saw for the first time this extraordinary land where there was no rain yet where through the life-giving river men lived in the midst of plenty. He saw a land of farmers, of compact villages strung along the valley, each one surrounded by fields assigned to the dwellers by the village sheik for cultivation.

Here life was controlled by the rise and fall of the great Nile. In the summer when the river was inundating, there was not much to do but eat and sleep; but when the flood subsided in the autumn, planting began. Men rowed over the shallow water in their boats of papyrus stalks, scattered seed broadcast and then led over the area a bunch of cattle, whose hoofs trod the seed into the soft soil. It was a case of follow the leader: a farmer in

Fig. 21. EGYPTIAN HOE.

the boat led a young calf at the end of a rope, or, as in the illustration, a man took a calf on his shoulders, the anxious mother followed her calf, and the gregarious herd thought it must follow the cow. Thus the shrewd farmer planted his fields by cow-psychology (Fig. 20). Where the land was not sufficiently inundated, or in case crops were planted after the river was down, a plow was used to break up the soil. The share was a piece of wood or bronze fastened to a long pole, which in turn was tied to a bar made fast to the horns of a cow which drew the plow. The farmer held it by a single handle. The Egyptians had also invented a "seeder." A hoe was a back-breaking affair because of its short handle; to this handle was fastened the wooden blade, and pressure on the joint was relieved by a guy-rope (Fig. 21).

The crops sprang strongly under the strong sun. But since there was no rain, man's wit must devise means for bringing water to the soil. Hence the vast irrigation canals—excavated by a corvée under whatever Pharaoh could command the situation; local branches dug by villagers under their sheik's direction, and a network of ditches that turned every man's field into a checkerboard; and lastly, the instruments for raising water from the fast-sinking river—buckets carried on a yoke by men, or well-sweeps (Fig. 22). The "sakkiyeh" or animal-driven wheel-and-bucket concoction which today makes raucous music from rise to set of sun was not yet invented.

In due time reaping followed. This was done with a small hand sickle, in more ancient days made of a series of flints set in a wooden frame [1] but in Joseph's day made of bronze. Threshing was accomplished by cattle—donkeys, cows, swine, etc.—who trod out the grain on the village threshing floor, a circular piece of hard-stamped ground with a raised rim to prevent the grain from being scattered. The farmer winnowed by throwing grain and chaff into the air with wooden shovels, so that the wind might blow away the latter. Lastly the grain was transported in baskets or bags on donkey-back for storage either in the householder's bin or in the larger "beehive" elevators of the overlord or in the royal store-cities (Gen. 41:48). The royal granaries were large bins or houses made of mud brick, conical in shape, with a trap door in the top by which the grain was poured in and a small opening at the bottom from which it was removed. These bins were grouped together and protected by a high wall. Remains of

---

[1] *Cf.* pre-historic sickle described on page 8.

FIG. 22.   A BATTERY OF WELLSWEEPS.

At the winter season when the Nile is low, it is necessary to use these sweeps to raise the water from the river to the fields. A channel is cut in the bank to conduct the river into a pool whence it can be lifted to a higher level, and so on. On the butt-end of the sweep is a ball of mud for a counterpoise.

many have been found and contemporary pictures are extant (Fig. 23). Keeping account of the yield in the fat years furnished plenty of work for the scribes.

In addition to cereal crops of barley and wheat, the farmer

raised lentils or beans for his own food and green fodder for his animals. Food was by no means monotonous. Bread, of course, was the foundation, made of millet or barley—unleavened bread like that made in Canaan. The flour was mixed with water into a stiff paste, the dough flattened and baked on hot stones or in a clay-lined oven. Vegetables were plenty: cucumbers of various kinds, onions, radishes, peas, lentils, beans, leeks, garlic, roots like carrot and turnip, egg plant, spinach and pumpkins. Fish was always plentiful, but was taboo by the wealthy. Meat from domesticated animals was easily available if one could afford it, as were duck, pigeons, geese and wild fowl. And for dessert, who could complain of watermelon, dates, figs, grapes, mulberries, pomegranates, syrups and sweetmeats made from dates or figs or honey. The Israelites looked back with longing to this menu when they found themselves free but starving in the desert (Num. 11:4-5). As for drinks, one might call for milk, wine made from dates or grapes, and beer made from barley or honey. If the records are to be trusted, the temptation to drink met with little resistance. The wise men of Egypt had a good deal to say about the evils of drunkenness.

The farmer's dwelling of mud brick consisted of one or two single-story rooms built on one side of a court. On the floor of one room the family slept, a piece of matting for a bed; or in hot weather they might sleep on the roof—always the coolest place. The chickens and pigeons roosted on sticks that projected a few feet over the courtyard from the wall. Dogs and cats stayed where they might. The donkey and a few goats used the court, though in general the livestock stayed in the fields, day and night. The other room in the house was for storage—jars for grain, boxes for the family clothes, and stacks of fodder. Cooking was done at a hearth in the court, where also was a large crock for water, filled twice every day by the women from the river or village reservoir. Household utensils were few; pottery bowls and saucers, gourds, metal or earthenware pots for cooking, knives of flint or copper. Not till the luxurious days of the XVIII Dynasty

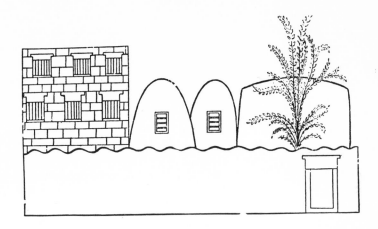

Fig. 23.   EGYPTIAN GRANARIES.

Upper register: A house, two granaries, a building of uncertain use, in a yard surrounded by a wall.

Lower register: Five grain bins, given in elevation in two registers and surrounded
by a wall given in plan. Three bins are seen to be filled; two are being opened so that
the man approaching the entrance may empty his sack through the upper "window".
Grain will be withdrawn through the opening at the ground level.

were spoons and ladles introduced. The only forks were large ones for lifting a piece of meat from the pot. Every house also had a stone mill which was always worked by the women. Of furniture as we know it, there was none in the farmer's house: a person squatted when he wanted to sit.

Farmers were the foundation of the state. They raised all the food, they starved when the Nile failed to do its part; in seasons of bumper crops the money-lender and the local noble got their share and the pharaoh in the Great House got his. So the farmer was always poor and seldom a free man. What happened to him in the seven-year famine of Joseph's time is vividly pictured in Gen. 47:13-26: all free men became slaves and the land became Pharaoh's.

THE NOBLES

Above the farmers and their village sheiks were the "counts" who ruled a fortress-city with its dependent villages; and higher still the "nomarchs" who ruled a whole province or nome. In former days they had virtually been the government as far as the common people were concerned; they had held law and order and property in their keeping. The biographies of some of these men as written in their tombs form an interesting parallel to the character of Joseph. Listen to what Ameni, nomarch of the Oryx-nome says about himself in his tomb at Benihasan:

There was no citizen's daughter whom I misused, there was no widow whom I oppressed, there was no peasant whom I repulsed, there was no herdsman whom I repelled, there was no overseer of serf-labourers whose people I took for [unpaid] imposts, there was none wretched in my community, there was none hungry in my time. When years of famine came, I plowed all the fields of the Oryx-nome, as far as its southern and northern boundary, preserving its people alive, and furnishing its food, so that there was none hungry therein. I gave to the widow as to her who had a husband; I did not exalt the great above the small in all I gave. Then came great

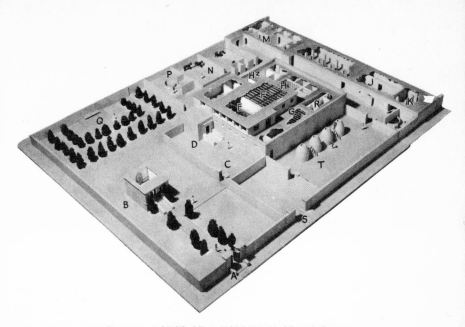

FIG. 24.   HOUSE OF A NOBLEMAN OF AMARNA.

Reconstructed on the basis of several hundred houses excavated at Tell el-Amarna.

A. Main entrance with porter's lodge.
B. Private chapel approached by steps.
C. Inner court reached by a walk at right angles to the first one.
D. Entrance to the house: a projecting porch having a brightly painted doorway.
E. The "North Hall" used by the family in summer to get the benefit of the prevailing north wind.
F. Central Hall with clearstory lighting. The roof has been partly removed to show the wooden pillars that support it. This was the center of family life.
G. Leading from F, the "West Hall" (used mostly in winter) surrounded by storerooms.
H. Inner sitting room surrounded by the women's quarters—small cubicles, and
H2. The Master's Suite of ample size and dignity: antechamber, bedroom with raised recess for the bed, anointing-room with appropriate apparatus, shower bath and toilet.
J. Stables for eight horses, and a long harness room.
K. Shelter for small wooden chariot; compartment for manure.
L. Servants' quarters—one large room.
M. Kitchen group with ovens, storeroom, etc., and a small suite of rooms for the chief cook or the steward.
N. Cattle byres.
P. Well with steps leading down.
Q. Garden. Trees are set in brick tubs that contain Nile mud. They must be watered daily.
R. Guest rooms.
S. Tradesman's entrance, leading to
T. Granary courtyard containing four conical grain bins, served by small brick stairs. (*Cf.* Fig. 23)

Niles, rich in grain and all things, but I did not collect the arrears of the field.[2]

During the prolonged struggle with the Hyksos, these families had been wiped out and their estates had passed to the crown— a change that the Bible erroneously credits Joseph with having achieved. Their lands were then administered by royal officials. Joseph himself was such an official. Potiphar who was Joseph's original owner was probably another, though he may have been a noble as well, the remnant of some old family, who possessed the empty titles that went with his ancestral estate but wielded no power except as the Pharaoh gave it to him. His job was a sinecure; underlings did the work.

Here we may well take a look at the house in which Potiphar lived and in which Joseph had his first exciting adventures, fortunate and unfortunate (Gen. 39:1–23) (Fig. 24).

THE COURT

The magnitude of the government business demanded a host of officials. At the head of the list stood the Grand Vizier He was selected for his administrative ability, may or may not have been of aristocratic family, and kept his position so long as he was satisfactory or until his rivals displaced him. On the opening of business each morning, he was the first to have an interview with the Pharaoh and present him with the details of current business from all parts of the kingdom. The Vizier was also the head of the judicial system and presided over what we might call the Supreme Court. He enjoyed among other titles that of "Mayor of the City." The next person to be interviewed by the Pharaoh was the Chief Treasurer, whose title was "Controller of the Double White House." He was responsible only to the king and to him even the vizier had to go for cash.

[2] J. H. Breasted: *History of Egypt*, p. 161.

Lower officials such as stewards of the vast royal estates cleared their business through the treasurer, who with the vizier decided which items should be selected for royal scrutiny. All local admin-

Fig. 25.   A SCARAB AND RING.

Left: Side view of the scarab beetle, represented as walking.
Center: The scarab mounted as the bezel of a ring, and pivoted to turn on its axis.
Right: Scarab turned to show the signet—in this case the name of Queen Hatshepsut "Beloved of Amon" (Dynasty XVIII)

istration whether civil or military, exercised nominally by local nobles was ultimately controlled by a royal Sheriff or "Herald," under whom worked a swarm of scribes, tax-gatherers and police. In Joseph's day the kingdom was not too large to be handled in this way, though as Egypt grew into an empire under the XVIII Dynasty, government became a bureaucracy with thousands of officials.

INVESTITURE OF A GRAND VIZIER

The first act of investiture was the presentation of a signet ring (Gen. 41:42), which was a scarab set with swivel on a band of gold. A scarab is a stone or pottery imitation of the black beetle *scarabaeus sacer* very common in Egypt. By a curious symbolism this beetle became the emblem of the sun-god in his function of creator and preserver; and by magic the sun-god was compelled to preserve whatever was inscribed on the base of the scarab. Names or other personal symbols were the most usual inscriptions, and thus the scarab could be used as a seal for stamping one's name on documents or other possessions. Kings gave validity to laws by using such a scarab seal, or conveyed authority to officials by giving them a ring on which royal insignia were engraved. A king had to have as many scarabs as he had responsible officials. In king Tutankhamen's tomb over 2000 rings were discovered. When therefore the Pharaoh gave a ring to Joseph, he was not presenting him with a gewgaw to please his vanity, but was empowering him to do business in the king's name; it was giving him complete royal authority (Fig. 25). Babylonian kings used cylinder seals for the same purpose (Dan. 6:17; Esther 8:8).

Robes and ornaments came next, distinctive of his high office. The garments were of linen, for the Egyptian despised wool and had not discovered cotton or silk. Linen manufacture had reached an unbelievable degree of perfection—540 warp threads to the inch and 110 woof threads. Weavers could make linen cloth as fine as silk. Not only have we pictures of this diaphanous material (Fig. 26) but actual samples have survived.

Decoration with gold chains or gold collars was the usual way of rewarding officers who pleased the king. They were sometimes thrown down to the recipient by the king himself from his throne or given to servants to distribute (Fig. 27). This distinctive honor was called "receiving gold." The cloth was plain white but necessary color was added by embroidered fittings, by elaborate collars of semi-precious stones and by an abundance of jewelry of which the gold chain placed about Joseph's neck was an example.

A chariot was a necessary accompaniment to high office. It was not used in Egypt before the coming of the Hyksos kings, nor were there horses in Egypt previous to that time. But henceforth chariots were the symbols of the conquering race and their use was limited to the king, the vizier, the army generals and a few other ranking officials. Surviving specimens show that the woods of which chariots were made came from the Asiatic homelands of the Hyksos people, namely, stone-oak, ash, hornbeam, and white birch bark. These trees do not grow south of forty

FIG. 26. DRESS OF A ROYAL LADY.

She wears a huge wig of black human hair and sheep's wool over her plaited natural hair. Around the top is a fillet of cobras with hoods expanded. The necklace consists of three rows of semi-precious stones. The garment is a single piece of exceedingly fine linen, pleated into a chevron pattern behind. The edge in front is fringed.

degrees of latitude; the nearest supply would be the Trans-Caucasus (Armenia) (Fig 28).

THE PHARAOH

At the head of this great hierarchy stood the Pharaoh. While the Hyksos kings under whom Joseph served were foreigners, they were shrewd enough quickly to adopt the language, the insignia and the social organization of the hereditary rulers of Egypt. A Pharaoh took his legitimacy from his wife, who must be a daughter of the preceding pharaoh. Though usually he was the pharaoh's son and consequently a brother or half-brother of his wife, by a fiction of the priests he was said to be the physical son of Ra the sun god. Accordingly the title "Son of Ra" was always prefixed to the cartouche or oval containing his individual or birth name. In addition he had a throne name given to him at his accession, to which were often prefixed several titles indicative of his state, such as "Lord of both Lands," "Lord of the Diadems" . One title, however, was always used, "King of Upper and Lower Egypt" . The two chief names of, say, the Hyksos king Khian (or Khayan), XVI Dynasty, under whom Joseph may have served, would read like this:

S-USER-EN-RAꞐ,   son of the Sun,   KHAYAN.

The king had three other names that need not concern us here.

HIS DRESS

The king had various crowns which were suitable for different state occasions. When officiating before gods of the southern kingdom, or personally appearing in the south, he would wear

Fig. 27.   IKHNATON DISTRIBUTING GIFTS TO HIS VIZIER EYE
AND WIFE.

The king leans from his cushioned balustrade and throws down gold collars, rings and
other valuable ornaments to his Vizier. The queen and three daughters assist. Above is
the emblem of Aton, the solar disc whose rays terminate in human hands and present,
the "key of life" to their majesties' noses.

the crown of Upper Egypt ⟋ ; when officiating in northern

temples, this fact would be indicated by the crown of Lower

Egypt. ⟍ ; or at mixed functions at his capital attended by

priests and officials of all Egypt, a combination of the two, the double crown, would be demanded . For symbolic evidence of his priesthood in various temples, he would assume a complex crown such as some particular god wore . His undress head-covering might be a pleated linen cloth that pro-

FIG. 28. AN EGYPTIAN CHARIOT.

An XVIII Dynasty chariot belonging to Yuya, father-in-law to Amenhotep III, and therefore measurably like one that a vizier would use. One mounts from the rear; the master then stands at the left in front of the little screen, the driver at the right. Frame of wood covered with embossed and gilded leather; floor a woven matting in lieu of springs; wooden wheels; leather tires. Since the chariot is smaller than usual it was probably made just as a part of the funerary equipment.

jected on the sides after the fashion of the well-known Sphinx's, or a balloon-shaped cap studded with gold or electrum ornaments. His head was shaved in order to accommodate readily all

FIG. 29. PHARAOH'S DRESS.

Seti I (XIX Dynasty) is here represented offering incense in his temple at Abydos. He wears a negligee cap with ribbon behind, a multiple necklace, a sheer skirt that clearly shows his legs. A kilt decorated with feathers and two serpents hangs in front.

these and many other crowns and elaborate wigs. In addition, he always wore on his forehead a golden cobra with expanded hood, symbol of the power of life and death wielded by the king.

As for garments, they were innumerable, one for each separate function of state or social occasion. In general they were scant, thin, and often translucent (Fig. 29). Broad jeweled collars, bracelets and earrings adorned the pharaoh on state occasions. On the arm of Tut-ankh-amen were found thirteen bracelets, and not only the quantity but the excellence of his jewelry is astonishing.

The Royal Palace

Almost no royal residences have survived. A pharaoh seldom occupied the palace of his father, but built a new one on a fresh site. This was easily done because all houses, even the king's, were built of mud brick. Valuable stone foundations, pillars and structural timber, if any, would be appropriated for the new work. The only good sample of a palace now existing is that of Ramses III, XX Dynasty, whose connection with Bible events is his defeat of the Sea Peoples, including the Philistines, off the coast of Syria in 1185 B.C. His palace stood within fortress walls and lay adjacent to the huge temple of Amon which is known as Medinet Habu at Thebes (Fig. 30). This palace was probably much more pretentious than that of Joseph's Pharaoh, but suggests the general idea. It is more like the one Moses saw at Tanis.

Priests and Temples

Gods like kings had to be served: they needed a house to live in, clothes to wear, food to eat, adoration and entertainment; and priests were servants who supplied all these things. As ritual developed under their hands, the priests grew in numbers and in differentiated functions until there was a vast hierarchy of them, rivalling the hierarchy of the crown, and an army of scribes, taxgatherers, farmers and slaves, to work and administer the god's

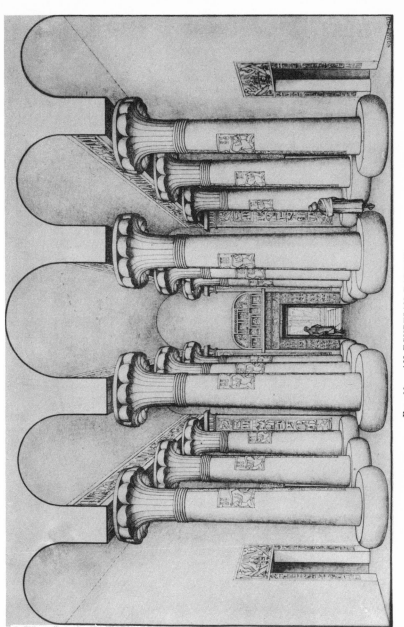

FIG. 30. AN EGYPTIAN PALACE.

This is the audience room of Ramses III (XIX Dynasty) in his palace at Medinet Habu,
Thebes. Bases, columns and palm capitals are of stone, the barrel vaults are of brick.

vast estates, which at one time embraced a third of the kingdom. The Bible story indicates that the temple lands were free from taxation, as from archaeological sources we know they were. In Joseph's day the city of On [3] was the center of the cult of Ra, and its priests were held in the highest possible respect. The king could confer no greater social honor on Joseph than to give him as wife the daughter of the priest of On (Gen. 41 :45).

Of the temples extant in Joseph's day we have hardly a trace. This is due partly to the war of expulsion waged against the Hyksos by Ahmose I and the vengeance wreaked on all they left behind; partly also to the fact that later kings had a way of using the buildings of former kings as quarries from which to get ready-cut stone for their own enterprises. But since the theory that underlay the service of the gods remained unchanged, the temple building would tend to remain constant in form through the years. We may safely say that a typical temple built by Joseph's Pharaoh would consist of the following (Fig. 31) : (1) A girdle wall of mud brick large enough to enclose not only the temple but the cluster of houses in which the priests lived. All the space within this wall was sacred to the god. (2) The stone girdle wall of the temple proper. The front section of this wall was pierced by a lofty portal flanked by two towers called pylons. Portal and pylons occupied the entire width of this inner enclosure. Passing through the portal one came to (3) an open court on two sides of which were colonnades surmounted by a flat roof. These furnished a grateful shade were priests might stroll and processions form. Straight ahead lay the temple proper (4) not touching the stone girdle wall at any point. Stout pillars on the façade supported the architrave and invited one to enter the cool shadows within. A pillared hall came next (5), beyond which was sometimes another similar but smaller one, or a series of vestibules, adding to the impressiveness of the approach. Finally a series of chambers (6) in which the treasure of the god was stored, together with the equipment for worship, processionals,

[3] Modern Heliopolis, 6 miles northeast of Cairo.

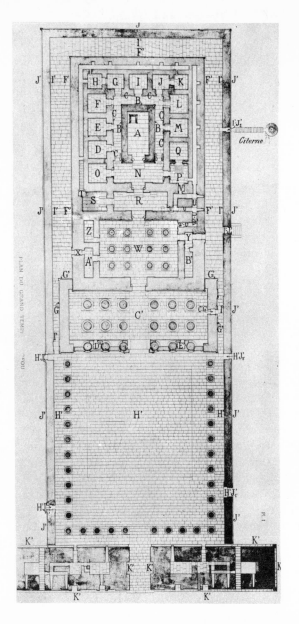

FIG. 31. PLAN
OF A TYPICAL
EGYPTIAN
TEMPLE (EDFU).

J′ The girdle wall

K′ The two towers
or pylons that
flank the entrance

H′ The fore-court
surrounded by
colonnades

F′, G′ The temple
proper, structur-
ally independent

G′ The first vestibule

W The second ves-
tibule

D-Q Service and
storage rooms sur-
rounding the
shrine

A The shrine or resi-
dence chamber of
the god

Not shown are the
out-buildings and
priests' quarters, to-
gether with the brick
girdle wall that en-
closed both them and
the temple.

etc. In the center of these rooms was the shrine, (7) usually cut from a single piece of stone. It was fitted with bronze doors and contained a statue or emblem of the god usually resting on a portable shrine or on a boat. Quite literally the god "dwells in thick darkness" (1 Kgs. 8:12–13). It is easy to see that Solomon's temple at Jerusalem was built with a similar theory of worship in mind.

EGYPTIAN BELIEFS AND PRACTICES

There are several features of Egyptian life that seem to have had a tremendous influence on rich and poor alike and that color vividly the Joseph story. One of these is a belief that dreams are significant. It has taken thirty-five centuries for psychology in the person of Freud and others to reach the same conclusion. The dreams of the butler, baker and Pharaoh express their subconscious wishes or fears in the imagery of their everyday life; but the imagery is a disguise and needs to be explained to the dreamer (Gen. 40:1–23; 41:1–8). To interpret these dreams and to furnish guidance in all important matters there grew up a class of Wise Men and of Magicians—wise men who dealt in the maxims of experience, magicians who dealt in occult powers. Throughout antiquity, Egypt was famous for both. Her wisdom has come down to us, some of it from the First Dynasty, accumulating like a snowball as it rolled through the generations, finding at intervals various names of sages to whom it attached itself. We still have for example the *Instructions of Ptah-hotep* in a papyrus of the XI Dynasty, the *Instructions of Ke'gemni*, the *Maxims of Ani*, and several others. In our Book of Proverbs the compiler has been strongly influenced by a selection from the *Wisdom of Amen-ope* (Prov. 22:17–24:22).

If a wise man had more than a local reputation he would be attached to the court. Magicians were to be found on every corner; in fact, magic underlay the entire thinking of the Egyptians, permeated all their life, found embodiment in all Egyptian art, and bridged the chasm of death to operate in the underworld.

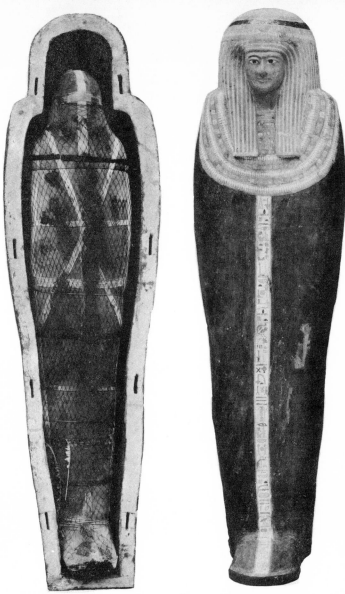

FIG. 32. A MUMMY (*left*)

This shows merely the outer wrappings. A royal mummy would have in addition **the** brilliant outer coating of plaster of Paris gilded and inlaid.

FIG. 33. AN INNER COFFIN (*right*)

The cover is painted and inscribed. One or more square boxes originally enclosed **it.** Joseph's coffin would be comparable.

The court of every Pharaoh had a battery of magicians, and what they could do was marvelous! Stories of their exploits are found in a XVII Dynasty papyrus now in Berlin. In one of them a magician cut off a goose's head, placed it at one side of a court-yard and the body at the other; then to the recital of his hocus-pocus the two parts hopped rhythmically towards each other, joined properly, and the goose went off cackling.

The physicians of Egypt (Gen. 50:1–3) were also famed throughout the ancient world. Seven hundred years later than Joseph's time, Homer could say, "Such cunning drugs had Helen, drugs of a healing virtue, which Polydamna gave, the wife of Thon in Egypt, where the fruitful soil yields drugs of every kind. . . . There everyone is a physician, skilful beyond humankind." [4] This was because the civilization of Egypt with all its arts had been continuous for many centuries; and though the physicians were not embalmers, except in the Joseph story, because of that art the Egyptians had a truer understanding of the human body than did any other people. The usual job of the physician was to heal and to beautify, to accomplish both of which a knowledge of magic was necessary. Their *materia medica* included powders and decoctions made from sycamore figs, dates and other fruits, the piths of certain trees, salt, oil, magnesia, honey and sweet beer; often mixed with such unpleasant ingredients as rancid fat, bone dust and the droppings of animals. Here for example is a prescription for inflammation of the eye: "Parts: 1 myrrh, 1 'Great Protector's' seed, 1 oxide of copper, 1 citron pips, 1 north-ern cypress flowers, 1 antimony, 1 gazelle's droppings, 1 oryx offal, 1 white oil. Place in water, let it stand overnight, strain through a cloth and paint it on the eye four days with a goose feather." Physicians please take notice!

EMBALMING

In the early dynasties there was no embalming; bodies were allowed to dry up. In the XI and XII Dynasties and presumably

[4] *Odyssey* iv: 227–231.

FIG. 34. AN "ANSWERER."

This little figurine has been impregnated with magic and placed in the tomb with his deceased master. His function is to do work of any kind and so spare his master that trouble. When he hears the call he is supposed to answer, "Here am I"—hence his name, "ushebti" or "answerer". He is made of pottery, has a green glaze with certain details set off in brown: wig, necklace, a hoe in each hand, a woven basket on his back, and an inscription down his front which reads: "Enlightenment (a) of the Osiris (b), the Royal Scribe of the Lord of the Two Lands (c), Pentaur (d)."

(a) "Enlightenment" means in this context "words of instruction." It is the first word of the usual inscription on a ushebti, calling upon him to serve the dead. All the rest of the formula is here omitted to save space. We should read, "Enlightenment, etc. . . . (you know the rest) . . ."

(b) A deceased person is spoken of as "the Osiris" because of his supposed incorporation with Osiris, the god of resurrection. We should say, "the late (Mr. Pentaur)."

(c) The deceased whom this ushebti is supposed to serve belonged to the court of the Pharaoh, one of whose many titles was "Lord of the Two Lands," i.e., of Upper and Lower Egypt. His work was no doubt like that of the scribe described in this chapter.

(d) Pentaur is the name of the deceased. It means "He of Taur(et)"; and Tauret was a hippopotamus goddess. Egyptian, like Biblical, names often contained the name of a god, as Elijah, or Meri-Baal.

(Translation supplied by Dr. John A. Wilson, Director of the Oriental Institute, Univ. of Chicago.)

through the Hyksos period, bodies were prepared with salt and soda (natron), while in the XVIII Dynasty myrrh and spices were added; in fact, after the various organs of the body had been removed, all the cavities were filled with gums and other preservatives such as the Ishmaelite caravan brought from Gilead (Gen. 37:25). The limbs and the rest of the body were wound with yards of linen bandages beginning with each digit separately. Amulets to protect and to give special powers were placed at proper positions in the swathing and sometimes a papyrus roll of the *Book of the Dead,* a kind of guidebook to the underworld, was placed between the legs. In the case of kings and other important persons a coating of white stucco was spread over the whole, engraved with suitable hieroglyphics, covered with gold leaf and varnished. The body was thus hermetically sealed in a work of art. But Jacob's mummy probably looked more like Fig. 32. Though the author of the Joseph-saga does not specify what method was used with Jacob's body, he does give fairly accurately the time consumed by the process. In the later days of the art's perfection forty days were usual, while the period of mourning extended to seventy (Gen. 50:3). When Joseph died (Gen. 50:26) he would naturally receive a more elaborate mummification than Jacob, since he was a Vizier; and for burial in Egypt he would have several coffins nested into one another; first, one or more wooden coffins following the shape of the mummy, and then two or three rectangular wooden coffins enclosing these. The inner anthropoid coffin or mummy-case would look like Fig. 33, while the outer rectangular wooden coffins would be painted to resemble a house, with painted offerings for the deceased and extracts from the *Book of the Dead.*

Placed with the body in a rock-cut tomb there would be an equipment for him to use in the future life: furniture, clothing, jewelry, food and drink, a chariot, a number of magic servants about six inches high ("answerers") (Fig. 34) and whatever Joseph loved to use in this life. Any one who is interested will find a complete description of a royal burial in the three volumes,

The Tomb of Tut-ankh-amen by H. Carter and A. C. Mace. Joseph's equipment, though much less costly and extensive, would be similar.

EGYPTIAN WRITING

Certain features of Egyptian life, though not specifically mentioned in the story, are necessarily implied. We shall therefore

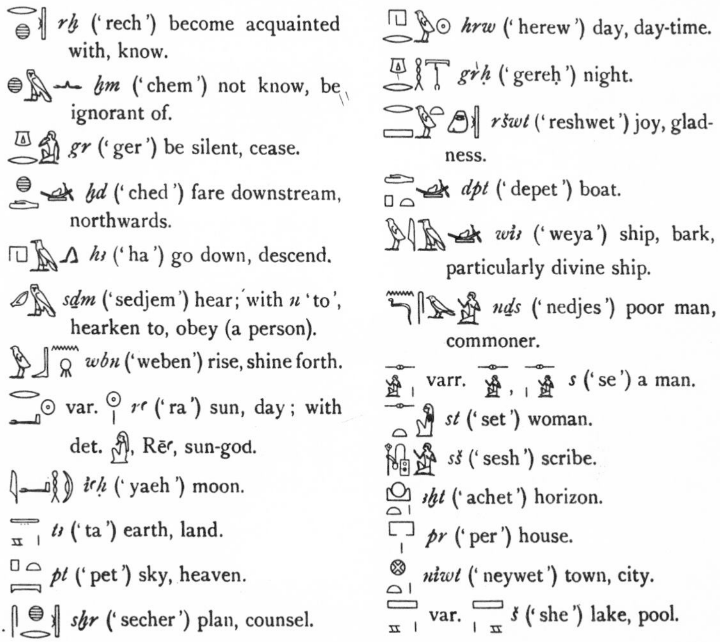

rḫ ('rech') become acquainted with, know.

ḫm ('chem') not know, be ignorant of.

gr ('ger') be silent, cease.

ḫd ('ched') fare downstream, northwards.

hɜ ('ha') go down, descend.

sḏm ('sedjem') hear; with *n* 'to', hearken to, obey (a person).

wbn ('weben') rise, shine forth.

var. *rʿ* ('ra') sun, day; with det. Rēʿ, sun-god.

iʿḥ ('yaeh') moon.

tɜ ('ta') earth, land.

pt ('pet') sky, heaven.

sḫr ('secher') plan, counsel.

hrw ('herew') day, day-time.

grḥ ('gereḥ') night.

ršwt ('reshwet') joy, gladness.

dpt ('depet') boat.

wiɜ ('weya') ship, bark, particularly divine ship.

nḏs ('nedjes') poor man, commoner.

varr. *s* ('se') a man.

st ('set') woman.

sš ('sesh') scribe.

iḫt ('achet') horizon.

pr ('per') house.

niwt ('neywet') town, city.

var. *š* ('she') lake, pool.

FIG. 35.   EGYPTIAN HIEROGLYPHICS.

The characters are made up of living things and inanimate objects or parts of them. Easily recognizable are an owl, seated man, hand, boat, hawk, chicken, lower leg, arm and hand, feather. In a regular text the signs are arranged in small rectangular groups which can easily be composed in a vertical or horizontal direction.

examine some of them. Every one knows the appearance of Egyptian hieroglyphics, perhaps the most picturesque and decorative writing ever devised. Its origin goes back to pre-dynastic times. Originally it was pure picture-writing; then the characters came to stand for syllables, and finally to a certain extent for letters, thus duplicating the evolution of cuneiform. This kind of writing, as its name implies ("sacred engraved writing"), was used only for inscriptions on temples, tombs, sepulchral stelae and monuments in general. The characters may be written horizontally or vertically, to be read from left to right or the reverse, depending on which way the animals and birds face (read toward their faces). At best it is a cumbersome language, as a glance at Fig. 35 will show. To facilitate quick writing on papyrus, the scribes developed an abbreviated script form of hieroglyphic known as hieratic, or "priests' writing." This was extensively used from Dynasty V (2700 B.C.) onward in copying literary works. In the ninth century B.C. a still further simplification took place called demotic; but this does not enter our picture. The forms used in the time of Joseph and Moses were hieroglyphic and hieratic. Joseph kept his accounts in the latter.

Let us look on while Joseph dictates his weekly report of grain stored in the city of Pithom.

Clapping his hands, the Vizier summons a scribe—a man of the lower class but intelligent, well schooled and experienced. The scribe is dressed merely in a short linen kilt. At his waist is slung his kit of writing materials. He seats himself cross-legged on the floor before Joseph, spreads his papyrus roll on his lap, places his ink pot beside him, selects a reed pen with a fine point, and looks up for the dictation to begin (Fig. 36). While Joseph is arranging his own notes, we may take a look at the equipment.

First, the palette, a wooden case in which he keeps his pens. It is rectangular, from 8 to 16 inches long and from 2 to 3 broad. Down the middle runs a groove, sloping at one end. The pens are inserted here, usually as many as ten; they are held in place by a piece of wood glued across the groove about half way, or by a sliding cover that protects the pens from injury. At one end is sunk an oval hollow, or sometimes a dozen or more hollows, to

Fig. 36. A SCRIBE.

This is one of the masterpieces of Old Kingdom sculpture (V Dynasty, c. 2700 B.C.).
The scribe sits cross-legged, spreads the papyrus roll in his lap, in his right hand holds
the reed brush, and looks up at his master to catch his first words.

hold ink or paint. As we look, the scribe fills one of these holes from the reservoir—the ink pot. Most palettes have two holes for red and black. Extra holes are for more ink or for different colors (Fig. 37).

Scribe Kaï picks up a pen. It is about ten inches long, made of a round reed about an eighth of an inch in diameter. We are surprised to find that one end of the reed has been bruised; it is not a pen at all, but a brush. The ink pot is made of faience (pottery) and the ink is a mixture of colored earths or minerals or vegetable dyes mixed with gum and water. The paper is made from the cellular pith of the papyrus plant that at that time grew luxuriantly in the marshes. Stalks that often reach a height of 20 feet or more are cut into strips. These are placed side by side horizontally until the total height is about 10 inches; then a series of 10-inch strips is laid on these vertically with gum arabic paste between. When pressed and dried .and pumiced, the sheets give a smooth, flexible surface that takes ink without spreading. Sheets are pasted together horizontally into strips of any desired length. The longest known specimen measures 135 feet. When written upon this sheet becomes a "papyrus"—the universal form for literary works in Egypt. It is rolled up and tied with a string. When written and illustrated with colored pictures by an expert scribe, a papyrus is a beautiful work of art.

Joseph begins to speak. Kaï dips his brush and writes with amazing swiftness and precision.

THE SCRIBE

Kaï arouses our interest so much that we make inquiry about him of the doorkeeper. We find that he comes from the artisan class: his father is a goldsmith, who, finding that his son has a taste for learning, used the influence of one of his aristocratic customers to get the boy admitted to a government school in the treasury department. There he learned both hieroglyphic and hieratic, then mathematics, accounts, business forms and model letters. It was a stiff school. The sessions began about sunrise and

FIG. 37.   A SCRIBAL PALETTE.

Egyptian scribal outfit of the first dynasty or later consisting
of a slate palette with restored water jug and a brush case.

lasted till noon; the chief incentive to learning and diligence was the stick. Lunch was served in the morning—three bread cakes and two jugs of beer, brought to the school by the boy's mother. When the master announced closing-time, according to a papyrus in the British Museum, "the pupils left the school with cries of joy."

Mastery of the curriculum fitted Kaï for almost any office in the civil administration. And now having reached middle life he finds himself private secretary to the Vizier. Look again at his face (Fig. 36) and you will discover the qualities that put him at the head of his profession—intelligence, alertness, discipline. In fact, his master was so well pleased with him that he wished to put a mortgage on his services for the next world, and so had this limestone statue made of him, impregnated with magic, and ordered it buried in his own tomb. Then he was sure of a good stenographer throughout eternity!

Kaï's father might have sent his son to a temple school. In that case his studies would have included besides writing, the copying and interpretation of religious texts in both characters, legends of the gods, funerary texts and the like. With this education he would have become a priest. In either case he would have made his way in the world, for the profession of scribe was honorable. Says an old Egyptian poem in praise of learning, "There is not an employment without a superior one except the Scribe, who is first." To be a scribe was the ambition of every poor boy with brains, and happy indeed was he when he could write after his name the hieroglyphic that combined the pen, ink bottle and palette slung together 𓏞 𓏛.

All of this material is woven into the story of Joseph so skilfully that we cannot escape one conclusion: the writer knew Egypt. Checking up on the details by means of the extant monuments and literature we find that each one is corroborated in some specific way. Egypt itself is the best commentary on the life that is unfolded in the saga.

Fig. 38. TEMPLE OF RAMSES II AT ABU SIMBEL.

This temple was cut from the solid mountain. Four giant portrait statues of Ramses adorn the façade, the temple entrance placed between each pair. A rock slide sheared off the head of number two. The temple is in Nubia nearly a thousand miles from the Mediterranean.

LIFE IN THE TIME OF MOSES

If we only knew what was the time of Moses![5]

Following the opinion of many competent scholars, we shall assume that Moses lived in the days of Ramses II and his successor Merneptah or perhaps Seti II. According to the account in Ex. 2:1–10, Moses was born a slave in Egypt but by an extraordinary turn of fortune became a prince. As such, he would have received the finest education possible (Acts 7:22), which involved the mastery of the learning and skill of the scribe, training in executive matters, and if Josephus is to be trusted, a military training as well.[6] He was familiar, then, with the court of Ramses II which in all essential ways was like that of previous kings already sketched above.

The Ramses of Moses' childhood and young manhood was primarily a self-advertiser and a builder. His long reign of 67 years gave him time to spread himself, with the result that his cartouches are blazoned on most of the extant monuments of Egypt. Either he built new buildings or restored or enlarged old ones. The great Hypostyle Hall at Karnak, for example, begun by his grandfather, continued by his father Seti but left unfinished at his death, was completed by Ramses; so also were Seti's mortuary temples at Thebes and Abydos. Original with him was the grand rock-cut temple at Abu Simbel far to the south, one of the most impressive shrines of the Old World (Fig. 38); his own mortuary temple at Abydos and an enlargement of the temple at Luxor. Far to the very north he built anew the old Hyksos city of Tanis (modern San el-Hagar) which he renamed after himself —the very city referred to in Exodus 1:11 (*cf.* Fig. 19). According to the remains excavated only a few years ago, Tanis was a monumental seaport city. Not only did Ramses build a magnificent temple but he placed before it a statue of himself

---

[5] Full discussion of data and theories is given by H. H. Rowley: "Israel's Sojourn in Egypt," in the *Bulletin of the John Rylands Library,* Apr. 1938.

[6] *Antiquities* II, 10.

made of a single piece of granite 90 feet high and weighing 900 tons! Fourteen obelisks he also erected in this city at different times. Since Tanis was the civic capital of Egypt during most of

Find two men getting water in jars from a pool (see the lilies); two men mixing the mud; a carrier; a man making bricks in a mould; a man laying the bricks in rows; a man mending his hoe.

Find two task-masters with sticks (Ex. 1:11; 5:14); men carrying and depositing mud; two men carrying dried bricks with a yoke; one returning with empty yoke.

Fig. 39.   BRICK-MAKING IN EGYPT.

this reign, Thebes serving as the religious capital, and since this is adjacent to Goshen, the land of bondage, we shall not be far wrong if we place here the activities of Moses.

SLAVERY

All this phenomenal building was in process while Moses was growing up. He not only saw it and was impressed by it, as we

are today, but he realized with indignation that the toiling slaves
who did the work under the taskmaster's lash were his brothers

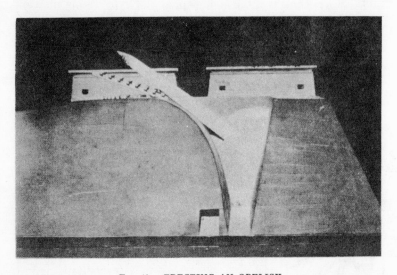

Fig. 40.   ERECTING AN OBELISK.

In front of the temple pylons where the obelisk is to stand, two huge piles of earth are
raised, leaving a well over the granite base placed to receive the huge shaft. The well is
now filled with sand. Up the bank from the left the obelisk is drawn, cradled on a
wooden sled with rollers beneath. When the butt of the obelisk overhangs the near wall of
the well, the lashings that hold the sled are cut and the base of the shaft is allowed to
rest on the sand. The sand is then withdrawn from the well by way of a small chamber
to the left of the bottom, and as the sand settles, the shaft sinking with it gradually
assumes a vertical position and finally rests squarely on the base.

(Ex. 2:11–12). The slaves did all kinds of work (Ex. 1:13–14),
but the making of bricks is particularly mentioned (Ex. 5:6–19);
and quite specifically they are said to have built the two delta
cities of Pithom and Ramses (Ex. 1:11). Fortunately we have
contemporary pictures or records that enable us to visualize these
processes. Though the temples themselves were built of stone, the
subsidiary buildings for the storage of temple revenues, products
of the land, were of brick, as were the houses of the priests built
within the girdle wall of the sacred precinct, and the wall itself.

Fig. 41.   INSCRIPTION OF THE OBELISK OF SESOSTRIS I
AT HELIOPOLIS.

Down the center of each face is a long line of deeply incised hieroglyphics.
Did Moses, like Plato, attend the university here (Acts 7:22)?

So there was enough to keep thousands of slaves busy. (Fig. 39).

Brick-making was the least objectionable of slaves' tasks. When Moses inspected the limestone quarries at Turra or the sandstone quarries at Gebel Silsileh or the granite quarries at Aswan, he found his Hebrews there also.[7] Then he began to realize what slavery meant. There human muscle did all the work that today is done by machinery; and the blocks cut out by these sweating, groaning slaves, far exceeded in weight anything handled in this day. Under a blazing sun, in a hole in the rock that quivered in the reverberating heat, with the dread hippopotamus-whip lash of the overseer cracking on the backs of those about to faint or die, Moses saw them cut out a thousand-ton block, put rollers under it, and with long ropes at which hundreds of men pulled and with levers to ease the mass along, drag it over a stone road-bed to the quay, and transfer it to a barge huge enough to carry it. Then he saw another set of slaves begin the 750-mile voyage to Tanis, the unwieldy barge towed by a dozen crews in boats and steered by other boats attached to the stern. At the destination the unloading, and miracle of all, the up-ending of the great block on its foundation called for a high quality of brain and a mastery of engineering principles (Fig. 40). How many thousand slaves died in the process—from sunstroke, exhaustion, beatings, crushings under unmanageable blocks of stone—no one will ever know. When today we look at the thousand-ton colossus lying on its back at the Ramesseum at Thebes, we think of it as a marvel of cunning workmanship; Moses saw it as a symbol of torture and death.

CRAFTS

Men as able as the Hebrews could not be kept down to merely muscular tasks. We know from Exodus 5:14 that the gang-foremen of the Hebrews were themselves Hebrews, and with such a demand for skilled labor many slaves must have risen to the pro-

[7] So Josephus, *Against Apion,* I. 26, quoting Manetho.

fessional class. Moses saw his countrymen engaged in decorating obelisks with superb hieroglyphics (Fig. 41), in sculpturing the reliefs with which every foot of every temple wall, pillar and architrave, was adorned; inlaying the copper doors with silver-gold metal (electrum); or making the thousand and one objects demanded by the ritual and by the physical service of the gods. These artist-slaves were too valuable to be whipped to death. No doubt they found life fairly pleasant, and when the rabble left the house of bondage under Moses' leadership they stayed behind. There were plenty of Hebrews in Egypt after the Exodus, as we know from the inscription of Ramses IV in the Wady Hamma-mat c. 1160 B.C.

This life of hardship in Egypt left an indelible impression upon the Hebrews. While it is probable that only a single tribe was enslaved, the memory of suffering coupled with the religion of Yahweh which this tribe adopted in the wilderness was trans-mitted by missionary zeal to all the kindred tribes in Palestine and under the teaching of the prophets was turned into a motivation for social justice:

You must remember that you were once a slave yourself in the land of Egypt (Deut. 5:15; 15:15; 16:12; 24:18, 22).

CHAPTER V

THEY THAT GO DOWN TO THE SEA

AT FIRST GLANCE one might think that shipping had little place in the life of Bible times, for the Israelites were not sailors. Palestine had no navigable rivers—only the crooked Jordan that could not compare with a camel as means of transportation. Of its lakes one was useless and the other seems not to have been used until late. The Mediterranean sea coast was not possessed by Israelites until the days of the Maccabees, c. 144 B.C., and had it been, the scarcity of harbors would have discouraged any attempt to exchange life on land for the doubtful gains of voyaging. To the Israelites the sea was a mystery like the judgments of God (Ps. 36:6), and the finest picture they have given us of it represents the terror of storm and the thankfulness of deliverance (Ps. 107:23-32; Jonah 1).

Nevertheless life in Israel was influenced by the sea. On the shores of the Mediterranean grew up the Canaanite civilization that was nourished always by a sea-borne commerce and that gave to the Israelites the earliest culture they knew. Along its coasts came and went the navies of great powers that helped shape Israelitish history and destiny. Out of it came from the west the sea peoples who made life miserable for them in the days of the Judges, and the Philistines who harried them through the books of Samuel. And later the triremes of Greece and the quinquiremes and merchant galleys of Rome brought culture and wealth, conquest and oppression and destruction. Except for one brief period in Solomon's day the sailor folk and the ships we shall consider are all foreign.

MESOPOTAMIAN CRAFT

Shipping began on the great rivers of Mesopotamia and Egypt. The most primitive form of boat was the raft. The Assyrian reliefs picture for us the little platforms floated on inflated skins and riding high enough to keep the cargo from getting wet. (Fig. 42). A variant on this is something that resembles the ship of the Three Wise Men of Gotham : a circular frame of wood or reeds covered with skins and then painted with bitumen. While such a bowl-contraption looks unmanageable—one wonders how it can

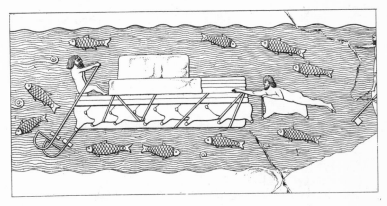

FIG. 42.   ASSYRIAN RAFT.
The raft consists of inflated skins placed together to support
a platform on which men and cargo can ride.

be steered—it has nevertheless persisted on the Tigris from As- syrian days to the present. On coracles like these the Israelite exile at Haleh brough his grain down to the nearest river-port whence it could be shipped to the Nebo-temple in Sargonsburg.

By Abraham's time large river and seagoing ships had been evolved. Practically all transportation within the alluvium was by water, on river and canal. We have record of a voyage made a little before his time from the island of Bahrein in the Persian

Gulf to Lagash on the great Shatt-el-Hai canal—a run of over six hundred miles; and the bill of lading of a sea ship that c. 2040 B.C. had come up to Ur from the Persian Gulf after a two-year cruise: it brought copper ore, gold, ivory, hard wood for the cabinetmakers, diorite and alabaster for the sculptors. Not all of these articles came from the shores of the Gulf but had been brought by other vessels from distant parts, and transshipped.

But the greatest evidence of the use of boats in Abraham's day comes from the Code of Hammurabi. Ten sections deal with shipping, of which the following are most interesting:

Sec. 235. If a shipbuilder builds a boat for a man and he does not make its construction seaworthy, and that boat develops structural weakness the same year and has an accident, the shipbuilder shall mantle that boat and he shall strengthen it at his own expense and he shall give the strengthened boat to the owner of the boat.

Sec. 237. If a man hires a boatman and a boat and loads it with grain, wool, oil, dates or any other kind of freight, and that boatman is careless and sinks the boat or loses its cargo, the boatman shall replace the boat which he sank and whatever portion of the cargo he lost.

Sec. 277. If a man hires a boat of 60 GUR tonnage, he shall pay 1/6 of a shekel of silver as its hire per day.

Sec. 240. If a boat going up or down stream strikes a boat going across stream and sinks it, the owner of the sunk boat shall establish before god what was lost in his boat and (the owner) of the striking boat shall replace that boat and whatever was lost.[1]

It sounds quite modern—fixed tariffs, traffic regulations, legal penalties on the Euphrates 4000 years ago!

EGYPTIAN CRAFT

The earliest river-craft in Egypt was made of bundles of papyrus reeds bound together so as to make a stem and a stern. Actual wooden boats also have survived from Pyramid days, 2800

[1] R. F. Harper: *The Code of Hammurabi*, Chicago, 1904.

Fig. 43.   EGYPTIAN RIVER BOAT.

One of eighteen found in the tomb of Tut-Ankh-Amen. This crescent-shaped keelless craft is fit only for smooth water. In the prow (right) and in the stern are small pavilions where the king may sit and enjoy the scenery. In the center is the King's cabin. Steering is done by the two huge paddles lashed to steering posts. Their tops are ornamented with human heads wearing crowns to show that this is a royal boat. A single mast holds a square sail that is bent onto an upper and a lower yard. The hull is brightly painted, mostly with checkerboard designs. No rowers or steersmen are needed in this case, for the boat is propelled by magic.

B.C. They were shaped as our boats are; the planks were held together with dowels inserted in the plank's edge, and with cramps that bound the planks together end to end. There were no ribs and only a few thwarts. Joseph used some such boat when he made his inspection tours up and down Egypt. In fact, the tomb of Tut-ankh-amen has yielded the model of just such a craft complete in every detail (Fig. 43).

Such boats might stand the gentle pressure of the Nile, but never the sea. When about 1490 B.C. Queen Hatshepsut sent her famous venture from Thebes through the Red Sea to the land of Punt (Abyssinia) she used a strongly constructed craft of considerable size. The lines of the hull are long and graceful, from the prow that rises high out of the water almost like a stout bowsprit, to the much higher stern that curved up to its termination in a lotus blossom. There was one mast a little aft of center, well stayed fore and aft; a big square sail hung from a yard, and there was ample space for a deck-load and two small cabins, one in the forecastle and one in the poop. Two steering paddles hung overboard from a steering-post in the stern. In order better to stand the shocks and strains of ocean storms, the hull was strengthened with big hawsers that ran over a couple of shears and so formed a sort of truss to give rigidity (Fig. 44).

Queen Hatshepsut's son-in-law and successor, Thutmose III, used ships like these in his seventeen campaigns against Syria and Palestine in which he annihilated the last vestige of Hyksos power in those lands. By them he saved himself and his generals many a weary mile of marching. We do not know how large these ships were. A thousand years before Abraham, King Snefru of Dynasty III built ships one hundred fifty feet long, and in an Egyptian fairy-story of about Abraham's day, the ship of the "Shipwrecked Sailor" was said to be two hundred twenty-five feet long. Perhaps from these we may infer what the dimensions of an XVIII Dynasty ship would be.

The most accurate idea of ships used along the Palestine-Syrian coast in Old Testament times comes from the picture of a sea-fight sculptured on the walls of the temple of Ramses III at Medinet Habu in Thebes. This work commemorates the battle of 1190 B.C. fought just off the coast, in which Ramses attempted to break up the invasion of the sea peoples who were trying to get a foothold in Egypt, Palestine and Syria. Prominent among the enemy are the Philistines from Crete, who are here depicted as wearing an imposing head-dress of feathers (Fig. 45). While the victory of Ramses prevented their invasion of Egypt it did not prevent their conquest of all the coast lands to the north. As a consequence Deborah and Barak had to fight them on the plain of

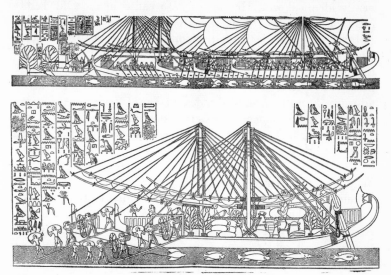

FIG. 44.   EGYPTIAN CARGO SHIPS.

These are two of Queen Hatshepsut's seagoing fleet which she sent to Punt (Somaliland?). The ships are braced with a hawser running two-thirds their length. The deck load reminds us of Solomon's cargoes—trees and apes besides gold, silver and incense in bales and jars.

Esdraelon forty years later, while Saul and Jonathan were slain by them on the heights of Gilboa not far from the year 1000 B.C. They finally became stabilized in southwestern Palestine.

PHOENICIAN CRAFT

The ships that most concerned the people of Israel were owned by the Phoenicians. This Semitic people had come in from the East with the Canaanites almost at the dawn of history, and finding the little pockets of soil at the foot of the mountains too meager for their support, took to the sea. Their first timid efforts

centered in the town called Kupna by the Egyptians who brought
from here the cedars for their ships and palaces. By the Phoenicians themselves it was called Gebal, and since their speech was
nearly identical with Hebrew, it is so called in the Old Testament (I Kgs. 5:18; Ezek. 27:9). The Greeks called it Byblos
(Map I, 149). With the destruction of Cnossos in Crete around
1400 B.C., the ultimate extinction of the Aegean civilization by
the Dorians around 1100 B.C., and the decay of the Egyptian sea-
power after Ramses III, the way was open for a Phoenician
advance. From then until the destruction of Tyre by Alexander
in 332 B.C., the Phoenicians were a dominant sea power in the
Mediterranean. They had a monopoly on the carrying trade;
their colonists dotted the shores as far as Carthage and Marseilles
and Cadiz; their fleets penetrated everywhere in search of raw
materials and markets—to the Black Sea, to the Scilly Isles off
Britain, to the Canaries; and at the instigation of the Egyptian
Pharaoh Necho, seventh century B.C., they even circumnavigated
Africa in a two-year voyage, coasting down from the Red Sea on
the east coast and returning via the strait of Gibraltar. They
certainly were an adventurous lot, expert in all matters of wind
and wave, skilled navigators and so well-disciplined that the
Greeks, with whom they ultimately fought for the supremacy of
the Mediterranean, were forced to admire them. Both their
chunky merchant vessels and the great liners—"Tarshish ships"
—were superior to those of the Greeks in equipment and speed.
The Phoenicians also kept their own secrets about routes and
harbors and thus held on to their success for many centuries. But
in the end, the Greeks took over.

In the days of the Israelite monarchy and of Assyrian supremacy on land the Phoenicians still kept control of the sea. Sometimes they had to pay a heavy "baksheesh" to Assyria for the
privilege of using ports that Assyria had conquered; but they
preferred payment and peace to war. Assyria needed their help
also. Not only did she use them to bring cedar from Lebanon to
some handy northern port like Ugarit, but she hired them to build

FIG. 45. AN EGYPTIAN-PHILISTINE SEA FIGHT.

This huge relief, contemporary with the fight itself, adorns the walls of Medinet Habu Temple at Thebes, built by Ramses III. It was fought off the coast of Palestine and Syria c. 1185 B.C. The Egyptians are here distinguished by round helmets, the Philistines by a crown of feathers, and the Sardinians by horns on their helmets (one of them is having his throat cut by a Philistine). The limp figures at the top represent bodies floating in the water beyond the ship.

boats on the Euphrates at Til Barsip (just below Carchemish, Map II, 151) to transport the timber down stream to Babylon and across to the Tigris, and even to transport troops into the marshes of lower Babylonia, as Sennacherib did. We have the provisions of a treaty between Esarhaddon of Assyria and Baal, king of Tyre: "If the ships of Baal or the men of Arvad are shipwrecked in Palestine, neither men nor property are to be seized, but they are to be sped safely on their way"; and the same is to hold true with ships belonging to Assyrian subjects.[2] But when Assyria slackened her grip on the coast-lands, Tyre knew how to take advantage of it, and she refused to admit Assyrian ships to her wharves. A certain piece of correspondence from the Assyrian financial agent at Arvad, dated 667 B.C., reads as follows: "Ikkilu [king of Arvad] will not let go the [Assyrian] ships; they cannot come to anchor at the wharf of the [Assyrian] king. Every wharf he takes for himself. Whoever comes to him, he establishes his feet [lets him enter and trade]; whoever comes to the wharf of the land of Assyria, he kills and his ship he destroys." Even the nobles of the Assyrian court have to pay blackmail to the Phoenicians to get their business transacted.[3] Assyria never did subdue Tyre. The best she could do was to besiege the city thirteen years at a stretch!

All of this enterprise and the wealth it brought made a tremendous impression upon Israel which was a sort of poor country cousin. Possibly because of actual harm done, including the introduction of foreign cults, but more likely through jealousy, the prophets are always threatening Tyre with doom (Is. 23; Ezek. 28; Joel 3:4–8; Jer. 25:17, 22; Amos 1:9–10; Zech. 9:1–4). It remained for Ezekiel to give us not only a pæan of rejoicing at the imminent downfall of Tyre, and a glowing picture of her present wealth, but a specific list of some of the places her merchants visited in the way of trade and the goods she brought from them (Ezek. 27).

[2] A. T. Olmstead: *History of Assyria*, p. 375.
[3] *Ibid.*, p. 418.

Unfortunately our data about the ships themselves are very limited. A relief of Sennacherib from Nineveh shows a Phoenician war galley of c. 700 B.C. The hull is low and cigar-shaped. It has

FIG. 46. PHOENICIAN WAR GALLEY, TIME OF SENNACHERIB
C. 700 B.C.

The ship has a long beak with which to ram the enemy. There are two banks of oars though only one line of rowers is visible between decks. The warriors are on the high top deck, their round shields hung over the side. Salt water is indicated by the crab seizing a fish.

a long straight ram in front at the water level. The super-structure is high and furnishes some protection for the seventeen (thirty-four) rowers, evidently arranged in two tiers, as well as deck-space for the warriors whose shields are hung along the sides. She apparently carries no sail, though the broken condition of the relief makes this uncertain (Fig. 46).

Another relief of Sargon II, now in the Louvre (Fig. 47), represents a freight boat bringing timber for the palace of Khorsabad. The details of the boat are obscure except that the prow and stern are very high, the former ornamented with a horse's head while the latter is a fish-tail. The rowers face front. The boat has no mast and the deck-load of logs is represented, by the usual rule of perspective, as being above the men. Each boat also tows three logs. The boats with a mast and two stays, going in the other direction, carry the government inspectors. Such a fleet brought cedars for Solomon's temple from Gebal to Joppa (2 Chron. 2:16).

From a tomb painting at Thebes comes a picture of a Phoenician merchant ship lying at the wharf at Thebes. She is round-bellied to carry a heavy cargo, and has a mast in the center that supports two spars at the top and bottom respectively of a square sail. Men are scrambling up the rigging and shouting at one another. Samples of the wares she brings are visible on deck.

With the coming of Alexander in 332 B.C., the Greek war-ships enter Palestinian waters. Previous to this date the Greeks may have made some attempts at traffic, but the Phoenicians were too strong to be trifled with. Accordingly the Greek traders and colonists sought the Black Sea and the shores of Italy, Sicily and the West. During the fight for supremacy between the Seleucid dynasty of Antioch and the Ptolemaic dynasty of Egypt that was waged intermittently in Palestine from 323–198 B.C., both contestants used Greek triremes, but Ptolemy with his fine naval base at Alexandria was able ultimately to control the sea. This fact interests us only so far as it affected his fitful rule over Palestine, or the sea-borne commerce in which Jews might be engaged.

A trireme represented the perfection of the ship-building art. She was stream-lined—long, narrow and low; her length about a hundred forty feet, her beam fourteen, and her upper deck about eleven feet above water. Her draught was slight, partly so that her crew might drag her up upon the beach almost every night. She had one large mast amidships and a smaller one near each end, though sails were merely an auxiliary, seldom used in voyaging and never in battle. Most of the interior was reserved for rowers. Running two-thirds of the length on both sides was a series of seats and foot-rests, three tiers high. The lowest man's feet were near the waterline. When he pulled his oar, his head and body swung backward between the feet of the rower behind and

a little above him. In the same way, man number two fitted into
man number three on the top row. The ancients were thoughtless
enough not to leave us any blueprints of their ships, so that we

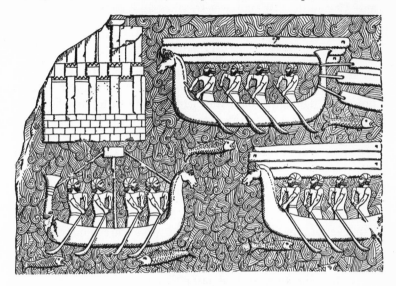

Fig. 47. PHOENICIAN FREIGHT SCOWS.

The two scows on the right are bringing cedar logs from Sidon, destined for
Sargon's palace at Khorsabad. The boat on the left carries inspectors.

are in the dark about just how the oar-benches were arranged and
how they managed the oars of three different lengths up to thirteen
feet. We have only pictures. The ship must have been crowded,
for within her narrow compass there were one hundred seventy-
four rowers, who of course had to be relieved every two hours;
besides officers, sailors and marines. The total complement must
have been not far from three hundred eighty men. The main
weapon of offense was the ship herself, which was hurled at the
foe at full speed in order to splinter his oars by a side-swipe, or
ram him broadside. For this last purpose the ship's prow was
provided with a bronze triple beak and the plank construction so

arranged as to distribute the force of the impact throughout the hull without crushing.[4]

Since in Paul's time most ship-owners and sailors were Greeks and Levantines, Roman war-triremes and merchant ships followed Greek models.

HARBORS

As long as ships were small, harbors also could be small. That was fortunate, for there are no large harbors on the Syria-Palestine coast. Though Mount Carmel thrusts its head into the sea at the southern end of a wide bay, it forms no shelter against prevailing winds. The only breakwaters that make a safe roadstead are blunt spurs of the Lebanon and allied coast-ranges, and the little islands or half-submerged reefs that at places lie off shore. The tiny ancient harbors of Gaza, Askelon, Ashdod and Jamnia had to be partly built, and they have been pounded to pieces by the sea and silted up. Jaffa harbor is made by a string of ledges a quarter of a mile long that lie about two or three hundred yards off shore, so low that the waves break over them in even a moderate sea. At Caesarea, which Herod the Great built on a virgin site thirty-two miles north of Jaffa, there was no harbor at all; so Herod built one of great blocks of stone sunk in twenty fathoms of water. At Dor and Athlit only a point of rock projects far enough to form a tiny shelter on one side or the other, and the moles made on them by the Phoenicians have long since been swallowed up. "Thus, while the cruelty of many another wild coast is known by the wrecks of ships, the Syrian shore south of Carmel is strewn with the fiercer wreckage of harbors." [5]

North of Carmel the possibilities for good harbors are more abundant. Acre was built on a genuine promontory, Tyre and

---

[4] If any reader wishes to follow the details of a sea-fight, which though imaginative are based on scholarly research, he may read Professor William Stearns Davis' account of the battle of Salamis in his novel, *A Victor of Salamis.* Informing also is the account of the life of a galley slave of Roman times in Lew Wallace's *Ben Hur,* in which the hero is a Jew.

[5] G. A. Smith: *Historical Geography of the Holy Land,* p. 131.

Sidon had little islands and reefs for shelter, Arvad was an island
which always had a lea side; and so up the coast to Ugarit there
was many a ledge or an indentation in the coast that offered a
refuge for craft under a hundred feet long.

FIG. 48. MODERN TYRE FROM THE AIR.

You are looking about west. The two curves on the north shore afford some slight
protection for craft and constituted the Sidonian harbor. In ancient times there were
probably breakwaters here. The Egyptian harbor on the south is faintly indicated by the
white lines of reefs.

But always man pieced out nature as best he could. If there
were ledges he filled in the gaps with masonry and from their
extremities he built out protecting arms to break the force of the
sea which in the winter storms is tremendous. It is not always
possible to trace this work, but a good beginning has been made
at Tyre, the most important of Phoenician ports and the most
closely connected with Israel.

Though Tyre now seems to occupy the end of a peninsula (Fig.
48), it once was an island about half a mile off shore. If one
were to dig into the sand along the backbone of that peninsula,
one would find the original mole built by the engineers of Alexander in 332 B.C. in order to bring siege-engines under the city
walls. Silt brought by currents and winds is responsible for the
growth of the wall to the present neck of land six hundred yards

broad in its narrowest place. Today there is an anchorage north
of this neck, and a smaller one south of it. These are relics of two
original harbors built in the time of its glory when Tyre was an
island, the Sidonian harbor on the north-east and the Egyptian
on the south-east. But the ancient ones were bigger than the present. While many generations of travellers have seen blocks of
stone lying on the sea-floor, not till the present century has curiosity brought about any action. During 1934–36 a Frenchman,
Father Poidebard, took aerial photographs which show the sea
bottom at greater depths and with greater detail than does the
eye at sea level; to this he added at first local sponge-divers and
then a deep-sea diver with a full modern equipment, including an
under-water camera. These revealed the fact of an ancient system
of breakwaters built out from the island on reefs or on the sea-
floor, at places fifty feet below the surface, forming an outer
roadstead and an inner harbor. There was also a northern harbor,
but this has not yet been investigated. With this equipment, so
tiny in comparison with the great harbors of modern times, Tyre
was able to send to sea hundreds of merchant craft and to gather
wealth that was the envy of the nations.

The Perils of Sea-Faring

We moderns who put to sea in the most luxurious floating
hotels that defy all the elements can hardly realize the conditions
of ancient voyaging. Except in Roman times the ships were tiny,
and that meant first of all cramped quarters that were exposed
to rain, sea and sun; restricted food, promiscuous not to say
dangerous company, seasickness and the constant danger of shipwreck. There was no compass and no chart; the pilot steered by
the sun and stars or felt his way along from headland to mountainous island, trusting to memory for the identification of land-
marks and the safe entrance to harbors. Then there were the
man-made dangers. Piracy was frightfully common—one might
almost say the rule; for the merchant was always tempted to eke
out his legitimate gains with stolen ones. To be captured by

pirates meant not only the loss of the ship's cargo but the seizure of all on board for sale into slavery. It was a common practice also to light beacon fires to lure ships onto the rocks so that they might be plundered and their crew taken as slaves.

We have seen above how dealing with petty tyrants in port cost plenty of money and sometimes life itself. But for a detailed picture of the perils of doing business by sea there is nothing to compare with the story of Wenamon, an Egyptian who went to Byblos to buy timber for the god Amon of Thebes. It is written in a papyrus of c. 1100 B.C. (time of the Biblical Samuel) and is now preserved in Moscow. It bears all the earmarks of being a true story; if it is fiction, the story-teller has merely compiled a series of incidents out of the experiences of many voyagers. It seems all the more probable when we recall that Egypt was then in a decline, and the coasts of Palestine and Syria were held by the Philistines and other sea peoples whom Ramses III had not been able to keep from settling there. The Egyptian buyer therefore was at the mercy of men who had no "fear of God." The story is too long to be retold here. Its various adventures include having Wenamon's gold and silver stolen by a fellow passenger; compensatory stealing from a stranger by Wenamon; being ordered out of Byblos harbor by the local prince; reprieve and the promise of the timber he came to buy, when fresh money came from Egypt; pursuit by ships of the sea people because of Wenamon's theft; double-crossing by the prince of Byblos; shipwreck on the island of Cyprus; danger of murder by the Cypriotes, and escape by the clever use of his tongue before the queen. We also learn that sea-captains sometimes threw overboard suspicious characters and confiscated their goods, and that several former ambassadors from Egypt had been murdered by the prince of Byblos, who used their graves to browbeat later messengers.[6]

Truly a tale of danger, treachery, thievery and inhumanity. But that was what men who went down to sea in ships had to expect in the days of Samuel.

[6] For the full story, see G. A. Barton: *Archaeology and the Bible.*

FIG. 49. GENERAL VIEW OF MEGIDDO FROM THE NORTHEAST.

This is a perfectly shaped "tell." On the terrace at the right of the mound are the buildings of the Oriental Institute that house the excavators. The little tell in the foreground is the dump for the rubbish of the diggings. Some day the mound will have been skived off layer by layer until all its secrets have been laid bare, and only the core of original rock with its prehistoric caves will remain.

CHAPTER VI

FROM NOMAD TO CITIZEN

THE HEBREWS first appear on the horizon of Palestine, or the land of Canaan as it was then called, in the early fifteenth century B.C.; and the people were not entitled to be called a nation until the time of David, c. 1000 B.C.

During this period of five hundred years occurred the process of transformation from nomad to citizen. This involved the stabilization of the tribes, the development of agriculture, of village life, of some of the skills that go with industry and trade. Contact with the more advanced Canaanites brought also revolutionary changes in point of view; the drift away from tribal organization and ethics to those of the city-state with its commercialism and class distinctions; the transformation of their paganism or primitive Yahwism into Canaanite nature-worship with all its complex and demoralizing ritual. There were both gains and losses in the change, but both were inevitable. Until this change had occurred, Israel was not ready for the kingship with its political, social, industrial and commercial ambitions.

Let us take a look at the Canaanite culture as it appeared about 1190 B.C.

A CANAANITE CITY

Megiddo may be taken as a typical larger Canaanite town (Fig. 49). It lay on the south-west side of the plain of Esdraelon just where the Grand Trunk Line from Egypt to Babylon emerges from a sword-cut in the long ridge of Mount Carmel. Having long occupied this site and been repeatedly destroyed, the present city lay on a mound of its own ruins perhaps seventy feet above its original stratum. As guardian of the pass, Megiddo was a fortress with strong walls of stone and mud brick, broad enough for soldiers to move in large numbers to any portion that was being hard pressed. There was only one entrance, a fortified gate on the north side. Climbing to it by a long ramp and entering the town we find a huddled mass of one-story houses separated by crooked lanes. The dwellings are mostly of brick with small pieces of stone added here and there. Since the outer door is open, as we pass by we catch a glimpse of a small court backed by a room or two. In the open the women are plying their household tasks —grinding, baking, washing—while children, chickens and goats run about at will, even into the street. Not far inside the city gate is an enlarged space where rough sack-cloth supported overhead on ropes and sticks furnishes shade for the peasants who bring the produce of their gardens here to sell. They and their wares are a colorful lot. On the edge of the voluble buyers and sellers stands a group of idle men waiting to be hired (*cf.* Mt. 20:1-7).

The most imposing building in town is the king's palace (Fig. 50). The lower three courses of the wall are of hewn stone (ashlar) upon which lies a course of cedar beams. Above this the wall is of baked brick to a height of twenty feet. The corners of the building are of ashlar, but the rest of the walls are plastered and painted. We knock at the door of cedar and bronze. A slave opens it and admits us to a foyer about 8 x 10 feet. The floor is covered with a mosaic of sea shells set in lime, while sunk in the center of it is a basalt basin in which we are invited to wash our feet. The attendant empties the basin by turning it over. A drain is under it.

We now enter the central paved courtyard about 35·x 65 feet and open to the sky. The walls that surround it are painted in brilliant red, blue, green, brown and yellow. From the court a door leads to the servants' quarters, the kitchen and other utility rooms; another door leads to the apartments of the royal family and another to the throne room where ambassadors are received and other business is transacted. On the roof is a summer parlor where the king can enjoy the broad view of mountain and plain, or enjoy the cool breezes that sweep in from the Mediterranean.

FIG. 50. MEGIDDO LARGE HOUSE.

This modernistic-looking structure was built on a substantial stone foundation, the walls above being of brick with a plaster finish outside and cedar within. Since it was placed hard against the city wall, the excavators think it was occupied by an officer in charge of defense. From the courtyard troops could easily mount the stairs to the ramparts and to the roofs of all the houses in that sector. Another stair leads to a tower from which one can survey the whole plain. Such a house gives a fair idea of what the larger royal residence looked like.

Through the courtesy of the chamberlain we take a look at the king's bedchamber, especially at the magnificent bed. The wooden portion is adorned with plaques of ivory carved with little scenes, some descriptive and some symbolic. One in particular shows a prince seated on a throne that is supported by two winged human-headed lions. Near the prince is a woman with a feather crown, evidently his queen, and a minstrel with a harp. Before the king stands a line of naked captives evidently about to be executed or else driven to the fields for forced labor.

We may take a look at the royal treasury—three underground rooms. Here is an astonishing collection of furniture and bric-à-brac: costly chairs used on ceremonial occasions; crowns, scepters and such-like regalia; silver statuettes of gods and goddesses; vases and bowls, gifts from kings, from the heads of transportation companies who desired his favor and protection, and especially from the great Pharaoh of Egypt. Here are bars of silver and gold that represent the yield of the king's fields, the village taxes and the tariffs levied on the merchants who make use of the caravan routes that pass the city. Here also are 200 or more pieces of carved ivory intended for various uses; some of them merely objects of beauty, like a little wand eight inches long, its four sides completely covered with animals and gods; other plaques to be used in adorning furniture (Amos 6:4). One group of objects is set aside by itself as if for some special purpose: two heads of gold adorned with solar-disc crowns—these from the Pharaoh; a cosmetic jar of serpentine and another of hematite, each trimmed with gold—also from Egypt (Fig. 51); a heavy gold bowl in the shape of a scallop shell, from the king of Hamath; an ivory tusk banded with incised gold, the small end carved into a human head —this from the king of Tyre; a few cylinder seals of lapis lazuli, an electrum ring on which was mounted an Egyptian scarab; and a dozen other miscellaneous objects of beauty.[1]

[1] Workmen of the Oriental Institute, Chicago, dug up this cache in 1937 absolutely intact; and in the rifled storerooms they found the few bits of wreckage left from the great looting, and the 200 ivories for which the barbarian invaders (Philistines and other sea peoples) had no use.

The wealth of these tiny cities was unbelievable. When Thutmose III took Megiddo in 1479 B.C. he records that the loot of this city plus what was brought by the king of Kadesh who had

Fig. 51.   COSMETIC JARS FROM MEGIDDO.

Found with a gold hoard hidden beneath the palace floor. The one on the left is made of haematite. It is now in the Oriental Institute, Chicago; that on the right is in the Palestine Museum, Jerusalem.

come down to help his friend included immense quantities of gold and silver, 924 chariots, 200 suits of armor, the magnificent household furniture of the king of Kadesh, including his gorgeous tent, his royal scepter, a silver statue, perhaps of his god, an ebony statue of himself inlaid with gold and lapis lazuli; besides thousands of horses, 113,000 bushels of grain, 2000 large cattle, and 22,500 small cattle.[2]

Other features of Megiddo engage our attention. There is the large residence of the military captain on the city wall, with adjoining barracks, and most remarkable of all, the water supply

[2] J. H. Breasted: *History of Egypt,* p. 292.

Fig. 52. THE MEGIDDO WATER TUNNEL.

This long tunnel, cut through the solid rock, runs from a point inside the city to a spring outside. It is tall enough for a woman to walk in it upright with a jar on her head. As usual in constructing such a shaft, the workers start from each end and if luck is with them they meet somewhere. This view shows how one gang had to change its course in order to make connection.

system. Formerly the water for Megiddo had been brought in jars on the heads of women from a spring outside the city to the south-west. An enemy could easily hold the spring which was beyond the effective range of slingers on the walls, and so compel the surrender of the town. But now the workmen have sunk a shaft perpendicularly within the city, a short distance from the

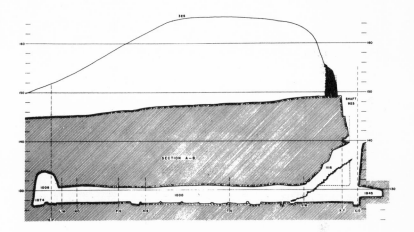

Fig. 52A.   SECTION OF THE MEGIDDO WATER TUNNEL.

Longitudinal, showing from right to left the well-shaft, the rough rock-cut stairs, the tunnel and the enlarged end where is the spring. The tunnel slopes toward the right to allow water to flow from the spring to the foot of the stairs.

wall nearest the spring (Fig. 52). They went down through loose rubbish, the debris of former cities, until after thirty feet or so they came to solid rock. On this rock for foundation a wall was built so as to construct a square well up to the surface some fifteen feet in diameter, with stone steps built in the sides so that women might ascend and descend. Rubbish taken from the pit was now put behind the wall, the top levelled off and the well mouth concealed by building a house over it. Next the excavation was continued straight down through the rock, stone steps being

left around the sides, as in the well. The projecting stairs gradually forced the sides of the well toward the center until it was
impossible to dig any further in a perpendicular direction; so the
vertical well was changed to a passage that sloped at 45 degrees,
steps were cut in the slope and enough headroom left so that
women could pass easily with waterjars on their heads. The engineers decided that they had now gone deep enough (120 feet)
and the axis of the tunnel was changed to horizontal and directed
toward the spring about 165 feet away. Here two gangs were
employed, one working from inside and one beginning at the
spring. The engineers used what instruments or horse-sense they
had in directing the two gangs toward each other; but as they
approached, some one's quick ears heard through the rock the
picks of the other gang approaching a little to the right. At once
the direction of the tunnel was changed so that the two gangs met
head-on. Then the spring was carefully walled up and camou-
flaged, and Megiddo could now rest confident. It was the finest
water system in Canaan.

After our trip through this town we are able to see why the
Israelite nomads were so long in conquering Canaan. Their arts
were no match for those of the older civilization, nor were their
resources great enough to hire help. According to the archaeologists the House of Joseph was in possession of the north-central
highland by 1380 B.C.: but Jericho was not taken until c. 1360,
Bethel c. 1300–1250, Lachish c. 1230, Megiddo, 1100. It took
the Israelites 250 years to capture the chief Canaanite strong-
holds. During all this time the cities acted as a lure. Their wealth
excited Israel's envy; their wide commerce kept them discon-
tented with their own backwardness and isolation; and they
therefore helped establish the Israelitish trend from the land to
the village and the city, from herding and farming to trading and
caravaning, from democracy to social stratification into rich and
poor, into ruling class and debtor class; to military despotisms and
finally to the destruction of the Israelitish states. We shall have to
examine these changes somewhat in detail.

FIG. 53.   INFANT BURIED IN A JAR. FOUND AT MEGIDDO.

Such interments are found not only in the cemeteries but beneath city walls or the thresholds and floors of houses and shrines. The victim is placed in the "embryonic" position and provided with food and drink for his journey. The whole is enclosed in an egg-shaped clay jar. The primary motive of the sacrifice was probably to protect the home or city. (1 Kgs. 16:34; Ex. 13:2; 22:29)

CANAANITE RELIGION

The religion of these Canaanite town-dwellers occupied a good deal of their thought, for it was vitally connected with their prosperity. There were gods many who had to be propitiated. The discovery of the bones of small children enclosed in oval clay jars is evidence that human sacrifices were sometimes performed to avert evil and secure the protection of divinities. Such deposits are found under the threshold of a house or under the city gate (Fig. 53). That such practices infected Israel is shown in 1 Kings 16:34: "In his days [Ahab's], Hiel the Bethelite rebuilt Jericho. He laid its foundation upon Abiram his first-born and set up its gates upon Segub his youngest son." But for the enlightenment of archaeology we should be· at a loss to explain this passage.

The chief divinity to be propitiated was Astarte, for as earth-mother goddess she controlled all fertility, animal and human. In recent years we have learned a good deal about this fertility cult, not only from the figurines and other cult objects dug up on all Palestinian and Syrian sites but from the ritual hymns supplied by the tablets of Ras Shamra.

To make vivid this seductive worship let us imagine that an Israelite named Joel is invited by a citizen of Megiddo named Peridia to attend worship at Astarte's temple during the great spring festival.

The ceremonies began on the day of the full moon nearest the spring equinox. All the city was in festal array. Brightly colored streamers fluttered from poles stuck in the clay roofs of all the houses. Children danced in the streets clad only in garlands of anemones and other wild flowers that carpet Esdraelon at this season, and all the men of the city crowded forward to the shrine of Astarte. This was a sizable building of brick on stone foundations, built near the city wall to the east. In front of it was a large open area where the present celebrations were· to be staged. Joel could not see much of the interior of the shrine, but it evidently consisted of a number of rooms. He noticed the door-posts on the

FIG. 54.   AN ALTAR OF INCENSE.

Reconstructed from pieces found at Megiddo in the Astarte temple. The four "horns" at the corners serve to hold in place any bowl or incense burner placed on the altar. It was to such an altar that Adonijah and Joab fled for sanctuary (1 Kgs. 1:49-53; 2:28-35) and it was such horns that they grasped in their terror.

top of which, like capitals, were stone blocks carved to represent an opening lily. For this occasion they had set up a small stone incense altar on the platform in front of the entrance. It had four horns on it (*cf.* 1 Kgs. 1:50) (Fig. 54).

Not all could get into the sacred area, but Peridia and Joel pushed along till they stood immediately in front of the entrance to the shrine. Behind them the court was densely filled. Little girls were elbowing their way through the crowd selling crude clay figurines (Fig. 55):·

"May Astarte be gracious! Buy a goddess for your wife. Astarte will bring children to your home."

While waiting for the ritual to begin, Joel had time to notice a number of strange things. In the upper story of the temple tower there were two large holes like windows. A few doves were roosting there or flying about to pick up the grains scattered occasionally over the court or thrown to the roof by some of the men. Peridia explained that doves were sacred to Astarte and that feeding them was sure to bring good luck. One or two men in the crowd drew considerable attention to themselves by allowing large snakes they had caught to stick their heads out from the sleeves of their tunics. Far from being startled, the crowd pressed closed to the men and tried to touch the snakes.

"The snake also belongs to Astarte," said Peridia. "He is her husband taking that form. Look over there on the wall beside the door and you will see."

Following the pointed finger, Joel looked and on either side of the entrance he saw some baked clay panels with figures modeled on them.

"That naked figure," the steward explained, "is the great Earth-mother, source of all life. Two snakes crawl up her legs and place their heads between her thighs. That means to us that out of the earth come the forces that make our goddess fruitful, that fill our barns with plenty, our byres with cattle and our homes with children."

In front of the altar Joel saw a strange clay object, a tapering hollow cylinder about 25 inches high.

FIG. 55.
CLAY FIGURINE OF
ASTARTE.

Such objects are turned up in abundance on all Palestine levels from 1600–1200 B.C. They were made cheaply and rapidly in molds. Possession of these figurines brought fertility to the land, the flocks and the home. They were often included in the household shrines along with the teraphim or family ancestors (*cf.* Gen. 31:19).

"That," said the steward, "is the stand where the 'man of god' places the offerings we bring. There are doves on that also looking out of the little window on the side and perched on the handle; and you see four snakes crawling up to the openings. All these things remind us constantly of the Earth-mother and her consort when we bring our gifts to the altar."

Joel followed this talk with considerable misgiving for nothing like this was carried on in the tents of Israel.[3]

As he spoke, the sacristan or "man of god" came through a side door and placed on the stand a beautiful bowl of electrum containing wine.

The trilling of female voices was now heard, and from the temple door issued a dozen "ladies of the chapels" clad in white, garlands on their heads, and in their hands castanets and tambourines. The audience pushed back as far as possible to give place for their sacred dance around the altar (*cf.* Ps. 68:24–25). Some of the ladies had roving eyes and were apparently more interested in the audience than in their ritual. Just as the dance finished, children issued from the temple with loaves of bread and jars of wine. These they placed on the altar and on little clay stands shaped like a temple—windows, doors, and all—while at the corners were cherubim. Those on the front of the stand had female heads, the body of a lion, and wings; those at the side were males (Fig. 56). Peridia explained that all the gods, male and female, were honored in this festival and so were here represented.

The high priest and soothsayer now entered chanting,[4]

---

[3] Compare the Hebrew commands: "Do not act perniciously by carving an image for yourselves in the shape of any statue like male or female, like any animal that is on the earth, or any kind that flies in the air, or any reptile on the ground. . . . Do not let yourselves be allured into paying homage to them or serving them." (Deut. 4:16–19.) The Yahweh worshippers were fighting a life-and-death struggle with the Canaanite Astartes and Baals, none of whose ritual practices could be tolerated.

[4] The ritual here given is Prof. George A. Barton's translation of a Ras Shamra text, *Jour. of Bib. Lit.,* 53:61–78 (1934).

I will summon the gods, gracious and beautiful, children of princes—eat of bread with me, and drink of wine, my weary ones!

FIG. 56.   CLAY SHRINE WITH CHERUBIM.

Restored from fragments found in the Astarte Temple at Megiddo. It is probably an incense stand shaped like a house. At the corners are two female cherubim (*cf.* 1 Kgs. 6:29). In the center of each side is a male cherub. They all have lion bodies and probably wings. They are the emblems of the fertility cult that dominated Palestine for many centuries. The cherubs represent the invisible deities that dwell within the shrine (*cf.* 1 Kgs. 6:23-28).

The audience was hushed. Peridia whispered, "The gods are now here to partake of the feast; they cannot resist the summons of the priest."

All faces were now turned to two groups of priests who came running from behind the shrine. They were dressed as laborers, and each carried a grapevine planted in a basket. Setting the baskets down on each side of the altar, the priests began solemnly to prune the vines; others propped up the stalks and tied them. Meanwhile another priest had entered and taken his seat on the ground in front of the altar. Ashes covered his face and his black robe, a broken reed was in his hand. He looked at the laborers with pretended anger, scowled and shook his fist.

"What is that fellow doing?" asked Joel.

"Hush! That is Moth the god of death, who is disappointed that he will not be able to kill the vines this season," explained the steward.

Undismayed at Moth's presence, the laborer-priests now began to pick small stones out of the baskets and throw them around the court, unmindful whom they hit. At this there was considerable laughter and shouting, and a scramble for the stones that would bring good luck to their vineyards.

Then the priest took up the ritual, in a song that every one evidently knew by heart, for all joined in at the top of their lungs, clapping hands rhythmically, stamping with one foot and swaying their bodies.

Moth shall sit; in his hand the scepter of bereavement; in his hand the scepter of silence. The pruners shall prune the vine; those who tie shall tie the vine; they shall cast the stones from its field as as did Gepen.

This they all chanted three times.

Now these laborers and Moth retired, while out of the house came a herdsman carrying in his arms a small kid and leading a she-goat. Following him was a priest with a clay stove and a bronze cauldron. The crowd became still again as the priest set the stove in front of the altar and blew up the charcoal fire with an eagle's-wing fan. The herdsman milked the goat and put the milk in the cauldron over the fire. The priest took the little kid and in an incredibly short time killed and dressed it; he placed it in its mother's milk now boiling merrily over the coals. While the odorous steam filled every one's nostrils, the priest raised a chant in which the laborers now in priestly costumes joined as they issued from the temple door:

As to the fields, the fields of the gods, the fields of Asherat and the merciful ones—over the fire remove the ashes; slay a kid in the milk, resting in the curds—

This they repeated a dozen times or more until the priest was satisfied with the boiling.

"The gods have come again to the feast," said Peridia; "they smell the boiling meat and are pleased. They will surely bless our fields and our flocks."

This act done, all the accessories were removed except the stove, and the sound of trilling again was heard.

"This is the last and best," whispered Peridia; "this blesses our homes. El and the mother-goddess will make our wives fruitful."

The chorus of women clad in a single garment of sheer white linen entered singing:

El will be merciful; the staff of his hand will he lift up—the bird he shall pluck, he shall put it on the coals!

The priest now entered dressed as the god El, carrying a staff in one hand and a bird of some kind in the other. An attendant took the bird from him, plucked it, placed it on the coals and fanned them to a heat. The women continued their chant, swaying and turning their bodies so that they could be seen by all, while El passed them slowly and touched each of them gently with his staff:

The women, as El shall pass by them, the women shall cry,
"O Moth, Moth, we shall set limits to thy scepter, tearing
away the staff of thine hand."
The bird shall warm at the fire, broiling on the coals.

(Here a slow dance around the fire and the altar)

> *We are women, each the wife of El, and his slaves.*
> *He shall cleanse their lips, shall lift them up.*
> *Their lips are sweet, sweet like the pomegranate.*
> *With them is kissing and conception.*
> *By embracing, she who is passionate shall bring forth—*

Having chanted this ritual three times the "ladies of the chapels" retired through the temple door, casting eyes over their shoulders as they did so. Several men, evidently of the well-to-do class, including Peridia, followed them into the shrine and the crowd began to disperse. Quite perplexed by all this strangeness Joel returned to his people.

The Social Transformation of Israel

The Hebrews had taken a momentous step. They had given up the life of marauding and were learning to depend more and more upon farming. But who should teach them the technique? They may have captured a village or two with its surrounding farm land and killed off the males, but that did not automatically make them farmers. Some of the surviving women folk, who regularly worked in the fields, made themselves useful by showing the Hebrew women some things and telling them more, and their tales had to do with the mother-goddess and the baalim and El-elyn and Moth, all of whom had more to do with bringing crops and increase of all kinds than anything men could do. From sheer necessity the Hebrews were slowly made over into the likeness of the Canaanites, and the El or the Yahweh they had brought in from the desert took on more and more the likeness of Baal.

The transformation of Israel involved also the point of view about property and social organization. Out in the desert the tribe held all the gifts of God in common; there was no private ownership in air and sun, water and grass. Now that the Israelites had become stabilized it was necessary for each family to work a specific portion of the clan-land; and while at first, no doubt, the land was assigned by a council of family heads for temporary use only and in accordance with the size of the family, as time went on occupancy tended to become indistinguishable from ownership. The Canaanite owned land, why not the Hebrew?

The Canaanites were commercial-minded; they bought and sold for money. Why should the Hebrews not sell their grain, butter and flocks to the town-dwellers and lay up for themselves treasure against a rainy day?

The Canaanites had kings who protected them in time of war, administered justice in times of peace, and as a reward were entitled to a portion of the produce of field and flock; why should not the Hebrews who showed ability be charged with similar responsibilities and receive a like reward?

The drift in Israel was steadily away from the loose agglomeration of tribesmen towards, first, a kind of farmer aristocracy to which Gideon and Saul belonged, that duplicated the commercial aristocracy of the Canaanite towns, and finally to a full-fledged kingship which was equally Canaanite and decidedly non-Israelitish. Events proved that this was not for the best interest of democracy. This later judgment is put into the mouth of Samuel in 1 Samuel 8:10-19, and his arraignment of the kingship is an accurate description of a Canaanite state: military organization, elaborate households, industrial and commercial exploitation, taxes, the corvée, confiscation of lands, slavery.

Another important social change had to do with housing. In the books of Judges and Samuel we see the gradual abandonment of the tents in favor of village houses. That change was not fully completed in the days of Saul 1 Chron. 5:10) or even in the days of Solomon (1 Kgs. 12:16)—though by this time the word tent probably was used figuratively for home. That means that tribal life was exchanged for a village life in which Israelites and Canaanites shared, and in which both intermarriage and social stratification were bound to occur. Sometimes the Israelites took over the actual towns as they killed off the former occupants or reduced them to serfdom (Jdg. 1:28); sometimes they rebuilt a destroyed town after the Canaanite pattern, and occupied it (Jdg. 18:27–28).

We shall now take a look at life in

A CANAANITE-ISRAELITE VILLAGE

Again let us use our imagination and say that the clan of the peasant Joel, in whose company we have seen a religious festival at Megiddo, decided to strike for a bigger and better living-space. Joining with a cousin-clan they attacked the Canaanite village of Dothan and after some stiff fighting they had seized and were holding it. This was a bold move, for it was a sizable town on a mound overlooking rich valley lands across which went the winter caravans from Egypt to Damascus. Several times that day the Canaanites had driven them out, but by nightfall the town was safely theirs. The fighters then mounted the roofs of their new homes, still carrying their clubs and other weapons against further surprise attacks. These houses were one-story affairs of rubble stone set in mud, plastered with mud, lime and chopped straw and then whitewashed. The roof consisted of beams on which reeds had been laid and the whole capped with clay. The stone rollers with which the former owners had rolled down the earth after a shower to keep it from leaking were still there.

One of the best houses in the village had been assigned to Joel as a reward of valor. It had a little chamber built on the roof (Jdg. 3:20), the furniture of which was still intact, left by the Canaanite owners when they hastily evacuated—a bed, a table, a chair and a lamp (2 Kgs. 4:10). This must have been the guest-chamber of a wealthy family (1 Sam. 9:25; 1 Kgs. 17:19). The former owners had evidently used the roof for a number of purposes: there were remnants of figs, raisins, peppers, flax (Josh. 2:6) and fuel which had been drying there. Since it had a parapet (later made obligatory, Deut. 22:8) it was a convenient place to walk (2 Sam. 11:2) or meditate or pray (*cf.* Acts 10:9) or enjoy the cool breezes.[5]

Fig. 57.   CLAY STOVE.

The original would be about a foot high, crudely modeled by hand and dried in the sun. The first fire put in it would harden the clay to stand the weight of a kettle. Charcoal is placed in the shallow top, draft comes up through the holes, and a grill or skillet or kettle rests directly on the coals. The stove can be moved even when hot by taking hold of the lugs on the side.

Joel climbed down the narrow stone stair built outside against the house wall, and entered the one door to find his wife and children inside. They were all there, safe and sound, praise Yahweh! What a spacious living room, ten feet square!—though

[5] The housetop was a place where everybody went in times of excitement (Is. 22:1–2a). That accounts for the 3000 spectators (no doubt exaggerated) on the roof of the Dagon temple at Gaza while Samson was making sport (Jdg. 16:27). The peculiar act of Absalom in connection with dispossessing his father took place on the roof as a publicity stunt (2 Sam. 16:22). To get news all over town one had only to "proclaim it from the housetops."

all his possessions had been dumped there hastily and were not yet arranged. He thought this room was all—and it usually would have been all; but behind it was another little room where the former aristocratic owner used to sleep (2 Sam. 13:10). He had not expected any windows; but this palace had two, with shutters on them (Jdg. 5:28; Prov. 7:6). They would let out the smoke, at any rate. The living room floor had two levels, both of them made of earth: on the upper one raised about 18 inches the family evidently worked, ate and slept; on the lower there were evidences that the family sheep, goats, donkey, chickens and dog made their home (2 Sam. 12:3). There were a couple of wooden mangers; likewise a good many household furnishings left by the late tenants, which, added to his own gear, made quite a respectable inventory. Things were looking up!

A couple of Canaanite slaves the family had had for some years now came driving in the few animals and bringing the last remnants of household gear from the old home. A donkey was staggering under the load of the tent, the poles of which perversely stuck into a house every time he turned a corner in the alley. Tents were now obsolete, but this one might be stored on the roof for use in case the Canaanites should ever turn out the Israelites—who knows? The women now milked the goats in the parlor, gave the children some curds and a little honey out of a jar (Is. 7:14-15), themselves ate curds and bread with a few figs, then prepared to sleep. The door was locked with the queer key that hung on a nearby peg. The rush mats that stood in the corner were unrolled on the floor, and all lay down on them, each man covered with his cloak (Ex. 22:26-27), the children covered with a quilt of goats' hair. But Gentleman Joel and his lady slept in the inner chamber where there was a bed (1 Sam. 19:13). Never before had the lady seen one.

Next morning at sun-up Joel went to the roof to greet his neighbors while his wife put the big water jar on her head, daughters number one and two put smaller jars on their heads and walked three hundred yards down to the valley spring. A caravan

FIG. 58.   A VILLAGE OVEN.

More correctly this is a bake-house. The oven is a clay jar half buried in ashes in the center of the floor. Around this focal point a ring of women squat and exchange gossip while the bread bakes. The smoke goes out the door.

was already there, "having come from Gilead, with their camels carrying gum, balm and laudanum, going down to Egypt." The females stood at a respectful distance behind a wall till the camel-men pulled out. They found the curb of the spring full to the brim; no need to let down the jar with a rope.

At home once more, sorting time—finding a place for everything and putting everything in place. First the fire. The place for it was on the lower level hard up against the higher, for there was the clay stove—the first they had ever seen. Joel explained that here was where you put the charcoal or sticks, here was the hole for the draught, and on top the hole where you set your pot (Fig. 57). The wife found hanging against the wall a clay ladle and a big bronze spearing-fork to lift the meat out of the boiler (1 Sam. 2:13). She had a smaller one of her own. She brought out her jar in which she kept her flint knives, and added to them a half-dozen bronze ones of different sizes which she found on the wall. No one had ever heard of spoons and eating-forks, so of course she didn't look for any. Next she found the black stone and roller with which she had always crushed the barley to make cakes; but Joel discovered in the corner a real mill made of two circular stones, the upper of which was rotated on the lower by means of a handle set near the edge (Jdg. 9:52-53). Both Mrs. Joel and daughter could now sit at ease, one on each side of the mill, and turn the stone by each grasping the tall handle with one hand and with the other feed in the grain at a central hole. Meal came out all around the edge and was caught by a projecting flange or by a cloth on the ground. The mother looked around for an oven, but did not find one. Later one of the Canaanite women who had been allowed to stay in the village showed her the village oven where all the women did their baking. It was just beyond the houses at the edge of the ash-heap. It was a rather small conical house made by leaning poles together tent-wise, filling the chinks with stones and plastering all tight with mud. A door about three feet high was in one side. In the middle of the floor was a clay bee-hive baking-pot and a circle beyond that where perhaps

six women could squat if it were a cold day (Fig. 58). By arrangement all the women of the village in groups of six had their turn
at the baking; and—so the Canaanite explained—the woman
whose turn it was to bake last of the group must furnish fuel for
all six! This prevented running short of fuel, for number six who
furnished it would not care to go home with her dough unbaked.
Number six was a different person each day. The dough was plas-

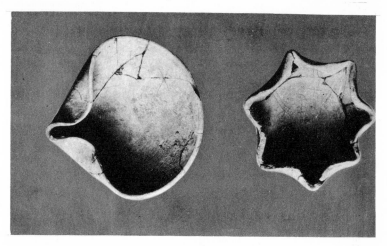

FIG. 59.   POTTERY LAMPS.

The clay saucers were found at Tell Beit Mirsim (the Keriath Sepher of the Old
Testament), and they date from 1200-900 B.C. The left one with the sides pinched to hold
the wick is the commoner form.

tered against the inside wall of the clay oven; the cover was put
on and the fire heaped over it. When the bread was baked it fell
off the sides upon some clean pebbles that covered the bottom.
Smoke went out the door. Mrs. Joel knew about fuel: she must
either gather thorn bushes from the hillsides (Ecc. 7:6) or make
it by mixing animals' dung and chopped straw, shaping the mixture into round patty-cakes ten inches in diameter and drying
them in the sun.

Pots of various kinds had been left in the house. Some were

simple and coarse, made evidently by the village potter; others
that were thinner and of more graceful lines came from some
large town, possibly Megiddo; but one was so beautiful in shape
and so skilfully decorated that Joel knew at once it came from
overseas. The steward in Megiddo had told him that one like it
in the palace had been brought from Mycenae.

She found four lamps also which might be placed in a niche
in a wall or hung from a beam. They were small, from four to six
inches long, and made of clay; shaped like a saucer with one side
pinched together into a kind of spout in which the rag wick might
lie (Fig. 59). In a little bronze case they found some needles of
bone and of bronze, and a pair of bronze shears. These things,
with a few other odds and ends, were the equipment of the new
house.

Joel, of course, returned to his old job of farming. His tools
had been brought to the new home and stacked in the corner with
those of his esteemed predecessor. The village lands were more
extensive and far richer than those he had formerly worked. In
fact, Joel could look forward to a prosperous future.

His plowing was done by a combination of crooked pieces of
wood (Fig. 60) drawn by a couple of donkeys, or a couple of
bullocks (1 Sam. 11:5; 1 Kgs. 19:19), or a team of anything,
human or animal, that could pull—even Joel's wife had helped
out on occasion. The use of an ox and an ass yoked together was
later forbidden (Deut. 22:10). The plow scratched the earth
six or eight inches deep.[6] He did his sowing by hand. Irrigation,
though an old art, Joel had never seen practiced in Palestine.
Here he was dependent on the rain and the underground rills,
and these, as all men know, were under the control of the Baal of
Dothan. All the processes of reaping, gleaning, threshing and winnowing (Fig. 61) he would practice unchanged, in the manner

[6] Early plows had shares of some kind, possibly of bronze, but in the
Philistine period, of iron. The Israelites were not yet smiths, for the Philistines who brought in iron kept to themselves a knowledge of how to shape
it (1 Sam. 13:19-21).

of farmers throughout the world at all times.[7] But where to store his enlarged harvest of grain—too great, he hoped, to be kept in a few grain-sacks? Joel's wife happened to learn from a Canaan-

Fig. 60.   A PALESTINE PLOW.

This immemorial implement is made wholly of wood, even to the pegs that hold it together. Lacking good timber the carpenter has learned to utilize short crooked pieces. In this case he has used three pieces to make a long pole, one for the beam, one for the upright and one each for the handle, the brace, and the piece that holds the plowshare. The yoke to which the plow is lashed consists of a beam with six pins: two pair to hold the yoke on the bullocks' necks, two to keep the pole in place.

ite woman that every house had a grain pit somewhere. So Joel dug in the corner of his "parlor" and soon came to a flat stone which covered the mouth of a dry well, the sides walled with stone and expanding at the bottom to about five feet in diameter. The bottom was floored with stone and the whole plastered with clay

[7] *Cf.* the description and illustrations of Egyptian farming in Chapter IV.

till it was as smooth and tight as the inside of a jug.[8] The pit was still about a third full of barley (Praised be Yahweh—or Baal!) Joel found that the village was surrounded by orchards and vineyards which had been parceled out to individual householders. The olives yielded oil, used in cooking; grapes were eaten fresh or were dried into raisins and pressed into clusters; likewise figs (1 Sam. 25:18; 30:12). Joel had been accustomed to these fruits ever since his people came to Canaan.

The only cloud on Joel's horizon was the almost certain knowledge that he would not be left in peaceful possession of his new riches. As his clan had treated the Canaanites, so strangers might treat him. It is true he did not live to see this calamity, but his grandchildren did. The Midianites, the Ammonites and the Amalekites who lived on the fringes of the mountains and vales of Ephraim, sensing the growing prosperity and power of the Israelite clans, began the raiding and furnished the incentive which the loose clans needed to combine and consolidate.[9]

Methods of Warfare

When the Israelite country was raided, the inhabitants often ran away if they thought the odds were against them; they took to the caves, the forests and defiles of the wilderness (Jdg. 5:6–7; 1 Sam. 13:6–7; 14:11, 22). But if they resisted, they placed themselves under the leadership of any one whom they trusted and went into the fray. There was not much organization or strategy—mostly hand-to-hand fighting with clubs, stones, slings, bows and arrows, flint knives and bare fists. In excavating towns

[8] Dr. W. F. Albright found scores of these pits in his excavation at Tell Beit Mersim, all of them at the early Israelite level. (*Archaeology of Palestine and the Bible*, 1933, p. 103).

[9] The book of Judges gives several samples of these "oppressions": by Arameans (3:8); Moabites, Ammonites, Amalekites (3:12–13); Canaanites and Sea Peoples (4:2–3); Midianites (6:1); Ammonites (10:6–8); and especially by the Philistines (13:1) who entered the maritime plain and gradually pushed their raids across the watershed which Israel had taken for itself.

FIG. 61.   WINNOWING.

The farmer stands back to the wind, and with his four-tined wooden fork throws a bunch of the chaff mixed with grain into the air. The breeze drives away the chaff in a puff of yellow smoke.

one often finds at important places just inside the walls little heaps of spherical stones a trifle larger than tennis balls. These are "ammunition dumps," the missiles provided in quantity for the defenders to throw either by hand or with slings. A home-made sling is one of the common implements of the Bible. Shepherd boys gather stray tufts of wool left by sheep on thorn bushes, twist them into thread and braid the strands into two stout strings. A flat expansion in the center holds the stone; one string ends in a loop that slips over the finger. The thrower rotates the stone around his head, then at the proper split-second releases one string, and the stone flies at the mark tangentially to the circle (*cf.* Jdg. 20:16).

Weapons of war such as the great nations wielded were quite beyond these villagers. In the days of the Philistine raiding, only Saul and Jonathan had a sword and spear (1 Sam. 13:22); on the other hand, the village of Gibeah in Benjamin had seven hundred left-handed men, "all of them accustomed to sling a stone at a hair without missing" (Jdg. 20:16). Personal bravery, physical strength, agility and endurance were the all-important qualities. The only strategy they seem to have practiced was laying an ambush, making divided attacks and strategic retreats (Josh. 8:3–7; Jdg. 7:16; 20:29; 1 Sam. 11:11). Their great enemies the Philistines, on the other hand, used some kind of battle formation (1 Sam. 4:2); possessed chariots, though the hilly terrain prevented their effective use (1 Sam. 13:5—discount the impossible numbers; Jdg. 1:19), and had coats of mail and a monopoly on the use of iron (1 Sam. 13:19–20) which gave them an advantage in war (Jdg. 4:2–3). War had not yet developed the deadliness or the cruelty of torture so frequent in later times. The only mutilations of captives recorded are cutting off the great toes and thumbs (Jdg. 1:6–7); and of the slain the foreskins were sometimes cut off as a trophy (1 Sam. 18:25, 27); or the heads of important persons cut off and exposed with the body to public gaze (1 Sam. 17:51; 31:8–10). In general it may be said that the earlier raids for plunder, and the corresponding defense, were fairly innocent affairs—a kind of rough sport; but when the existence of a clan was at stake or when the necessity or ambition for conquest aroused blood-lust, there was no limit to the process of extermination (Josh. 6:21; 8:24-26; Jdg. 18:27; 1 Sam. 27:9).

In this early period of settlement therefore we find the Israelites getting a toe-hold in the relatively open highlands of Ephraim, while around the edges of their territory remained the uncon-quered cities of the Canaanites. Their problem was first of all to get a living, then to expand their domain, and finally to imitate whatever Canaanite arts and practices seemed to be advanta-geous. That they should take over also most of the religion and the shrines of the older inhabitants was inevitable; and therein lay a peril that was not fully recognized until the prophets of the ninth century discovered its economic bearings.

CHAPTER VII

CAMEL TRAILS AND CARAVAN FOLK

TO A WESTERN mind, the word "road" means a surveyed and engineered construction; it means foundations, materials, surfacing, easy gradients, bridges and tunnels where necessary. But an Eastern road is a thing to marvel at, it is so simple. Nobody ever did anything to it, not even to roll the boulders and pick the stones out of the way. Camels go round a boulder. If a donkey is thrown by a rolling stone, that is merely an occasion for a good beating and much cursing. If the winter rains turn the plain into a marsh, there is dry though rocky ground a mile away. So the ancient trail drifts along, slouches along in a kind of shiftless freedom, up hill and down dale; only in general its eye is fixed on the far-off goal.

The appearance of the road differs with the terrain. On the plains the track is multiple; for while camel number two in the caravan usually follows camel number one, and all together their noiseless feet tend to create a path a foot wide, there are some wayward camels who follow their long necks a yard to the right for a while and then cross over to the left for better air or scenery. Then one caravan turns out for another when passing, and so widens the maze of interlacing paths to a rod or more. That is the look of the Grand Trunk line across the plain of Sharon. But when the line enters the hills, the thronging feet of men and animals fall century after century in the same narrow path; the rocks are worn slippery by the attrition of hoofs and pads, and stained brown by the mud traipsed on them from the patches of soil between. Now and then where the stone is soft the caravans wear the rock away. At the Ladder of Tyre, for example, where the trail clings to the side of the mountain a couple of hundred feet above the pounding surf of the Mediterranean and there is no chance for a caravan to spread itself, the road at places had been worn to a U-shaped trench six feet deep; one who was walking could not see over the parapet to the water below (Fig. 62). Now a macadamed auto-road covers the old trail!

Rivers cannot stop a caravan—there is always a ford somewhere within a hundred miles. High mountains will deflect

Fig. 62.   THE LADDER OF TYRE.

Taken not far from the present boundary between the British Mandate and the French. The limestone of the mountain is here soft and chalky and therefore is worn in places into a deep U-shaped trench. Along this road have marched the armies and caravans of all past time. Now the trail is buried beneath a macadam auto-road.

caravan to the nearest pass, but hills, steep though they be in places, are easily surmounted; a trail goes from Beth-shan to Jenin right over Mount Gilboa. Deserts are not impossible, thanks to the storage tanks wise nature has given a camel, and to wells that have been sunk at intervals. Thus an ancient trail ran from Basra on the Persian Gulf to Aleppo in North Syria, seven hundred and fifty miles entirely through the desert, without touching the Euphrates or a single town.

In general then we may say that wherever the caravan has a will there is a way; the will is provided by human desire, and the way is the result of trial and error, the successful solution being made inveterate through use.

CARGOES

It is now in order to find what were the desires that spurred the ancient Egyptian and Mesopotamian to travel away from his village and his fields. In general they were for metals, stone and timber. Metals, especially copper, bronze or iron, gave him tools and weapons more efficient than flints; gold and silver furnished ornaments for his person, his house and his tomb. Stone and timber gave what he could not find in the alluvium where he lived: hinge sockets for doors, foundations that rain or the river could not dissolve, alabaster slabs for sculptured dadoes, diorite and basalt for statues to adorn his temples and for stelae on which to engrave his laws and the record of his conquests; timber for palace roofs and for ships.

We know most of the ancient sources of metals within the range of Bible lands.

Gold: Nothing in any quantity nearer than Nubia, though a little has been mined in Armenia near Erzerum.

Silver: Mines worked from prehistoric times are found in Asia Minor just north of the Cilician Gates.

Copper: The island of Cyprus was the earliest and most abundant source; next, the peninsula of Sinai. Mines between the Dead and the Red Seas were worked sporadically; considerable amounts were found in Armenia west of Harput.

Tin: (Necessary for making bronze): a band running southeast through Persia, starting north of Lake Urumia.

Iron: Chief source, the southern shore of the Black Sea.

When wealth increased and luxury set in, kings and nobles wanted exotic foods and clothes and all the gewgaws that foreign men had invented to delight the eye. We have only to turn to Assyrian tablets and stelae to extract a list of these "peculiar treasures of kings." Among the tribute exacted by conquerors are found: censers, cauldrons of copper with handles of gold, fly-flappers of gold, bowls, cups, rings, pails, ladles, tripods, brace-lets, armlets, chains, horses, asses (domesticated and wild), mules, camels, buffalos, cattle, sheep, goats, gazelles, monkeys, stags, panthers, rhinoceroses, wild bulls, elephants, elephant hides, ele-phant tusks, ivory, scepters, wands and couches of ivory, lions, dolphins, partridges, ostriches, peacocks, purple dye from the murex shell, myrrh and other aromatic spices, conch shells, blue faience, oriental sweetmeats.

Considering the limited number of these objects that are native to Babylonia, Egypt and Palestine, the list opens up a vista of world-wide traffic, from.Persia, Armenia, Asia Minor, the islands of the sea, North Africa, the Sudan, Southern Arabia, and India.

The Bible contains frequent references to trade. By the time the Israelites became interested, the carriers and merchants were Canaanite and Aramean on land (Hos. 12:7) and Phoenician on the sea (Is. 23:1-12). Solomon's various business ventures were carried on through these people: he was the financier and gambler, they the executives (1 Kgs. 9:26-27). In the list of cap-tives carried from Jerusalem by Nebuchadnezzar, no mention is made of the merchant class (2 Kgs. 24:14) ; and even after the Exile the fish and other businesses in Jerusalem were handled by Tyrian rather than Jewish merchants (Neh. 13:16). Usually the word "merchant" in the Old Testament means Canaanite, and vice versa (Zeph. 1:11) ; the Jews became merchants only under the impetus of the Dispersion. Nevertheless, as a study of the trade-routes will show, Palestine was the bridge by which the Sudan sent gold and elephant-tusks to Assyria, Arabia sent spices to the Hittites, and Asia Minor sent silver to Egypt. That trade, as we shall see, powerfully affected the life of Israel.

Most of these objects existing in innumerable out-of-the-way places, gravitated like little rills towards a few Grand Trunk lines that carried them to the two earliest centers of civilization, Egypt and Mesopotamia. These lines, among the most ancient known to man, are given in detail in Maps I and II.

THE ORGANIZATION OF TRAFFIC

Not every man who owned a camel could run a caravan. Transport was a highly specialized industry that depended upon knowledge of sources, of markets, of routes covering a thousand miles or more, of shifting political conditions that often affected the routes to be taken, of arranging convoys of troops and the payment of tariffs at frontiers and towns along the way. Many of the wars with foreign states probably began with the seizure of caravans, or the levying of exorbitant tolls; and where distance or heavy odds made war impracticable, "presents," "tribute," and "treaties" had to be arranged. To be the organizer of caravans one must combine the strategy of a general, the guile of a diplomat, and the effrontery of a brigand. One became incidentally an internationally known character. Such a person was Labaya of the Amarna tablets (c. 1400 B.C.) a Hurrian. At the time of the letters he was living in Palestine in or near Shechem. The correspondence shows him to be the head of a caravan and courier firm so important as to be entrusted with private dispatches between the Pharaoh of Egypt (Amenhotep III?) and the kings of the Hittites. He controlled routes sufficiently to get business done from Thebes to Babylon, some 1400 miles.[1] In the time of Abraham, the caravan business was practically a monopoly of the Hurrians, though on southern stretches other people had a hand in it: Midianites (Gen. 37:28a, E document) or Ishmaelites (Gen. 37:28b, J document). But later the Arameans pushed the Hurrians out of their home in the bight of the

---

[1] C. L. Woolley: *Abraham*, p. 141 note. Woolley, the excavator of Ur, mentions a contemporary master of transport, a Hajji Mohammed ibn Bassam, Damascus agent for the Anezeh and the Ruwla and most of the tribes of Arabia and controller of all trade routes in the interior. When the motor service between Beirut and Baghdad was inaugurated, it was necessary to pay a subsidy to Hajji to safeguard the cars from attack by the Bedouins.

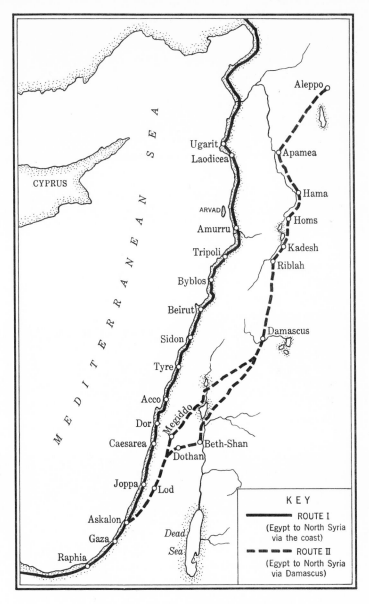

Map I. NORTH-SOUTH TRADE ROUTES.

Euphrates,[2] took over the bulk of their business and became powerful enough to maintain a political empire also, centered in Damascus from about 900 B.C., till Tiglath-pileser III destroyed it and deported the Damascenes in 733 B.C. That the Arameans were particularly interested in trade is seen in Benhadad's forcing Omri to give him trading rights in his new capital Samaria (I Kgs. 20:34). The records indicate that the Arameans were partly pastoral nomads and so were in a position to breed camels for their kinsmen who organized caravans.

CARAVAN DETAILS

The animals used were originally asses, as in the tomb of Khnumhotep at Benihasan (Fig. 17a), and in the case of Joseph's brothers. The Hurrians of that period bred asses in Edom (Gen. 36:24). This fact restricted the range of caravans, for donkeys must have water every day and their route must be determined by the presence of springs or wells. According to W. F. Albright [3] the camel was not domesticated until the eleventh century B.C. When therefore the Bible speaks of Abraham and Jacob as having camels (Gen. 12:16; 24:61; 30:43) we must understand that the story-tellers of the period of the Monarchy took the camel for granted without knowing the facts. Camels are rarely mentioned until the period of the Judges.

With camels, caravans can now range over long desert sections and establish new lines of communication. The Queen of Sheba rode on camels a thousand miles, bringing products of her country to Solomon (1 Kgs. 10:2). Most of these animals came from the fringes of Arabia where Bedouins of various brands bred them for this work. Midianites and Amalekites owned them "as the sand upon the sea for multitude" (Jdg. 7:12). These Arabian camels are tall, thin, long- and slender-legged and have one hump and a soft brown coat which is usually clipped short for cleanliness and comfort (Fig. 63). They are rubbed with tar to keep off vermin and galls; which, added to the natural aroma of the

[2] Text of Tiglath-pileser I, 1100 B.C.
[3] *Stone Age to Christianity*, p. 120.

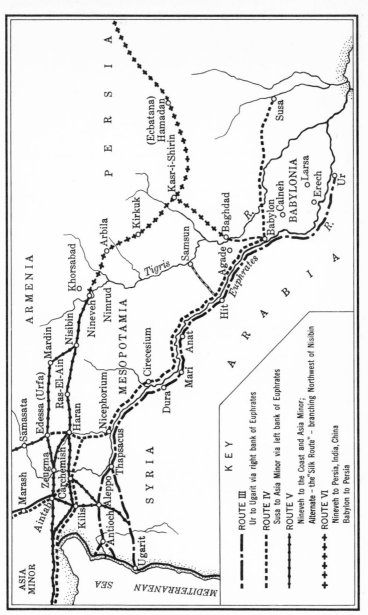

MAP II. EAST-WEST TRADE ROUTES.

camel, furnishes the public a unique olfactory experience. There is a very different kind that must have been used frequently on all northern routes: the Bactrian camel with two humps, short stocky legs that can plow through deep snow, a heavy, hairy neck and face, and great wads of black hair on its shoulders and front legs. It is practically never seen today south of Aleppo (Fig. 64).

Let us watch the camel men load and drive these animals. A light tap on the neck is signal to kneel down—though a little downward tug on the halter is a stronger reminder. The camel drops on his front knees first, then on his hinder knees, then by a series of lurches gradually settles himself down on his belly with both sets of legs tightly folded. Tie a rope around the folded front leg above the knee and the camel cannot get up. The loading now begins to the accompaniment of gurgling growls from the camel. This remonstrance makes no difference with the driver, for he knows that the beast will growl just as continuously when he is being unloaded. We admire the skill with which the men pack the goods. They divide the load into two equal parts, stow it tightly in rope crates or goat-hair bags ("sack-cloth") which are always part of the caravan equipment, and then tie them to the oak saddle that straddles the camel's hump, so that the weight on one side exactly balances that on the other (Fig. 65). The ropes are of goats' hair or wool or fiber, twisted in the long "rope-walks" under the trees that surround Damascus or some other town. And the saddle has longitudinal and upright projections about which hitches can be made; the rope renders through a wooden hook cunningly worked out from a forked branch instead of through a pulley. The saddle is of course padded to fit the camel's hump and to distribute the pressure. The load varies from three hundred to six hundred pounds, depending on the nature of the road.

When all the camels are loaded, an upward jerk on the halter, and the guttural word "khikh" bring the camels to their feet, a process that severely tests whether the load is properly tied on. Then the string of units is made into a caravan by the simple process of tying the halter-rope of each camel to the saddle of

Fig. 63.   ARABIAN CAMELS.

This picture might have been taken at one of a dozen places on the coastal trunk road. Whenever the terrain above the shore is steep and rocky and the beach itself is sufficiently broad, caravans take to the sand. Here the south-bound caravan loaded with sacks of grain has turned out for the north-bound "empty" by taking to the water. Both trains consist of Arabian camels, which are all but universal in Palestine. Their characteristics are sufficiently shown.

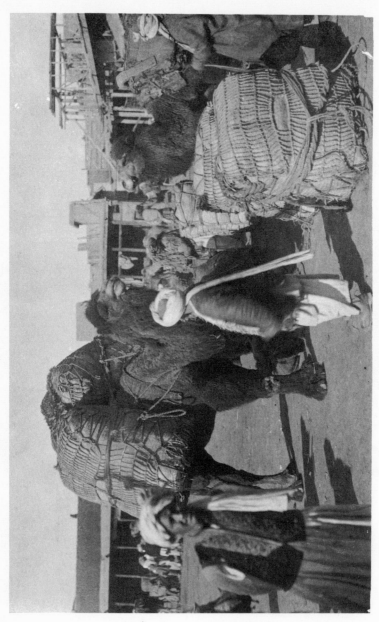

FIG. 64. BACTRIAN CAMELS.

The native home of this stout freight-carrier is central Asia. Shorter legged and more ponderous than the Arabian variety, it grows a long thick coat of hair as protection against the snows and cold of northern mountains, and sheds the same in great masses along the way in spring. Two big humps characterize this species. They will carry a load of 500 to 1000 pounds 25 miles a day. Incidentally, note the interesting rope-crates. The khan, though in India, is in arrangement like all the ancient ones in the East.

the camel in front. The rope of camel number one is hitched to the saddle of the donkey that carries the caravan-leader. So out of the khan or warehouse or loading-place silently draws the procession for its long trek, first the donkey with its rider, then

FIG. 65.   CAMEL SADDLE AND HOOK.

Saddle. The essentials of a freight saddle are two forked pieces of oak or other durable wood which ride the camel's backbone, one before and one aft the hump. These are united by two straight horizontal poles, one on each side of the central axis, which protrude far enough to furnish good tie-places. Naturally the camel must be eased against this wooden framework by thick padding. A riding saddle has a similar frame, only protruding from each end is an upright stout stake usually surmounted with a knob. These stakes keep the rider from being catapulted off the hump in emergencies, and may be grasped with the hands. This saddle is permanently

padded. *Right*. The pulley-hook is made of oak; cut from the tree at a natural crotch; finished smooth so that a rope will render across it as if it were a pulley.

the freight carriers with their drivers—one man to every five or six animals. If the caravan has a long way to go, through danger-ous country, a rendezvous is appointed where a dozen or a hun-dred caravans will assemble on a given day. Then under a convoy of soldiers the vast multitude sets forth, sometimes numbering two or three thousand camels.[4]

[4] C. M. Doughty says in his *Arabia Deserta,* that the Mecca-pilgrimage caravan he accompanied consisted of ten thousand camels, mules and asses; six thousand men, more than half of whom were serving-men on foot; and that the procession was two miles long and a hundred yards wide. But such aggregations are of course unusual.

On the road there are various things to consider, chiefly food
and drink. A camel has a supplementary pouch for water which
he can store, absorb or pass into the alimentary canal at will. He
needs a filling station every five days or so, though in a pinch he
has been known to go without water for three weeks. The men of
course must drink oftener; hence the need for frequent wells along
the route. Secure camping places for the night must be arranged
every fifteen to twenty-five miles, which are the usual limits of
a day's march. These places may be simply convenient spots
where men and animals may lie down, or they may be inns or
"khans" made for the express purpose of shelter. Khans take the
form of a walled hollow square with a single gate. Sometimes all
around the square, on the inside, is a kind of cloister, or a series
of rooms, in which men and goods may find shelter from storm
(Fig. 66). The innkeeper lives here with his family and collects
the requisite fee for the owner or the government. When a caravan enters, the animals are made to kneel and four to six of the
drivers—two or three on each side—untie the saddle and lift it
and its load bodily off the camel's back. In the morning therefore
the loads do not have to be reassembled and tied on; they have
not been taken from the saddle at all. After unloading, food and
drink are supplied to man and beast, camels are hobbled, the
campfire is lighted, the day's adventures are recounted or the
champion story-teller among the drivers—or perhaps mine host
—regales the company out of his repertory. Then the men wrap
themselves in their great-coats or a piece of gunny-sack and lie
down on the ground to sleep. The khan gate is bolted and the
guard set.

None of the very ancient inns has survived. But the califs,
governors and pious rich men of the Mohammedan era served
Allah and the faithful by building huge caravanserais of stone in
the cities and along the major routes. It is the ruins of these that
dot the present-day landscapes of the Near East.

Along the trail accidents are bound to happen. The broad,
tough foot-pads of the camel are excellent for stony or sandy

FIG. 66.   A KHAN.

This is the "Khan of the Good Samaritan" on the Jerusalem-Jericho road. The need of
some such protection is hinted by the wild and desolate terrain. The khan has only one
entrance. Within the gate on either side are rooms for the keeper and his family, and a
place where (in these days) camel men may loaf, drink coffee, smoke a hubble-bubble and
listen to a gramophone or radio. The great square is left open for animals. The smaller
square seen within the larger one is for further protection for valuable cargoes.

ground, but worse than useless .on slippery; and when a camel sprawls with his five hundred pounds of load, it takes a vast amount of swearing to get him up. Sometimes a camel takes fright and bolts, which means an hour's chase with portions of his load. littering the way. But what causes the most anxious thought is the constant danger of brigandage. In ancient texts we have numerous references.

The Song of Deborah tells us of brigandage so severe in central Palestine as to put caravans out of business (Jdg. 5:6). One of the provisions of Hammurabi's code (102, 103) indicates that robbery in poorly policed countries is to be regarded as a necessary risk. Worse than that is personal indignity and even murder. During the reign of Ikhnaton (1377–1360 B.C.) when Egyptian authority had been greatly weakened in Palestine, the king of Babylon complained that the caravan of his ambassador had been twice plundered. Some of his merchants traveling under the protection of another ambassador had been killed and their money stolen. The local king-bandits had cut off the feet of one and put the other on exhibition in a jar![5]

But in spite of all hindrances and dangers, the caravan men have never for long ceased to ply their profession.

SOCIAL INFLUENCE OF CARAVANS

Before the days of newspapers, telephones and radio, before the days of universal education, how could people know what was going on in the world? In the little villages that dot the slopes or crown the hills of Palestine, the mental horizons of the women were ordinarily limited to the gossip around the village oven and at the village spring; and the elders sitting in the town gate talked of crops and droughts and sheep-shearing, births, deaths and marriages—and taxes. But when a caravan came to town, the camel-men became centers of attraction because of the news they brought. We can imagine how eagerly a peasant like Amos

[5] A. T. Olmstead: *History of Palestine and Syria,* p. 177.

of Tekoa (Amos 1:1) would absorb the items he heard over a series of years:

A Syrian raid on Gilead, with its accompaniments of fire, rape and murder.

The vicious kidnappings carried out by Gaza on the trunk line to Egypt, and its wholesale slave trade with Edom.

Piracy by the men of Tyre—whole towns wiped out; and Edom's ready market for the slaves to work her copper mines.

The implacable cruelty of the men of Edom.

Gilead again a victim, this time of the Ammonites, who ripped up pregnant women in their bloodthirsty desire for conquest.

Moab burning the bones of the king of Edom.

Judah running after false gods while the temple of Yahweh languished.

Israel, crazy after money—get-rich-quick at any price; bribing Yahweh with a share of their ill-gotten gains.

Turning these events over in his mind, pondering them in the night watches, the inhumanity of such conduct finally so overwhelmed him that on his next trip to Bethel to sell his wool he went to the sanctuary where rich worshippers were buying Yahweh's favor with their gifts—"garments taken in pledge, and the wine of those who had been fined" (Amos 2:8), and standing in some conspicuous place let the word of Yahweh roll like thunder from his impassioned lips:

> Thus saith the Lord:
> For the three transgressions of Damascus
> And for the four, I will not turn it back;
> Because they have threshed Gilead
> With threshing tools of iron.
> So I will send fire upon the house of Hazael.
>
> Thus saith the Lord:
> For the three transgressions of Tyre—of
> Edom—of Moab—of Judah—of Israel.
> (Amos 1:3—2:8)

Thus the first "radio commentator" of history gathered his data from the only press bureau then in existence, the caravan men, weighed them in the balance of his own conscience and hurled his judgment at his public in the name of God.

Not only was news brought by the caravan men with their cargoes; but everything that civilization had developed in the way of ideas, skills, religion, art, passed from land to land on the backs of camels. Things both good and bad became part of a universal heritage. The early traders from Akkad scattered everywhere the cuneiform script, the art of keeping accounts, the methods of doing business in foreign lands. Merchants brought their gods with them and set them up in the little shops where their agents resided: gods of good luck, gods of fertility—Baals and Ishtars, Marduk, El-elyon, Zebul, Mot and Maat and Yahweh; it paid not to offend any of these. How to foreclose a mortgage safely at just the right time, how to make an extra penny by using heavy weights when buying and light weights when selling, how to imitate an expensive Mycenean vase and save the local market from being flooded, how to carve ivory so that a *nouveau riche* customer would think he was buying an original Egyptian inlaid couch instead of a native one—all these little tricks of the trade were passed on from town to town deliberately, or were absorbed spontaneously when some alert merchant saw an imported article and realized his opportunities. Thus the men of Israel were gradually made over not only by pressure of the immediate environment but through foreign ideas: they changed from pastoral to agricultural, from peasants to townsmen, from food-producers to manufacturers and traders, from hide-bound Yahweh worshippers to cosmopolitan liberals at home in any temple, and finally, from free men to slaves and exiles. The caravan is a symbol of all these things and in large part was the agent of transformation.

CHAPTER VIII

LIFE AT SOLOMON'S COURT

THE CITY bequeathed to Solomon by his father David lay along a finger-like hill between the valley of the Kedron on the east and a nameless valley on the west, later called the Tyropean. The rocky sides of this hill they cut down steeply so that there was no foothold by which to climb. Above this scarp the walls and towers were set like a crown. Towards where the finger joined the more rounded hill to the north—the present Temple area—the Jebusites had cut a deep trench crosswise, made the wall doubly strong at that point; and later they built another wall about sixty feet farther north. This finger, to that point, was the site of the city which David captured. It was a microscopic city, perhaps 1250 feet long and an average of 300 feet wide. Its area was therefore about eight acres, or less than that occupied by the Great Pyramid of Egypt.

Under Solomon, Jerusalem had become a great capital. The bazaars had expanded northward up the Tyropean valley and then had begun to climb the western hill. Here new houses had sprung up also, where the breezes from the sea swept away the odors of an undrained city and where there was an inspiring view eastward past Olivet to the deep gulf of the Dead sea and the opalescent ramparts of Moab. Solomon saw that these hundreds of new homes needed the protection of walls. Accordingly he threw a rampart around them, not far from the lines laid down in Fig. 67. At the same time he added a large area to the north of Davidsburg, doubling the size of the old fortress, and reserved it wholly for a new palace for himself (1 Kgs. 3:1). This area that roughly corresponds with the present Temple grounds was also enclosed with a wall. Jerusalem was now larger than any city in the East except the monster capitals of Egypt and Assyria.

The king's expanding power and wealth was the focus of popular talk. Through the gates every day came not only foreign emissaries on missions of state, but pack-trains loaded with tribute, new recruits to be trained for the army or new mercenaries for the king's bodyguard. Swarms of bureaucrats went through crowded streets to their offices, proud of their new-found dignities, while their wives spent lavishly in the bazaars. Trade zoomed. Local weavers, potters, cabinetmakers, smiths, jewelers, could not keep pace with the demand; the king therefore sold bazaar concessions to foreign merchants, who brought in articles of luxury that became the envy of the poor and the opportunity of the nouveau riche. When Solomon began his huge building enterprises there was an influx of skilled workers from abroad, for no Israelite could undertake the construction of a big house that required hewn stone for foundations and cedar beams for sills, rafters and pillars. King Hiram of Tyre supplied these craftsmen and overseers (2 Sam. 5:11). They had to be housed and fed all within easy distance of the Royal Quarter where work was destined to go on for twenty years. To supply these builders with material and to do the heavy work of transportation and lifting, scores of thousands of peasants were forced into service—the dreaded corvée that had been introduced in a small way by David (2 Sam. 20:24), but was now enlarged to huge proportions (1 Kgs. 9:15, 20–21). It was an era of expanding markets and rising prices; Jerusalem was a boom town.

THE PALACE BUILDINGS

Let us take a look at the royal structures that made Solomon's name synonymous with magnificence. Perhaps the best way will be to transport ourselves in imagination to Solomon's city and listen in while Ahijah, a royal scribe, escorts the visiting Crown Prince of Tyre on a sight-seeing tour.

Ahijah. "Your Royal Highness, I propose that we begin our tour at the northern end of David's old city that adjoins the palace on the south."

Presently they come to a lofty gate. It is flanked by two towers which on their north face have stone steps leading to a second story. The prince can see the bronze helmets and spears of the guards behind the battlements.

Ahijah. "His Majesty king Solomon built this towered and fortified gate which we call 'the Millo,' or 'the Filling,' in the first year of his reign (1 Kgs. 9:15). It was here that his father David personally led the attack against the city of the Jebusites and broke through the wall. The breach was never properly repaired; but His Majesty ordered the whole north wall to be strengthened and this gate to be erected as a memorial to his new reign. Here on the end of this stair you can see painted the figure of Astarte,[1] to whom His Majesty has dedicated the Millo. Beyond is the old city, two thousand years old, they say. It was once called Salem (Gen. 14:18), or in its longer form Urusalem. Inside towards the center is a citadel which contains David's palace, now disused, and his sepulchre. Since there is nothing further of importance there, we shall turn our attention to the newer buildings.

"The place occupied by the new Royal Quarter was once a hilltop an acre or so in extent, much smaller than you now see. His Majesty had first to build retaining walls on the east and west sides and fill in the slopes of the hill to make this broad platform. The northernmost part of the area had been sacred to other gods before David's day, so the Temple was placed there, and the empty space between it and the Millo of the old city was just the site His Majesty needed for his palace."

They now come to a large building, the first one encountered by people who ascend from the Millo to the higher level of the Royal Quarter.

[1] R. A. S. Macalister and J. Garrow Duncan: *Excavations on the Hill of Ophel.*

Ahijah. "His Majesty has named this first and largest building 'The House of the Forest of Lebanon.' Your Highness may have heard your father speak of this and the other buildings, for only through his cooperation were they built" (Fig. 67a).

Prince. "Yes, in our archives I have seen copies of the treaty made by my father with His Majesty (1 Kgs. 5:12), and the accounts of the lumber operations in the Lebanon (1 Kgs. 5:6, 13–14). It cost His Majesty 225,000 bushels of wheat and 180,000 gallons of olive oil per year (1 Kgs. 5:11). Our men felled the trees, sluiced them down to the sea, tied them together and towed them to Joppa (Fig. 47), from which port Israelite workmen pulled them up to this mountain (1 Kgs. 5:9).

Ahijah. "You will see plenty of those cedar trees in this building. Before we enter I want you to notice the size of these foundation stones, many of them 12 to 15 feet long (1 Kgs. 7:9–12). These were obtained locally, about ten miles north of here. His Majesty had an army of workmen in the quarries—they say 80,000; and it took 70,000 more to drag the stones to the building, though I think these figures have been stretched. (1 Kgs. 5:15–17). There were also 3300 overseers, a good many of whom were your countrymen; for our men could not have done this work without expert advice. Even so, it took thirteen years to build only the palace and seven years more for the Temple" (1 Kgs. 7:1; 6:38).

By this time they had ascended the stone stairs and were standing in the great hall.

Ahijah. "Now you see how the hall gets its name—'The Forest of Lebanon'; here are three rows of cedar columns each made of a single tree-trunk forty-five feet high (1 Kgs. 7:1–5). The rafters are also single timbers of cedar. The hall is well lighted from the three tiers of windows on each side and the three sets of doors which give easy admission to the crowds of people who come here to see the court ceremonials. The chief decoration is that double row of gold shields and bucklers hung around the walls and on the pillars (1 Kgs. 10:16–17)—the envy of all ambassadors who behold them. I saw the Egyptian ambassador taking

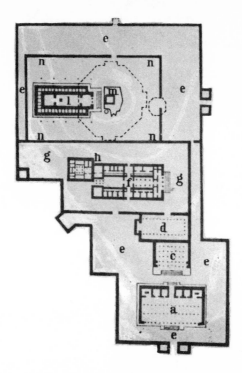

Fig. 67.   PLAN OF SOLOMON'S BUILDINGS.

a. The House of the Forest of Lebanon
c. The Hall of Pillars
d. The Throne Room
e. The outer court of the palace and temple areas
f. The king's residence
g. The middle court surrounding the residence quarters
h. House of Pharoah's Daughter
l. The Temple
m. The Altar of Burnt Offering
n. The inner court of the Temple

The rock terraces rise steadily from 2390 feet at the south entrance of these buildings, to 2430 feet, the highest point, where the Altar stands.

special note of them the other day." (In 1 Kgs. 14:25-26 we have an account of how Shishak, king of Egypt, captured Jerusalem in Rehoboam's time and carried off all these decorations.)

They now cross the hall and leave the north door. Facing them is a second building (Fig. 67c).

Ahijah. "This is called the 'Pillared Porch' because there are pillars in front above the entrance steps, and as we pass through you will see pillars supporting the roof. This is a kind of waiting room where those stay who have business with the king or whose cases at law are to come up for trial."

They now pass to the last of the public buildings on a still higher level—the Hall of Judgment, or Throne Room (Fig. 67d) to which the Pillared Porch is an anteroom.

Prince. "Oh yes, I remember this place well. Here is where His Majesty gave me audience when I arrived two days ago. It was really a very dramatic show—guards, courtiers, fan-bearers, liveried servants with gold-dust sprinkled in their long hair, musicians and all. I was especially interested in the throne, which looked as if it were Phoenician work, but I could not examine it carefully, of course."

Ahijah. "This will be a good time to do so."

They pass along this really regal hall, sheathed from floor to ceiling with cedar, ornamented with pilasters of sweet-smelling sandal wood (1 Kgs. 10:12), and equipped with bronze braziers for heating, golden lamps, and tripods on which vases of flowers or other ornaments might be placed. On either side of the throne were raised balustraded "boxes," in which ladies of the harem, ambassadors or courtiers might sit and view the show. The chairs were all inlaid with ivory.

Ahijah. "Here is the throne. Isn't it magnificent! There are six steps, as you see, broad enough for six lions on each side to crouch on guard, their mouths snarling defiantly. If I may guess, I think the lions stand for the majesty of the king (Prov. 30:29-31). See how the idea is repeated on the arms of the throne where lions ramp on each side. Those heads of bullocks carved on the

Fig. 68.   PHOENICIAN IVORY BORDER
FROM SAMARIA.

The design consists of a rhythmic arrangement of
lotus buds and flowers. The florid central units represent the flower in full bloom, the petals conventionalized into a semicircular coronet, while the sepals curl
at the ends into a primitive Ionic volute. From the
expanded base of the stalk spring pairs of buds, alter-
nately shut and half open.

tall back of the throne are associated with the fertility cult of both our peoples. They insure by their magic that the king's lands shall be more fruitful. All these details are overlaid with gold; but the most beautiful decorations are the sculptured inlays of ivory which I confess I do not understand."

The prince bent to examine them with care and found them all to be of Phoenician workmanship (See Fig. 68).

Ahijah. "You should have been in this hall last year when His Majesty entertained the Queen of Sheba! (1 Kgs. 10:1-13) Her visit had more behind it than we knew at the time. You see, her kingdom lies in the extreme south of Arabia and she has control of all the caravans that bring the wealth of that country to Jerusalem, Damascus, Syria, Phoenicia and Egypt. She also receives and transships the costly goods from farther south and east, from Ophir and India—rubies, emeralds, pearls, ivory, incense, strange animals and plants, silver and gold. Now His Majesty had recently acquired control of the caravan routes from the Red sea northward, and had put into commission a fleet of ships on the Red sea itself built and navigated by your Tyrian seamen, and that was ruining her trade. She was frightened enough to take a fifteen-hundred-mile trip by camel to see if she could make some kind of living arrangement. Of course we only saw the entertainments His Majesty put on for her; what went on behind the scenes we do not know. But something satisfactory was evidently patched up, for the lady went home happy." [2]

Prince. "They say she could put on quite a show all by herself! Did she bring a respectable train with her?"

Ahijah. "You ought to have seen it!—a thousand camels. We couldn't house them within the walls, so a special camp was set up in the Upper Kedron valley and a guard of soldiers was detailed to keep them safe. The camels were laden with royal

[2] An explanation not found in the Bible but based on archaeological discoveries about Solomon's business enterprises. See N. Glueck: "Ezion-Geber," in *Biblical Archaeology* I. 3, 14.

presents, tons of spices and more gold than our treasurer had ever seen at one time, and precious stones that no one could name. They say the gold weighed one hundred and twenty talents! [3]

"But the entertainments! The queen had heard in her far country of the wisdom of His Majesty and resolved to put it to the test. We were assembled here one morning for the audience when the queen suddenly announced that she had an insoluble problem for His Majesty. At a clap of her hand the guard opened those doors yonder and we could see that the steps and the Pillared Hall were filled with children dressed all in white, just alike. They began to file into the Audience Room, which could not contain them all.

"'Your Majesty,' said the queen, 'here are five hundred boys and five hundred girls of the same age, dressed all alike. No doubt your Majesty will be able to separate the boys from the girls!'

"In a flash His Majesty ordered, 'Bring in a thousand basins of water and let them wash!' While riddles were being exchanged to fill the time—and the queen had some good ones, (1 Kgs. 10:1, 3)—the basins were brought and the washing began. All the boys washed their faces directly with both hands, as boys always do; the girls as they had been taught, poured the water from the left hand to the right and with it washed their faces.

"'That is easy!' said Solomon, and the queen had to join in the laughter." [4]

Prince. "Speaking of riddles, did you ever hear that King Solomon and my father used to exchange riddles in their younger days? They had an arrangement whereby the one who could not guess a riddle should pay a fine. My father was not so shrewd as

[3] Value: A Babylonian "heavy" talent weighed 909.600 grains Troy, or 130 lbs. avoirdupoids, equal in weight to 4,230,000 United States gold dollars, and in purchasing power perhaps twenty-five times that, or $105,750,-000 = £21,150,000. See 1 Kgs. 10:10.

[4] This of course is a late Arabic legend, but it serves to show the popular impression left by this shrewd monarch on contemporaries, and by them transmitted to posterity. Many much more wonderful feats are recorded by Gustav Weil in *Biblical Legends*.

Solomon and the fines he had to pay finally went beyond the joke stage. So what did my father do but hire a bright young Tyrian named Abdemon to solve the riddles for him and to invent some that Solomon could not unravel. Then the money flowed the other way till the score was even! But don't tell His Majesty. I think he never found out what made my father so suddenly brilliant." [5]

Ahijah. "Yes, I heard of that famous contests of wits. However, what impressed the Queen more than Solomon's wisdom was the elaborate state he kept. She was not used to such a highly organized establishment. More than once she spoke of the great variety of viands on his table, of the prompt and skillful attendance of his waiters and the splendid liveries of his servants, of his cup-bearers, and of the huge burnt offerings he made at the Temple. As she put it on one occasion, 'There is no spirit left in me! The half was not told me.'

"These are all the palace buildings we can see. Beyond are the king's private apartments (Fig. 67f). I am not allowed to enter there."

THE TEMPLE

Following the court just within the eastern boundary wall they came to the most northerly building in the Royal Area (Fig. 67l). (For the Biblical description of the Temple and its appointments, see 1 Kgs. 6:1–38). It did not compare in size with the palace buildings, but a boundary wall of large dressed stones in three courses surmounted by a single course of cedar beams formed a court about it and gave it isolation and prominence. The fact that it was covered with gold leaf made it resplendent in the morning sun. The men entered the enclosure.

[5] Related by Josephus on the authority of a Phoenician historian named Dius. See *Antiq.* VIII, 5,3. The so-called Number Sonnets in *Proverbs* are properly answers to riddles. For example: "What are four intolerable things?" Answer, Prov. 30:21–23; "What are four little wise things?" Answer, Prov. 30:24–28; etc.

Ahijah. "This large altar of burnt offering stands on the exact site of the ancient High Place that had been usurped by Auraunah the Jebusite for a threshing-floor (Fig. 67m). You will be inter-

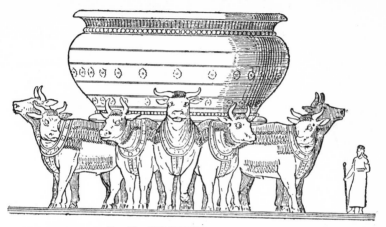

FIG. 69. SOLOMON'S BRAZEN SEA.

It is 15 feet in diameter and 7½ feet high; weight, 25-30 tons. The triads of oxen face each point of the compass. The fact that in making these creatures, the cherubim and various plant forms, Solomon broke the second commandment, is indication that in his day the Decalogue as we know it was not yet in existence.

ested in the great bronze "sea," as they call it, where water is stored for various uses (Fig. 69). There again we are indebted to your country. The man who cast it in the clay of the Jordan valley was a certain half-breed named Hiram, part Tyrian and part Israelite. It is the largest basin ever cast and it has the shape of a lotus blossom. That curious mounting on the backs of twelve bulls, three facing each of the cardinal points and symbolizing the four seasons, together with the double row of gourds cast under the lip of the basin, are all evidences that Yahweh as a cosmic deity has absorbed the functions of the Canaanite fertility cults with their bulls and floral symbols. You will find plenty of other evidences on the Temple itself. Over there by the building are ten small lavers on wheels, so that they can be moved wherever there is need. They hold only 360 gallons as against the sea's 15,000. They also are ornamented with lions, oxen and cherubim (Fig. 70).

As they advanced towards the temple porch, some priests approached to warn them that this was a forbidden area. But Ahijah had provided himself with a pass signed by the king's own hand.

Ahijah. "On the terrace at the top of the entrance step you will notice two curious pillars that stand free like sentinels. They are giant incense burners that in addition to their proper function also remind us of the 'pillar of cloud by day and of fire by night' that guided our fathers through the wilderness. We call the pillars 'Boaz' and 'Jacin,' from the first words of two oracles that guarantee the eternal continuance of the Davidic dynasty.[6] Hiram cast them also, and plenty of bronze they took, for including bases and capitals they are thirty-seven feet high and six feet in diameter."

Prince. "I imagine His Majesty got the idea for these when he visited Tyre. We have two splendid pillars like them in the temple of Baal-Melkart that my father built. One is of gold and one of emerald glass." [7]

Ahijah. "No doubt that is true. But His Majesty found plenty of suggestions in our own country. There are standing pillars at every Canaanite 'high-place,' only they are made of plain stone. They are the abode of Yahweh in his function of life-giver, the male principle, as the sacred pole or sacred tree is the abode of his consort Anat (Astarte, Ashtoreth). His Majesty is a great devotee of this cult and goes frequently to Gibeon to sacrifice on the high-place there. He sometimes offers a thousand bullocks at a time (1 Kgs. 3:4). Those bronze capitals above the pillars are ornamented with trellises on which are lotus flowers and two rows of pomegranates. These also are fertility symbols."

[6] W. F. Albright: *Archaeology and the Religion of Israel*, pp. 139, 144–8.
[7] On the authority of Herodotus (2:44) who personally saw them. Of the emerald pillar he says that it shone with great brilliance at night.

a. The much-traveled candlestick, or more properly a lamp-stand, here shown, is from the triumphal arch of Titus at Rome. Were it not for this relief we could not be sure how the seven branches were arranged.

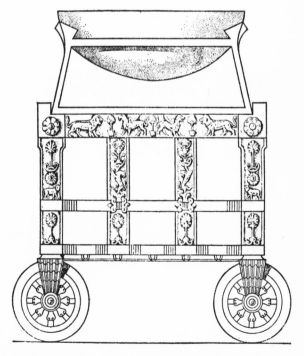

b. Smaller basins placed upon wheeled stands. They could be easily moved from one sacrificial animal to another. All the decoration consists of fertility symbols.

Fig. 70.   LAVER AND THE SEVEN-BRANCHED LAMP.

They now mounted the ten steps to the porch. The priestly guardians told them they could enter the first room only; the holy of holies was reserved for the High Priest. They passed the great doors to the vestibule, and then another set of doors carved and inlaid with gold, and when their eyes were accustomed to the dimness they could make out a room 60 feet by 30. The floor was of cypress, the walls and ceiling of cedar. A little light came in through latticed windows near the ceiling. At the farther end stood a small altar used for burning incense; it was plated with gold. On the right was a table on which bread was placed for Yahweh's eating; on the left a seven-branched lamp-stand. Beyond in the wall were double folding doors of olive wood. On them were carved palm trees, open flowers and cherubim.

Ahijah. "Of the inner shrine I know only what my friend Azariah the High Priest has told me. It is cubical in shape, lined with cedar, the walls carved with symbols like those you have seen. But the most striking objects are two huge cherubs fifteen feet high, made of olive wood and covered with gold. They look like winged lions with a human head; they stand upright and hold their wings horizontally with a spread of fifteen feet. That means that each cherub touches the Temple wall with his outer wing and the inner wings touch each other. Beneath the inner wings is the Ark, which has had a unique history, too long to be repeated here. (For adventures of the Ark, see 1 Sam. 4:1b–7:1; 2 Sam. 6:2–19; 1 Kgs. 8:1–9).

Prince. "What does the Ark look like?"

Ahijah. "It now is a gold-plated box of acacia wood about four feet long, fitted with poles on each side by which the priests carry it. But this is His Majesty's casket for the real Ark inside, which I suspect is a rude thing made of baked clay in the form of a sanctuary. There are many such about; every high place has one. (1 Sam. 14:18; called "ephod"). There is some doubt whether Yahweh resides in the Ark or in the cherubim. I personally think he can transfer himself from one to the other at will."

After examining the objects in the holy room, all of which had to do with food, drink, or odors for Yahweh, the pair returned to the light of day. Then the prince made a cynical remark:

Prince. "It is easy to see what His Majesty values most highly: he spends thirteen years in building a huge palace for himself, and seven years in building a small shrine for his god. In Tyre we put the emphasis differently. My father lives in a small house, while the temple of Baal Melkart is the largest and richest in Phoenicia."

COURT BUSINESS: AN IMAGINATIVE RECONSTRUCTION

If we could wave a magic wand and find ourselves present at Solomon's monthly business session with his ministers, we should doubtless see and hear something like the following:

Scene, the Throne Room of the palace. Tables and chairs have been arranged in a semicircle before the throne. Secretaries and messengers are assembling with their records and accounts on papyrus rolls carried in baskets. Enter the ministers and take their places in order of rank, the prime minister Jehoshaphat first. (For a list of all the officers see 1 Kgs. 4:1–19.) A blare of trumpets. The doors are flung open and Benaiah appears clad in the insignia of Commander-in-chief. Behind him a troop of splendidly accoutred soldiers each one nearly seven feet tall, wearing a crested gold helmet and cuirass of bronze and carrying a sword, a spear, and a gold-plated bronze shield. These form a double rank between the entrance and the throne.

With a fanfare of trumpets the troops present arms, and His Majesty enters, preceded by his major domo Ahishar, a black eunuch. The princes bow low, the underlings touch the pavement with their foreheads. Solomon mounts the throne, all resume their places, the guards form lines about the sides of the room, doors are closed and the business begins.

First the Commander-in-chief, Benaiah, reports on the state of the defenses. The boundaries of the kingdom are secure. Prince Hadad of Edom tried to make trouble (1 Kgs. 11:14) but he learned his lesson, so that business from the port of Elath now comes in as usual. The six fortified cities are proving to be strategically placed to levy tariffs on the caravan trade and to deal with any possible disaffection among the people (1 Kgs. 9:15c–19). In these fortresses are 12,000 horses and 1400 chariots, besides a reserve of 40,000 horses (1 Kgs. 4:26; 10:26).

Next the reports of the administrative districts into which the kingdom has been divided.

Governor Baanah of Megiddo and neighboring cities reports with satisfaction the completion of the outer wall of defense that practically doubles the area of the city and makes capture by assault impossible. He tells of the erection of the chief captain's headquarters on the easterly wall, and in particular the new arrangements for stabling horses, four hundred fifty of which have been assigned to Megiddo.[8]

Governor Jehoshaphat from the district Issachar reports on the supplies collected and distributed for the past month—for each governor in rotation must deliver all the food necessary for the upkeep of the royal establishment monthly. Here is the list:

Barley and straw for the horses in each of the six guard-cities (1 Kgs. 4:28), in addition to Tanaach, Lachish and Jerusalem; and food for the king's household at Jerusalem. The daily receipt of the latter has been

Fine flour, 337½ bushels; meal, 675 bushels; fatted cattle, 10; pasture-fed cattle, 20; sheep, 100; delicacies like harts, gazelles, roebucks and fatted fowl, more than could be used and no account kept (1 Kgs. 4:22–23).

The governor from Gaza, in whose hands have been placed the royal monopolies in horses and chariots, reports unusually fine business on account of military preparations in the north. Having prevented news of a rising market from reaching Egypt and Cilicia, the chief sources of supply, he has been able to buy

[8] See Fig. 71 and the report of excavations by the Oriental Institute. Philip L. O. Guy: *New Light from Armageddon.*

FIG. 71. MODEL OF SOLOMON'S STABLES AT MEGIDDO.

Reconstructed from the remains found in the Solomonic stratum of Megiddo. It shows a central passage through which the grooms cared for the horses; a row of square stone posts on each side to support the roof, each of which had a tie-hole through a corner; between these posts, stone mangers; a flat roof of mud, arranged with a clerestory for light and air. Each unit accommodated 24 horses. In the same part of the city stables for over 300 horses have been discovered.

chariots from Egypt at the old rate of 600 shekels of silver, horses from Cilicia at 150 shekels (1 Kgs. 10:28–29) ; and to sell the entire consignment to petty kings of the north who are conspiring against Assyria, for more than double the cost. After paying transportation charges and a few tariffs in Syria, he is pleased to report 100% profit for the month. (Applause from the throne, echoed by all!)

The military commander at Baalath that guards the rocky road to the Red sea, announces that in the preceding year the copper mines in the Arabah south of the Dead sea (at modern Umm el-Amad and Mrashragh), were opened up and reduction furnaces installed, and that plenty of metal was now being shipped into Elath. His special job for this year has been to devise furnaces to handle more efficiently the ore refining. At last he has succeeded. Just outside of Elath the wind blows strongly and steadily from the north and there he has erected a plant that utilizes this natural blast. By a series of chambers, blow-holes and vents, he can now obtain pure copper in half the time. A manufacturing plant has been set up adjacent where they can turn out any commercial bronze article from fishhooks to plowshares and arms. These goods are in great demand farther south on both sides of the Red sea, in Ethiopia and lands east, so that the Red sea fleet is kept busy, and profits flow in from both ends of the deal.[9]

He reports further that the Tarshish fleet, built and navigated under Phoenician direction, has just returned from a three-year voyage (1 Kgs. 10:22). Trading has been completely successful, especially in the matter of gold and silver bullion. For the sake of a diversion for His Majesty, the commander now begs to show a few samples of foreign curiosities; whereupon the doors open and in comes a procession of coal-black Abyssinians, each with some special object.

First a group of six men clad in loin-cloths of brightly colored

[9] N. Glueck: "Ezion-Geber," in *Biblical Archaeologist* I 3 (Sept. 1938) pp. 13–16.

straw, their curly pates decorated with a standing ostrich feather, bear on their shoulder a huge elephant's tusk seven feet long. Next come four men whose long hair is done up in knots pierced with ebony bodkins knobbed with silver; they lead apes of various sizes which strain at their leashes in excess of energy—one little one even hopping on his keeper's head, to His Majesty's great delight. Other men bring bars of sandal wood, the odor of which fills the house; peacocks both white and blue, one of which is induced to spread his tail, to the wonderment of all beholders; gems of various hues carried on small ebony trays. Last of all comes a procession of living almug trees, each one with its roots in a basket slung on poles and carried on the shoulders of four bearers.[10]

His Majesty is vastly entertained.

Last of all, the Treasurer begs to report that His Majesty's receipt of gold the past year has been 666 talents (bullion value, $20,000,000 or £4,000,000, in purchasing power equivalent today to twenty-five times that amount). In addition are the unstated profits from the king's business ventures and the gifts from various kinglets who find it profitable to show friendship (1 Kgs. 10:14-15, 21, 24-25).

No wonder the king listens to these reports with a satisfied smile.

After making appointments for private audiences with some of the ministers he adjourns the session.

Nevertheless, things were not so bright as they seemed. Future historians looking back from harsher times upon this period of expansion thought that it was a kind of Utopia and that Solomon was the wisest and happiest of mortals. The truth is that Solomon was a spendthrift who did not pay his bills. Over a period of years, Hiram of Tyre loaned this royal four-flusher $3,750,000 (£950,000) on the collateral of twenty towns in Galilee. When

[10] For picture of trees carried in this fashion, see relief from the temple of Hatshepsut at Thebes, A. E. Bailey and C. F. Kent: *History of the Hebrew Commonwealth*, p. 136.

Hiram finally called the loans he discovered that Solomon could not pay and that the collateral was worthless (1 Kgs. 9:10-14). These same historians did realize, however, that Solomon destroyed the liberties of Israel. When the king's building operations were at their peak, in addition to the Canaanite slaves, 30,000 free men of Israel were forced from their farms and transported to Lebanon to assist in cutting timber. In the quarries near at hand were 70,000 burden-bearers and 80,000 hewers of stone, many of them Israelites whose fathers had been free men since time immemorial (1 Kgs. 5:13-16). Then fell the taxes with crushing force—a tenth of the grain crops and the vineyards, a tenth of the cattle; at last, bold confiscation of the best lands in the kingdom; and worse still, the seizure of a man's slaves, and then his children, and then himself. (1 Sam. 8:11-18).

In view of the collapse and the depression that followed Solomon's death, this record effectively contradicts Solomon's claim to be a wise man.

WIVES AND GODS

In all oriental states the size of a king's harem was an index of his power and glory. David started his marital career with one wife, Michal the daughter of Saul. By the time he became king over Judah in Hebron he had acquired six wives, while other wives and concubines were added during the Jerusalem kingship, exact number not stated (2 Sam. 3:2-5; 5:13-16). But Solomon made his father look like a rank amateur. The wife of Solomon's youth was daughter of Hiram of Tyre.[11] In the fourth year of his reign he made a treaty with Shishak, Pharaoh of Egypt, and received a royal daughter for wife to bind the bargain (1 Kgs. 3:1), while Pharaoh captured the city of Gezer and gave it to Solomon as a wedding present (1 Kgs. 9:16-17). Solomon was so elated over this recognition by one of the great kings of the earth that he built a large palace for her and her servants adjoining his own in the new royal grounds (1 Kgs. 7:8. Fig. 67h).

[11] On the statement of 1 Kings 11:1, where she is called a Sidonian, and of Clement of Alexandria in his *Stromata,* I. 21.

Every time he made a trade treaty with a foreign king he seems to have sealed it with a marriage, till the harem swarmed with all nationalities and all kinds of girls. The official record gives a total of 700 wives and 300 concubines (1 Kgs. 11:3). The personality problems involved in such a household must have kept Solomon busy, especially when children began to arrive and complicate the already existing jealousies with intrigues for the advancement of each wife's son and his succession to the throne. It may truly be said of Solomon's modest outfit what the biographer of the Mogul emperor Akbar said of his harem of 3000 or so: "It furnished His Majesty with many opportunities to display his wisdom."

But this is not all of the problem. Whenever a new wife came, a horde of merchants came also to set up their shops in the bazaar—which was not so bad; and the new wife and the merchants brought their gods along—which was wholly bad; for it complicated the people's loyalty to Yahweh and especially the loyalty of the king who was guardian of the state religion. During Solomon's reign these foreign gods became a real menace, for their shrines occupied conspicuous places about town and in the suburbs. On Olivet was the shrine of Chemosh, god of the Moabites; on its southern spur, Milcom, god of the Ammonites. Down the valley of Jehoshaphat amid the pleasant walks and groves of the king's gardens, rose the horrid statue of Moloch of Tyre, to whom human sacrifices were offered. These and many lesser gods stole the king's heart and drew away many people from the simpler and more austere faith of their fathers (1 Kgs. 11:4-8). Israel never recovered from these debasing contacts until the Exile wiped out idolatry once for all (Jer. 7:30-31; Hos. 8).

This was Jerusalem during its one great period of inflation. After Solomon, came the crash and the depression that, with varying ups and downs, continued for three hundred years until Nebuchadnezzar destroyed the city altogether.

CHAPTER IX

LIFE IN THE TIME OF ISAIAH, 760–700 B.C.[1]

(In Part an Imaginative Interpretation)

ISAIAH'S father was Amoz, a citizen of Jerusalem. Already there were six children in the family, for large families were the rule. Since the struggle for existence was not so intense as in Gideon's day, his·record of 70 children (Jdg. 8:30) was not now likely to be duplicated; Jesse's number, 8 sons, was nearer. the average (1 Sam. 16:10–11). Amoz felt as did the Psalmist (Ps. 127:3–5):

> Lo, children are a heritage from the Lord.
>
> .   .   .   .
>
> Like arrows in the hand of a warrior
> So are the children of one's youth.
> Happy is the man whose quiver is filled with them!

For economic reasons, Amoz, like most of his neighbors, kept only one wife.

At the time of Isaiah's birth, the only help the wife received was from a midwife whose professional training consisted of having herself been a mother and having had some experience in assisting other women. Usually not much help was required. Israelite women learned to look after themselves (cf. Ex. 1:19). When Isaiah was born he was washed and then rubbed with salt to ward off the attacks of evil spirits, and wrapped in swaddling-

---

[1] The aspects of life portrayed in this chapter characterize all the period roughly from the division of the kingdom, c. 933 B.C., to the destruction of Jerusalem, 586 B.C.

clothes (Ezek. 16:4). When Amoz was sent for he at once named the child, for at this period fathers usually assumed that obligation (Is. 8:3c–4a; Hos. 1:4, 6, 9). The new boy was named *"Yesha'-yahu"* which means "Yahweh is salvation." No family name was given, as the practice was to say "son of Amoz" if any differentiation from other Isaiahs was necessary (Is. 1:1). The name was always an important protection, especially if some form of Yahweh was incorporated into it, as Eli-jah, Adoni-jah; or in case the father was a Baal worshipper, Jerub-baal (Jdg. 6:32), Meri-baal (2 Sam. 21:8).

Word of the arrival of the seventh son spread quickly by way of the housetops, and friends began to arrive to congratulate the father and to partake of the good cheer that was always provided on such occasions (implied in Jer. 20:14–15).

On the eighth day little Isaiah was circumcised (Lev. 12:3), and thereby inducted into his membership in the household of Israel. The rite was performed at home by Amoz who used a flint knife such as all his ancestors had used (Ex. 4:25; Josh. 5:2). Prayers and blessings were then recited, after which family and friends feasted together. Amoz also placed tattoo marks on his son to protect him still further from demons (Is. 44:5; Deut. 6:8. This custom was later forbidden, Lev. 19:28).

The house in which Isaiah was brought up lay on the western hill where were the better residences. It was built of cut stone inasmuch as Jerusalem was now too important and prosperous a city to use the old mud brick. Since Isaiah was an aristocrat, very likely related to the royal family, he lived in a finer house than the average, with cedar for the ceiling beams (Is. 9:10), cypress instead of clay or flagstones for flooring; the rooms large and supplied with windows (1 Kgs. 6:15; Jer. 22:14).

Amoz's wife managed her household. The work was done by herself and her daughters together with one or more household slaves—for slaves were used in all the well-to-do families. In the old days Amoz would have captured these slaves in war (2 Kgs. 5:2), but now it was easier to take some one's children for debt

(2 Kgs. 4:1; Neh. 5:5) or to buy in the open market (Is. 50:1). The value of a slave at this time (*cf.* E document, Ex. 21:32) was 30 shekels of silver, or about $10 or £2-2-0. With a decent master slavery was not so bad. The slave was assured of food and shelter as long as he was serviceable, was regarded as a member of the family even to the extent of being circumcised if a male, and admitted to all the religious ceremonies of the household. He was increasingly protected by law (Ex. 21:20-21, 26-27; even runaway slaves, after the promulgation of the Deuteronomic law, Deut. 23:15-16); nor could a slave be worked on the Sabbath (Deut. 5:14). Foreign slaves had usually a hard time, but Israelite slaves were especially protected from harshness and in addition, had the right of freedom, with all their children, in the year of Jubilee.[2]

The details of household life have not come down to us; such well-known trivialities were taken for granted by the Bible writers. But from widely scattered hints we can reconstruct some of these facts. The food eaten in Isaiah's home was like that of the Patriarchs, described in Chapter III. Grain was still the foundation; ground into meal or finer flour, mixed with water or oil, baked, or cooked in oil and eaten with oil as we eat bread with butter. The use of oil was inevitable in a land where the olive tree flourished.[3] Honey was also a constant article of food, both bee honey and fruit honey (Is. 7:15; Ezek. 16:13). Fruit juices were the universal beverages: pomegranate juice (S. of S. 8:2) and especially the products of the vine. Some wine was sweet (Is. 49:26); some was sour (Ruth 2:14); some was mixed (Prov. 9:2); some of it foamed, evidently because it was mixed (Ps. 75:8); some was spiced (S. of S. 8:2). Wine from Lebanon was especially prized for its fragrance (Hos. 14:7). For special occasions however they had hard liquor made from wine-grounds, dates and honey (Is.

---

[2] For these various protections, see Lev. 25:25-28, 35-55; late however.

[3] *Cf.* the annual export of 16,000 gallons of oil to Tyre in Solomon's time, 1 Kings 5:11; the widow's meal and cruse of oil, 1 Kings 17:12; and Elisha's provision of oil to pay a widow's debt, 2 Kings 4:1-7.

5:22; forbidden to a Nazirite along with wine, Num. 6:1–4).
It was chiefly this "strong drink" rather than wine that was
responsible for the drunkenness against which Isaiah and other
writers declaim (Is. 5:11; 24:9; 28:7; 56:12; Prov. 20:1;
31:4, 6).

Isaiah came directly under his mother's jurisdiction while he
was an infant. His mother nursed him till he was two or three

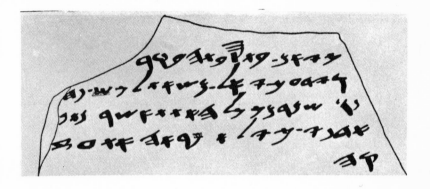

FIG. 72.   LETTER FROM LACHISH.

One of 18 "ostraca" or inscribed potsherds found in the guardroom at the gate of
Lachish. They were part of the evidence used in the military trial of the sender who was
apparently in sympathy with the peace policy of Jeremiah. They were written a few
months before the capture of the city by Nebuchadnezzar the second time in 587 B.C. When
found they were covered with the ashes of a great conflagration. The translation reads:
"Investigate, and (my lord) will know that for the fire-signals of Lachish we are watch-
ing, according to all the signs that my lord has given, for we cannot see (the signals of)
Azekah" (*cf.* Jer. 34:7).
The scribe used a reed pen, and ink containing carbon (lampblack) and iron. The
characters are not the square kind used in engraving on monuments, but a flowing script
used in writing on papyrus or parchment. In this case potsherds were used because of the
expense and war-time scarcity of the other materials.

years old (*cf.* 1 Sam. 1:23) and taught him to be useful about
the house as he grew to boyhood. At 6 or 7 he came more under
his father's tuition, who taught him to work. How he learned to
read and write we do not know. There were no schools at this
period. Nevertheless there were some people, probably many,

who knew how to write. Extant from Isaiah's time is the inscription on the walls of the Siloam tunnel under David's city, and in the book of Isaiah we find mention of "Shebna the secretary" and "Joah the recorder" (Is. 36:3). A hundred years later king Joash could read (2 Kgs. 23:2) while a professional writer or scribe was among his officials (2 Kgs. 22:8-10). Letters of this later time, 589 B.C., found at Lachish, show that men in the army or in government service could read and write. The materials used were pottery sherds (ostraca) and ink [4] (Fig. 72). Probably all these writers as well as the young Isaiah were privately taught by other writers.

As for the general rules of living, Amoz himself instructed his son. He instilled into him the necessity of respect for his parents (Prov. 30:17), of obedience (Prov. 1:8; 4:1-9; 13:1) and industry (Prov. 22:29), and enforced his teaching if necessary with a stick (Prov. 23:13-14). A good many of the maxims now preserved in our book of Proverbs were current in the days of Amoz and served the father in establishing right ideals in his son. Until the book of Deuteronomy was written after Isaiah's death there were few if any definite subjects of instruction; but after that date there was the Law. By that time parental authority was breaking down to such an extent that there was need to bolster it up by something sterner: the punishment for incorrigibility was written into the law of the land—and it was death! (Deut. 21:18-21)

The Industries of Jerusalem

As part of his son's practical education, Amoz took Isaiah about town to see the different industries. By this time Jerusalem was too large to be fed by the few square miles of its environs, and therefore it had to import supplies from distant points. Practically all of the lower town—between the eastern and western hills—was one bazaar where on the one hand the necessities of life were

[4] See *The Lachish Letters*, Oxford Univ. Press, 1938.

sold by near-by farmers directly, or by middlemen who represented Transjordan, the south country, Philistia and Egypt; and on the other, those products were manufactured and sold that made life more agreeable for city dwellers and villagers alike. Not only did Isaiah with a boy's curiosity see all these industries in full swing but he was able in his manhood to draw upon their technical terms and their imagery for some of his most brilliant prophetic utterances.

First there were the smiths, makers of "heavy goods," workers in iron, copper and its alloys of bronze and brass, and the precious metals. Most of the smelting (Job 28:2) was done near the mine as in Solomon's day (Chapter VIII). But the alloying, casting and shaping of products were done in the Jerusalem bazaars, each industry occupying its special quarter, and each individual manufacturer with his helpers occupying a separate stall, as any one may see today in Jerusalem. There Isaiah learned about the processes and the tools: furnaces, alloys, dross (Is. 1:25; Ezek. 22:18–22; Prov. 27:21); bellows (Jer. 6:29); casting and overlaying (Is. 40:19); smoothing with the hammer and riveting with the mallet (Is. 41:7); tools for carving and engraving (1 Kgs. 6:29, 32–36. A fairly complete picture of the smith at work at his anvil is given in Ecclesiasticus 38:28).

On the artisan's shelves in the brass bazaar Isaiah would see exposed for sale weapons such as helmets, scale breastplates, greaves, javelins (1 Sam. 17:5–6); fetters (Jdg. 16:21); cult objects and implements (1 Kgs. 7); plates and bars for city gates (Is. 45:2; Ps. 107:16); musical instruments such as cymbals and trumpets (1 Chron. 15:19, 24). In the iron bazaar he would find farming tools that had iron fittings, such as threshing sledges, wagon wheels and harrows (Is. 28:24, 27); flails (Amos 1:3); plowshares, coulters, mattocks (1 Sam. 13:19–21); sickles, axes (2 Kgs. 6:5; Jer. 50:16) and saws (2 Sam. 12:31). Here too would be instruments of war: chariots (2 Kgs. 9:27), spearheads (1 Sam. 17:7), swords (Ezek. 5:1), fetters (Ps. 105:18), prison bars (Is. 45:2). And in both bazaars he would see household utensils: pans, pots, kettles, cauldrons, forks (Ezek. 4:3; 1 Sam. 2:13–14), pens for writing (Jer. 17:1; Job 19:24), and razors (Is. 7:20; Ezek. 5:1). The mention of all these objects would imply that many score of men would be engaged in smithing in Jerusalem.

Potters also were a numerous lot because every household needed clay vessels—and clay is breakable.[5] The demand was constant. While Jeremiah speaks only of one potter whom he visited (Jer. 18:2), there must have been a ceramic quarter in Jerusalem; and to judge by the Chronicler there were guilds or families of potters in other places (1 Chron. 4:23). Potters were of necessity high-grade men, for the art calls for creative skill. Some details of the craft have come down to us. Clay was kneaded at the pit by being trodden under foot (Is. 41:25); probably there was additional kneading by hand at the pottery to keep it in workable condition. Jars and other utensils were made on a potter's wheel, or on wheels (Jer. 18:3) which were worked by the feet so that the hands would be free for manipulation. When shaped, the vessel would be glazed (Prov. 26:23), though water-coolers were left unglazed; and then came firing to fix both form and color. (These details are expressly given in Ecclesiasticus 38:29–30). What impressed both Isaiah and Jeremiah, as it impresses every one, is the absolute dominance of the will of the potter over his clay, and the mystery of creative skill (Is. 45:9; 29:16; Jer. 18:4, 6) (Fig. 73).

Potsherds have received a new significance in our day when they have proved to be the most reliable means of dating a given level of excavation. A comparative study also shows that as a rule Israelite pottery was inferior to Canaanite or foreign ware, and that the potters constantly tried to imitate the better foreign work, especially at this date the pottery of Cyprus and Phoenicia.

Since houses were constructed of stone or brick, in the carpenters' bazaar Isaiah saw only house furnishings and other objects

---

[5] The city gate that led to the refuse dump in the valley of Hinnom was called Potsherd Gate (Jer. 19:2, Amer. tr.) .

made of wood: tables, chairs, inlaid work and veneering. Of
farm implements he saw the framework of the plows, the yokes
and the three-pronged forks with which winnowing was done
(Fig. 61). The rural population usually bought these articles in
Jerusalem where division of labor and consequently greater skill

Fig. 73.   ISRAELITE POTTERY.

These samples were found in a tomb at Beth-shemesh (Ain Shems) and date from the
8th century. Throughout the period of the Monarchy, Israelite pottery was inferior in
design and crude in execution, as these specimens show. It could not compare with vases
of the Myceneans, 1400-1200 B.C. nor of the Greeks, 600-200 B.C. In the days of Isaiah
the most highly prized pieces were either imported from Cyprus and Phoenicia or imita-
tions of such by local potters.

prevailed. Much of the finer work of all sorts was done by
Phoenician artisans. In Solomon's day all the carpenter work on
the Temple had been Phoenician, but by the time of Jehoash
(ninth century B.C.) temple repairs were made by Israelites (2
Kgs. 12:11). A later "Isaiah" took note of the tools the first
Isaiah had seen in the carpenters' bazaar: measuring line, pencil,
planes, compasses (Is. 44:12-13).

In the cloth bazaar Isaiah learned that while in the country all the cloth was made by women in the home, in Jerusalem subdivision of labor had built up a suplementary craft of weavers. Isaiah watched all the processes. First the countryman or the villager brought in his clip of wool to sell. In the wool merchants' bazaar this was weighed—sometimes on scales of doubtful accuracy—and turned over to the fuller for cleansing and bleaching. The fuller soaked it in a solution of lye, beat it or rubbed it and dried it in the sun. For this work he required an open space, a vacant town lot or a field just outside (2 Kgs. 18:17; Is. 7:3; 36:2). The fuller's next process was to fluff up the wads so that spinning would be facilitated. This he did by using a cord stretched on a frame like a harp. With a mallet he struck the string and forced it to vibrate violently, then held it against the pile of wool. The vibration, oft-repeated, filled his shop with music and finally separated the hairs until the matted wads became light and homogeneous.

Now the spinners transformed the snowy mass into thread. The primitive method was still in use: a bunch of wool held under the arm or on a stick called a distaff (Prov. 31:19); continuous small tufts twisted by the fingers into a thread and kept tight at the lower end by a spindle attached to a small weight or "whorl" that acts as a balance-wheel to keep the twisting motion steady; the thread periodically wound up on the spindle when two or three feet had been spun. Later some one invented the spinning jenny whereby the thread was twisted by turning a crank; and a time saver for winding bobbins. All this seems elementary in comparison with modern mechanized procedures.

The thread now passed to the dyers, who wrung out from their vats the skeins of yarn, and incidentally colored their hands and their arms to the elbow a rich indigo or turkey red. In one end of a room about 10 by 20 feet were two large vats each hollowed out of a single stone about three feet each way, the shape of the excavation being spherical with a six-inch opening at the top. A deep circular channel around the rim of the stone caught what-

ever dye was spilled and conducted it back to the vat. Adjoining **were** shallow basins of cement and a number of hole-mouthed **jars** containing the lime necessary to fix the color.[6] For many garments however the native color of the wool or the goat's hair or the camel's hair sufficed.

All this was preliminary to the weaving, practiced by men in the bazaar. To make a loom, two stout posts were driven into the ground. Between these near the bottom was a horizontal roller to which the warp threads were fastened and on which the cloth was wound up as woven. The warp threads then went horizontally under another roller, up to the ceiling in the farther corner of the shop, and there were tied in a hank and weighted to keep the threads tight. The warp threads were alternated by two harnesses worked by treadles, and the shuttle containing the woof thread was thrown by hand from side to side. The operator sat on the floor with his feet in a pit where were the treadles. After a few shots with the shuttle the worker took a wooden "pin" shaped like a long blunt-edged knife, and with it beat the woven threads close together to make the cloth firm.[7]

Cloth was not woven in a piece and sold by the cubit; each garment was separately woven. In Isaiah's day native wool and flax were the common materials for textiles; but finer linen was made in Egypt (Ezek. 16:10. Silk was not introduced until Roman times). A further extension of this industry was needlework or embroidery. This art was as old as Babylonia, whence doubtless it came to Palestine (Josh. 7:21). Long ago Sisera enjoyed embroidery in bright colors (Jdg. 5:30). The late account of the Tabernacle (Ex. 39:3) mentions "violet, purple

[6] So W. F. Albright found them at Tell Beit Mirsim. See his *Archaeology of Palestine and the Bible*, pp. 119–121.

[7] This process is hinted in the story of Samson and Delilah, where the girl wove Samson's long locks into the cloth she was making and "beat them in with the pin" to hold them firm. When the strong man awoke he could not pull his hair from the web, but instead pulled up the loom by the roots and walked away with the whole contraption dangling from his hair behind him! (Jdg. 16:13–14.)

and scarlet material, and fine twisted linen, in variegated work"
(Ex. 26:36); and cloth of gold was reserved for God's house and
for royalty (Ex. 39:3; Ps. 45:13).

Isaiah was especially interested in the Tyrian quarter where
"royal purple" garments were on sale. The shopkeeper told him
that the famed purple dye came from a certain shellfish (murex)
found along the Phoenician coast and especially in the western or
Laconian [8] sea. The fish secretes only one tiny drop: hence the
labor involved in gathering many shells and extracting the dye—
and the consequent cost. How the color was fixed was a Tyrian
secret.

Near at hand in the Phoenician quarter were the cabinetmakers who turned out goods for the luxury trade. They specialized in the intricate process of inlaying with cedar, ebony and
sandalwood (1 Kgs. 10:12), or with ivory and opaque glass.
Phoenician jewelers also so far surpassed the native smiths that
they had a practical monopoly on delicate work. Isaiah saw them
sitting cross-legged in their tiny shops, blowing with a goatskin
bellows their little clay furnaces the size of a quart-pot; lifting
the tiny clay crucibles with bronze tongs and pouring the contents into moulds; or with blowpipe and tweezers soldering
minute globules of gold in a spiral design on a breastplate. Their
designs were mostly not original. Wherever Phoenician ships or
Aramean caravans went they brought choice pieces—Babylonian,
Elamite, Hittite, Cypriote, Mycenean, Egyptian, Arabian—and
the artists copied what they liked, combining the elements into
new forms. Such goods captured the fancy of the world; they
could be bought in all the cities of the East.[9] Isaiah's memory

[8] Possibly the "coastlands of Elishah," Ezek. 27:7.

[9] The Achaeans and other pre-Greeks looked upon Phoenician wares
with such wonder that they thought the gods must have made them.
Menelaus says to Telemachus (Odyssey iv:615 ff.): "I will give you a well-
wrought bowl. It is of silver, its rim finished with gold, the work of Hephaes-
tus (Vulcan). Lord Phaedimus, the king of the Sidonians, gave it to me,
when his house sheltered me on my homeward way." Homer must have seen
Phoenician work before he wrote his description of the shield of Achilles in

stored up all these articles of finery, and the enumeration of them constitutes a vivid part of his later denunciation of the aristocratic ladies of Jerusalem (Is. 3:16–24).

COUNTRY OCCUPATIONS

But Jerusalem was not the whole of Judea; there was the country lying at its very doors. Isaiah could leave the teeming city and in fifteen minutes find himself among the vineyards of Rephidim or among the flocks on the slopes of Olivet. These two occupations, vine-culture and shepherding, were and always had been the backlog of Judea's wealth.

Vineyards were found chiefly on the slopes of hills (Is. 5:1; Jer. 31:5). There the labors of successive generations had built retaining walls of stone and made level terraces for the vines by filling in with earth from the hillsides or from the valley whither it had been washed. Each vine was trained as a separate stock, pruned back each season to the parent stem, and propped up to keep the grapes above the soil. Nothing else could be planted in a vineyard (Deut. 22:9). The whole property was surrounded by a wall or a briar hedge, or both, to keep out thieves or nibbling animals (Is. 5:2, 5; Ps. 80:12; S. of S. 2:15); and was provided with a watchtower in which the keeper might stay, especially as harvest time approached (Is. 5:2; Job 27:18; 2 Chron. 26:10). There was always a winepress hollowed out of the solid limestone of the hill. There the grapes were trodden by naked feet (Is. 63:1–2) and the juice ran into a vat hewed out on a lower level. The "must" was allowed to clarify by settling, and the clear liquid was drawn off into jars or skins (Jer. 48:11–12; Job 32:19; Is. 25:6). Many a time in the vintage months of

---

Iliad XVIII. Also he writes about the prize offered by Achilles for the foot-race at the funeral games of Patroklas (Iliad XXIII:741 ff.): "A mixing bowl of silver, chased; six measures it held, and in beauty it was far the best in all the earth, for artificers of Sidon wrought it cunningly, and men of the Phoenicians brought it over the misty sea." Phoenician textiles were also famous: "embroidered robes, the work of Sidonian women" (Iliad VI:289).

September-October Isaiah went with other boys of his acquaint-
ance to join in the merry-making of the ingathering of grapes.
This festival had a religious significance, a time of thankfulness
for the bounty of God, and was called the "Feast of Booths." It
was a time of unrestrained joy, dancing and singing (Is. 16:10;
Jer. 25:30; 48:33; Jdg. 9:27)—one of the relatively few
occasions when the animal spirits of the Israelites were allowed
full sway.

Another occasion of joy was sheep-shearing. On this occasion
the master gave a feast to his shearers, servants and members of
his family. So Nabal in David's day (1 Sam. 25:4, 11), and so
Absalom (2 Sam. 13:23, 27, 28). This custom came down from
nomad days and continued as long as men kept sheep. Isaiah
would often be invited to such a merry-making; in fact, his
father may have owned a sheep ranch in the country and have
sent Isaiah to inspect, oversee and report. All the details of shepherding would correspond to those given in Chapter III.

MARRIAGE

Isaiah has now reached marriageable age. Amoz and his wife
have long been on the outlook for a suitable wife for their promising son and, while Isaiah may have had some preferences of his
own, he had no voice, or perhaps only small voice, in the decision. His parents finally selected a girl of good family of the
priestly class who had a reputation for piety. Since wives were
regarded by the law as property, the girl was bought—yet not
quite in the sense that a slave is bought. Amoz solemnized the
betrothal by paying a "bride price" to the bride's father as com-
pensation for his loss of a valuable helper in the home; and the
amount was determined in view of the bride's social status.[10]

The bride's father was supposed to give part of the purchase
price to the bride as her dowry—a very useful provision in case
of divorce or the death of the husband. The bride's father also

[10] David thought he could not afford to marry a king's daughter; but
Saul named a price that David was able to meet. 1 Sam. 18:22-27.

gave her a slave as personal attendant (*cf.* Gen. 29:24). So every one was satisfied, especially Amoz who thus acquired another worker in his household; for Isaiah brought his wife home to be ruled by her mother-in-law, just as he continued to be subject to his father as long as Amoz lived.

On the wedding day, first came the procession. Isaiah and his friends went hilariously to the house of the bride and returned with her and her girl friends. The bridegroom was dressed in his best and was garlanded with flowers and crowned for the festival by his mother (S. of S. 3:11); likewise the bride was "on exhibition," adorned with all the finery her economic status afforded—gold-embroidered robe, sash, jewelry (Is. 61:10; 49:18; Ps. 45: 13-15). Impromptu dancing and shouting made known to all the bystanders in street and house that this was a wedding and not a funeral. The young men also flourished weapons [11] to frighten away evil spirits who might spoil the fun.

The marriage ceremonies at Amoz's house were joyous and expansive, all of the neighbors participating. Amoz kept open house for a week,[12] with the marriage feast the culminating feature. This was an occasion of mirth (Jer. 16:9), with games, jokes, dancing and an exchange of gifts. Our only real glimpse of the joy of the dance is given in the Song of Songs 6:13-7:1

> Turn, turn, O Shulammite;
> turn, turn, that we may gaze on you.
> Ah, gaze on the Shulammite,
> in the Mahanaim dance.
> How beautiful are your steps in sandals,
> O rapturous maiden!

The music was an important feature of the wedding (Is. 5:12). There was singing, always in unison, the words supplied by memory and resembling some of the lyrics preserved to us in the Song of Songs. Accompanying the song was a variety of instru-

[11] *Cf.* 1 Macc. 9:39; S. of S. 3:7-8.
[12] If we may judge by the custom of earlier times, Jdg. 14:12.

ments (Amos 6:5). Isaiah himself had a harp, one of the large ones that stood on the floor and had 47 strings. Half a dozen of the young men brought smaller ones (Is. 23:16), some with three or four strings arranged above a sounding board out of which two horns grew, as on a Greek lyre; some had a triangular sounding board across which 6 or 8 strings were stretched, as in our modern zither. One very expensive one was made of sandalwood (1 Kgs. 10:12). Another boy brought a flute (Is. 30:29) and a couple of lads who looked out for the sheep at Amoz's farm were very skillful at playing the strident reed pipes that all shepherds know how to make and play. Most of the girls brought timbrels (Ps. 68:25) and sistrums (1 Sam. 18:6). The former were bowl-shaped drums held in one hand while the other hand struck the drum-head with a slap, or pattered with the fingers. A variant on this type was what we know as a tambourine—a hoop-shaped band of wood 10 inches in diameter with skin stretched over it, while in five holes cut in the band were little metal discs that jangled (Job 21:12; Jer. 31:4; Is. 24:8). Still more jangling came from the sistrum made of metal in the shape of a small Badminton racket, with wires playing loosely through holes in the loop. Altogether it was a noisy but not disorderly crowd that produced more rhythm than harmony and more recitative than melody.[13]

While Isaiah's wife legally was a piece of property, practically she was valued in her home and in the community for her personal worth. She no doubt proved to be another "Virtuous Woman" like the one described in Proverbs 31, worth "far more than corals." Later she was called a prophetess, but probably because she was a prophet's wife (Is. 8:3). Perhaps her practical wisdom gave her more than a local reputation, like the diplomat of Abel-beth-maacah (2 Sam. 20:16-22) or the hospitable matron

---

[13] The other musical instruments mentioned in the Old Testament are late in origin, and perhaps foreign: psaltery, sackbut (trigon), cymbals, lute, dulcimer (bagpipe), horn (cornet), trumpet, etc. See Ps. 150:3–5; Dan. 3:5; 2 Chron. 5:12–13.

of Shunem (2 Kgs. 4:8) or the courageous actress of Tekoa who put across some skillful business with David (2 Sam. 14:1–24). These women had personalities that enabled them to hold their own in a man's world. At any rate we shall believe that she and her husband experienced in their home the joys of true companionship and love based on the recognition of equal worth (S. of S. 8:6–7; 1 Sam. 1:8).

DEATH AND BURIAL

Not long after Isaiah's marriage his father Amoz died. There was loud mourning for the departure of this good man. Friends and relatives crowded into the house and showed all the customary signs of grief. Some rent their clothes (2 Kgs. 2:12); some put sack-cloth next their bodies (Amos 8:10); some took off their sandals (Ezek. 24:17) and sat in the courtyard with dust and ashes on their head (Ezek. 26:16; 27:30); others beat their breast and sides (Is. 32:11–12) and even cut themselves (Jer. 41:5; 48:37). Isaiah and all his brothers shaved off hair and beard (Is. 22:12; Jer. 16:6). All the company now and then uttered cries of grief throughout the seven days of mourning (1 Kgs. 13:30; Jer. 22:18; Amos 5:16; Zech. 12:11; 1 Sam. 31:13). On one of these days there was a funeral meal (Jer. 16:7; Hos. 9:4), but otherwise the family and guests fasted.

Since the Israelites lacked the arts of embalming, the burial occurred on the day of death. Amoz was taken by his sons to the vineyard he owned west of the city and there interred in the family tomb (1 Kgs. 22:50) which had been made by enlarging a natural cave in the back wall of a terrace. The body was dressed in a single mantle, one suitable to wear in Sheol whither his soul had gone (1 Sam. 28:14), and a small supply of food was placed on pottery vessels to comfort his journey.[14]

*   *   *

[14] As shown by excavations.

Isaiah had always been a thoughtful young man, and deeply religious; but after his father's death his personal grief coupled with his anxiety over his country's future when king Uzziah died, accentuated in him his sense of mission. One day while praying in the Temple he had a vision of Jehovah and heard a call to preach a message of doom to his people (Is. 6:1-13). Henceforth he devoted himself to the task of warning and reformation—a fifty-year ministry that led at last to a martyr's death.

Spiritual Deterioration

There was plenty to reform in the religious and moral life of Judah. One particular feature of which Isaiah disapproved was worship at the "high places," the Canaanite shrines that the Israelites had taken over. They were the seats of popular worship, whereas the Temple at Jerusalem was little more than a royal oratory. The high places were on hills, as at Gibeon—2565 feet above sea level—or in the highest part of the towns (2 Chron. 14:5). One speaks always of "going up" to them (1 Sam. 9:19, 25). When Isaiah went to Gibeon he could see at a glance the whole equipment. There was a huge altar for burning sacrifices, a smaller one for incense (1 Kgs. 3:3-4) and a shrine to hold the images. These were carved stones, and figurines of metal (Num. 33:52; 2 Chron. 34:3), fertility symbols under whatever name, male or female. In addition he found certain standing pillars of stone about two feet in diameter and eight to twelve feet high (Fig. 74), in which the Baal of the shrine resided. In some of them and in the rock on which they were erected there were cup-shaped hollows in which broth from the sacrificial meal was poured (Jdg. 6:19-20). Next to these and towering above them were several "Asherah" or sacred poles of wood, capped with some symbol to represent the female fertility principle, as the pillars usually though not always represented the male. In Jerusalem king Asa's mother had once erected an Asherah carved as an obscene image (1 Kgs. 15:13), but this was before Isaiah's day; and later Manassah erected another, the memory of which

FIG. 74.   STANDING PILLARS ON A CANAANITE HIGH-PLACE, GEZER.

These are three stones out of seven, ranging in height from 5'5" to 10'9". The divinity was supposed to reside in them. In the soil about the high-place large numbers of phallic emblems were discovered, and terra cotta plaques stamped with representations of Astarte, the Semitic mother goddess of fertility.

inspired a certain vision of Ezekial (2 Kgs. 21:3; Ezek. 8:3). Isaiah may not have known that the Asherah were survivals of tree worship, found throughout the ancient world; but he did know that they were sensual in their implication.[15]

If Isaiah happened to be at Gibeon on a festival day he would find the poles and the shrine gay with flowers and streamers. The Priest of the shrine would officiate, the invited guests—elders of the town or notables from far away—would assemble in the "sacred hall," and a meal would be served (1 Sam. 9:22-24) in which the god and his worshippers would become united in spirit and personality by partaking of the same food. All of this seemed crude to Isaiah, whose ideas of divinity were far above those of the common herd. The God who had spoken to him in that majestic vision in the Temple (Is. 6) could not fail to be grieved and disgusted by this travesty of religion, not only intellectually primitive but morally degenerate.

When Isaiah went to the Temple at Jerusalem on the Sabbath, he was no less perturbed; for not only had the old Canaanite Baals reasserted themselves in a Baalized Yahweh (2 Kgs. 21:3, 11), but Assyrian influences were now gathering head to inundate Jerusalem with foreign gods—less sensual than the Canaanite but equally subversive of Israelite loyalties. There, following his submission to the Assyrian Tiglath-pileser III at Damascus, Ahaz caused an Assyrian altar to be erected (2 Kgs. 16:10-14); by which we must understand that Ashur became a royally patronized rival of Yahweh as the state god of Israel (2 Chron. 28:21-25). Worse than that, the priests had lost all sense of the dignity or significance of their high office and were often drunk while offering sacrifices. The so-called prophets were no better: the state religion had become an orgy (Is. 28:7-8). No wonder the prophet's wrath blazed forth against the system and against the individuals who ran it. We can well imagine the sensation created, the increasing crowds, their vehement ejaculations and oaths, the

[15] Isaiah's judgment on this popular cult of Baal-Yahweh is perfectly expressed by a post-exilic writer—the Third Isaiah?—found in Is. 57:3-13.

cries, "Down with the traitor!", as Isaiah stood by the smoking
altar of Ashur-Yahweh and uttered his denunciation (Is. 1:4–
17):

> Ah! sinful nation, guilt-laden people,
> Brood of evil-doers, children who deal corruptly;
> Of what use is the multitude of your sacrifices to me?
> I am sated with the burnt offerings of rams.
> When you spread out your hands I will hide mine eyes
>   from you;
> Your hands are full of bloodshed.

Isaiah saw also the rising tide of Assyrian cult practices within
Yahweh's own precincts that reached its flood in the days of
Jeremiah. We can judge what these innovations were from the
records of what Josiah did in the way of cleaning up, and from
Jeremiah's preachments. In the Temple area was now established
the Assyrian worship of the heavenly bodies—the sun, moon,
planets and constellations. As part of their paraphernalia were
"sacred poles and sun pillars" (Is. 17:8), stables for the horses
and chariots of the sun, with altars to all these divinities. In
particular Ishtar now appeared as the Queen of Heaven—our
planet Venus—who as morning star was goddess of war and as
evening star was goddess of love and harlotry. She was worshipped on the housetops of the city; altars were there set up and
the whole family was employed in her ritual—the children to
gather fuel, the fathers to kindle the fires, the women to knead
the dough and to make cakes in her honor (Jer. 7:18). How
strongly her worship was rooted we may judge by what the
exiled Judeans in Egypt said to Jeremiah: "When we worshipped
the Queen of Heaven we were prosperous; when we turned to
Yahweh he destroyed our nation; henceforth the good old Queen
for us!" (Jer. 44:16–18).

In the temple court also were the "houses of the devotees of
the fertility cult," where the women wove tunics for Asherah. In
the city at the entrance to the governor's house by the gate were

"high places of the Satyrs"; in the valley of Hinnom, the shrines to the abominations of the Moabites and Ammonites, and the horrid image of Moloch where children were burned in sacrifice (2 Kgs. 23:4-15). In the temple also the prophet saw "women weeping for Tammuz"—practicing the Syrian cult that repre-. sented the birth, death and resurrection of the god of vegetation (Ezek. 8:14-15). Seeds were sprouted in a pot, the plants were tended carefully till they were six inches or more high, then allowed to die to the accompaniment of women's wailing. Isaiah called them "Gardens of Adonis." [16]

Isaiah developed some unique methods of getting his message across to the apathetic inhabitants of Jerusalem. On one occasion he took a harp, twanged its strings as he walked through the bazaar, picked up a following of men and boys who were curious to know what this crazy prophet would do next; then mounting some merchant's counter where he could be easily seen and heard, he sang a "Song of the Vineyard" (Is. 5:1-7). It started somewhat like a love song; it paused after the second stanza for a reply—and no doubt the interested audience gave him many a suggestion; then he continued his song still in symbolic language till finally he turned it into a fierce denunciation of his hearers.

Another publicity stunt was to give his children outlandish names. One he called "A-remnant-will-return" (Is. 7:3); another, "Speeding-is-the-spoil, hastening-is-the-prey" (Is. 8:3-4); and either a son of his own or of Ahaz he said would be called "God-is-with-us" (Is. 7:14). Whenever in the future any one should call these children by name he would necessarily remind every one of the political prophecies which called forth and explained the names.

Perhaps most freakish of all and most calculated to get the prophet and his warnings talked about was the device of walking about town for three years stark naked. Nor would he explain what it was all about until the period was complete and he had

---

[16] Is. 17:10, American Translation. In other lands similar worship was paid to Osiris and Isis, Venus and Adonis. Attis and Cybele, Dionysus, *et al.*

the whole town by the ears. Then the citizens learned to their dismay that the men of Egypt and Ethiopia, who king Hezekiah expected would save Judah from the Assyrian armies, would themselves some day walk as naked captives all the weary way to Nineveh (Is. 20:1-6). That was political propaganda with a vengeance!

ECONOMIC DETERIORATION

But the social and economic conditions in Isaiah's day far outweighed in importance any cultic or political matter; and they affected both the northern and southern kingdoms. The troubles had their roots in the Canaanite civilization to which Israel had become assimilated.

When the Israelites had taken possession of central Palestine as a ruling aristocracy of farmers (Jdg. 6:27; 1 Sam. 1:24; 9:1) they had reduced to serfdom the former Canaanite inhabitants (Jdg. 1:28, 30, 35). They had held the land as a tribal inheritance, not to be alienated from the family that occupied it (1 Kgs. 21:1-3). But the unconquered Canaanite towns had an aristocracy also, and these men held the commercial as opposed to the agricultural or pastoral point of view; they bought and sold everything, even land. In the life and death struggle that Israel waged with the Philistines, David had made friends and confederates of these Canaanite cities (2 Sam. 5:6-9; Josh. 15:63) and by intermarriage (2 Sam. 5:13; 3:3; Jdg. 3:6-7) and amalgamation of customs, the Canaanites and Israelites became one people. But the Canaanite ideology proved the stronger, and David began to play the grand monarch. He broke over the communal land taboo; seized estates even in northern Ephraim and gave them to his sons and supporters (Absalom, 2 Sam. 13:23; Joab, 2 Sam. 14:30) and in general acted up to the kingly part as the Canaanite lords played it, even to keeping a mercenary army in case his people should revolt (1 Sam. 22:7; 2 Sam. 15:18; 20:7). Under Solomon the process of seizure, of impressment into the army and the corvée, of personal enslavement, went still further (1 Kgs. 5:13–17). In the 200 years that elapsed between Solomon's day and Isaiah, the commercializing of the pastoral Israelites and the baalizing of their god Yahweh went on apace; with the result that the brotherhood-justice of the desert gave place to the doctrine that opportunity gave power to the fortunate. The growth of a rich land-owning, slave-owning, commercial aristocracy that lived mostly in the cities was the result, accompanied by the impoverishment and final enslavement of the less fortunate Israelite. These are the progressive steps in the downfall of the "people of the land," operative over two centuries:

Conscription of farmers and shepherds into the corvée gangs and the standing armies of kings (as above).

The burden of increased taxes to keep up the royal state.

To pay these taxes the less fortunate Israelites had to borrow from the more fortunate.

When interest or principal could not be paid, the creditor took away the debtor's mortgaged land (Is. 5:8; Mic. 2:1–2; Amos 2:6–7a) or took the debtor and his family as slaves (2 Kgs. 4:1–7).

Honesty in trade became a byword. Excavators have found under the counters of the merchants two sets of weights: a heavy set to use when buying, a light one when selling (Hos. 12:7).

No recourse to the law was possible. Law was on the side of the capitalist who made the law and executed it (Hos. 5:11; 12:8; Amos 5:6–7, 10–12; 6:12–13; Micah 3:9–11).

There was no help in religion, for Yahweh had been baalized and now was lined up as the guarantor of baalistic commercial law (Hos. 2:16; Amos 2:8; 5:21–24; Micah 3:11).

The remedy the prophets saw was a return to the original brotherhood-justice of the desert for which the un-baalized Yahweh had formerly stood (Micah 5:14–15; 6:8c) and to apply it to city life as well as country. Yet such was the power of the ruling class that a prophet's only safe course lay in keeping silent—for it was indeed an evil time (Amos 5:13). Amos was railroaded

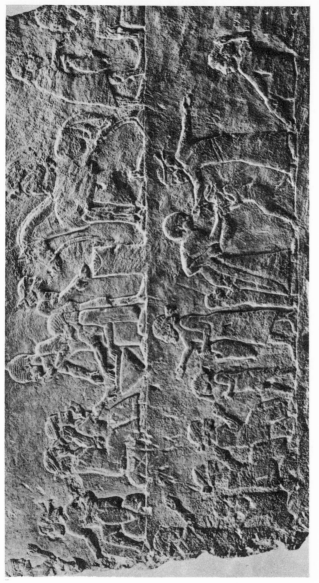

FIG. 75.   PRISONERS CAMPING ON THE MARCH.

The upper register shows the guard of soldiers eating supper out of an iron pot. They reach in with their hands. Next, a man pours grain into a manger for his master's horse. At the right, a soldier with a wine-skin presents a drink to his seated captain.

The lower register shows the prisoners eating. On the right is a family group. A mother gives her older son a drink from a skin while the younger reminds her that it is his turn next. The father is saying something dramatic while the seated man evidently enjoys the fun.

out of Bethel the first time he opened his mouth (Amos 7:12–13) ; so he and the other prophets of northern Israel were driven to the private circulating of written messages. It was under the terrible Jehu dynasty lasting one hundred years that the earliest written prophecy took shape—the stories of Elijah and Elisha, the Ephraimite document known as E, and the prophecies of Amos and Hosea. While therefore in all other countries the poor were sunk without a trace, both the ruling class and the gods being against them, in Israel they left behind them a magnificent series of protests, both in the northern and the southern kingdom. Nothing in literature is more scathing than the denunciations of the injustices of their day, by Isaiah and his contemporary Micah, their predecessors Amos and Hosea and their successor Jeremiah; and since they were all prophets of Yahweh, in reality their indignation bestowed upon their god a morality they had never before supposed him to possess. This is the great contribution of these prophets to the religious conceptions of mankind—they endowed Yahweh with a moral nature and ranged him on the side of the poor and the oppressed.

Added to this economic exploitation by their rulers and commercial tycoons were the further dislocations caused by war. In the century and a half ending with Sennacherib (c. 700 B.C.) Assyria had been advancing in three great tidal waves, each coming nearer the little Israelite kingdoms. The first to suffer was the northern kingdom. When Tiglath-pileser exacted a thousand talents of silver from Menahem, the latter assessed 60,000 landholders, small and large, 50 shekels each (2 Kgs. 15:19-20). That was the beginning of annual tribute that sucked the peasants dry; and when there was no more to pay, the Assyrian king again raided Israel and carried away "the Rubenites, the Gadites and the half-tribe of Manassah and brought them to Halah, Habor, Hara, and the river Gozan" (1 Chron. 5:26). Again in the days of Pekah of Israel, "Tiglath-pileser captured Ijon, Abel-beth-maacah, Janoah, Kedesh, Hazor, Gilead and Galilee, all the land of Naphtali, and carried the inhabitants captive to

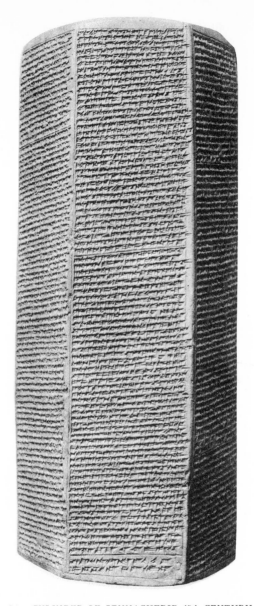

FIG. 76.   CYLINDER OF SENNACHERIB (7th CENTURY B.C.).

Contains a cuneiform record of the western campaigns of Sennacherib, including the
expedition against Palestine on which he lost his army, as narrated in the Old Testament.

Assyria" (2 Kgs. 15:29)—according to his own records, 16,751 persons. The final deportation of Israel came in 721 B.C., when after a siege of three years Sargon II carried Israel away and settled them among the earlier captives of the time of Menahem (above) and in the cities of the Medes (2 Kgs. 17:6; 18:11). According to Sargon's records these consisted of 27,290 of the leading citizens of Samaria (Fig. 75).

When these poor countrymen were wiped out, Assyria turned her attention to Judah, attracted first by the bribe offered by Ahaz for protection against Damascus (2 Kgs. 16:7-9). That too was the beginning of annual tribute, all of which came ultimately out of the farmers and shepherds. These taxes increased their poverty and their enslavement for debt. A little later Hezekiah tried to evade payment, but he was made to "pay through the nose" (2 Kgs. 18:14-16). He too passed the burden on to his people: again debt, foreclosure, bondage (Is. 3:14-15) while their absentee landlords and creditors in Jerusalem suffered hardly at all. When tribute at last stopped, down came Sennacherib with his army to collect in person; he took away all the stored-up cash of the nation: 300 talents of silver (Sennacherib says 800) and 30 talents of gold, equivalent in purchasing power today to over $22,000,000 or £4,400,000. Sennacherib's famous cylinder recording this campaign says that out of forty-six strong cities and fortresses and innumerable small cities he took, besides the people, countless live-stock; and from Hezekiah himself he took in addition to the money above mentioned, "precious stones, eye-paint, ivory couches and thrones, hides and tusks, precious woods and divers objects, a heavy treasure, together with his daughters and the women of his palace, and male and female musicians" (Fig. 76).

So the long trail of the Canaanite-Baalistic system of exploitation led from the comparatively high level of a free country-aristocracy that used foreign slave labor, down through various levels of impoverishment to economic slavery, to foreign invasion with all its slaughter, and to deportation for the survivors.

Fig. 77. LACHISH RESTORED.

The walls here pictured follow the lines laid down by Rehoboam (2 Chron. 11:5-12) when he established fortresses on the borders of his kingdom. After the destruction by Sennacherib (700 B.C.) and Nebuchadnezzar (597 B.C.) they were restored on the same stone foundations. The mound has been deserted since the 4th century B.C.

The Assyrian invasions bring us face to face with the horrors of warfare. We cannot do better than to study the siege of Lachish by Sennacherib in the time of Isaiah, c. 700 B.C.

THE SIEGE OF LACHISH

Lachish was a strong fortress-city 16 miles due west of Hebron, commanding the maritime plain and the road to Egypt. Now that the excavators have definitely identified the town as the modern Tell ed-Duweir, we are able to reconstruct it with considerable accuracy. At the time of its destruction in 700 B.C., the city might well have been considered impregnable, for it was surrounded by a double wall strengthened at short intervals with towers (Fig. 77). No general would think of leaving such a strong city in his rear, and therefore since Sennacherib was aiming to crush Egypt he must needs reduce Lachish. Not only is the account of the siege given on Sennacherib's cylinder and mention made in the Bible in two places (2 Kgs. 18:14, 17; Is. 36:2), but in the magnificent reliefs that once adorned Sennacherib's palace at Nineveh we can follow this siege in detail.

The first move was to surround the city to cut off all supplies and all possible outside help; the next was to bring up battering rams. Since the town was on a high mound the soldiers built a brick runway and on it pushed up the lumbering siege engines, a kind of primitive tank within which those who manipulated the ram were protected. To support the tank, bowmen advanced in pairs. Meanwhile from the walls and towers the defenders are shooting arrows, throwing down missiles and firebrands on the attackers; per contra, an Assyrian is pouring water on the firebrands from a long-handled ladle.

In spite of a vigorous defense the city is at last taken and the destruction begins. Some of the defenders are impaled on poles as a punishment for their valor, others are roped together and marched out of the city: a wretched procession of captives—a woman with all her belongings in a bag on her shoulder, a small son tugging at her skirts; a soldier decapitating one of his prisoners while two other prisoners stoically walk on; then march the triumphant Assyrian spearmen and bowmen, each holding aloft one of the two gory heads he has cut off in order to collect a bounty on them. In a grove of palms interspersed with

Fig. 78. THE TREK TO ASSYRIA.

A bullock wagon is loaded with bags of spoil on which the younger children ride, the smallest quite naked. In front walk father, mother and two children, one of whom judging by her long head-cloth is a girl. Each carries a bag over the shoulder and in one hand a skillet or a wallet. The woman has a long head-cloth similar to the girl's, and a simple sleeveless tunic reaching from neck to heels. These are true contemporary records of how Israelite town-dwellers dressed.

well-laden vines Sennacherib has set up his throne. The general and his lieutenants report the capture of the city; the Israelite elders of the town kneel in submission. Meanwhile the city is being looted and set on fire. Shortly a pageant of spoil will pass before the king for his delectation. Then begins the long trek of the captive families to their future house of bondage in Assyria (Fig. 78).

CHAPTER X

CHILDREN OF THE EXILE AND THE DISPERSION

IN THE HILLS OF ASSYRIA

WE MUST follow these wretched people into their new home.

Sargon used some of his Israelite captives in the fields and others in building his new capital, Dur Sharrukin, now occupied by the village of Khorsabad twelve miles north-east of Nineveh. It has been partly excavated several times, most recently by the Oriental Institute of Chicago. The city, approximately a mile square, was surrounded by a wall of sun-dried brick on a stone base eighty feet thick. Along its course were more than 150 towers and 7 gates, the gate towers gloriously ornamented with reliefs in enameled brick and flanked with colossal sculptured bulls. Astride the north-east wall was the citadel with its own wall and gates (Fig. 79). Within it, besides a temple to Nebo and several large homes belonging to major court officials, was the king's palace on a terrace of about 26 acres, large enough to take in two and a half cities the size of the Jerusalem of David's day.

The entrance to the palace was a huge triple gate, ancestor of the triumphal arch of Roman times. Colossal winged bulls stared fiercely at those who entered (Fig. 80), beautiful colored tiles framed the archway, above in the wall was a tiled relief and on each side rose battlemented towers with loggias near the top. Within, the largest of the courts with its magnificent entrance was the center of royal ceremonies and business of state. The walls were richly adorned with alabaster reliefs, a mile of them all together, colored tile and fresco (Fig. 81). The reliefs found here and in other palaces represent invariably the chief interests of the king—war, building enterprises and hunting. They constitute the finest works of Assyrian art that have come down to us. In spite

Fig. 79. KHORSABAD: RECONSTRUCTION DRAWING OF SARGON'S PALACE 705 B.C.

Main entrance is on the left. The palace is a series of open courts surrounded by rooms. The sacred quarter is marked by a ziggurat.

of the stylization imposed by two-dimensional design they tell a story with clearness and dramatic force, they give us intimate details of costume, and in the hunting scenes they portray animals with an accuracy and power that have never been surpassed in any age. See Figs. 82 and 83 and their captions.

Israelite captives from Samaria would be used on all this work except the sculpture, for which they had no training. Similarly employed were Sennacherib's captives from Judah, for this king's building enterprises surpassed that of all other Assyrian kings. Nineveh was largely his creation. The platform he built for his palace comprised about a hundred acres; it required the equivalent of 10,000 men for 12 years to deposit the 15,000,000 tons of brick and earth that composed it. On this job he must have used the descendants of the earlier Israelite deportees, together with the captives from the fortified cities of Judah mentioned in 2 Kings 18:13-16, numbering 200,150. We are told that at work these slaves wore short tunics, were shackled at ankles or legs and had a bar or long rods attached to their waists—not a comfortable working equipment. Other captives cut huge blocks of alabaster in the mountains, dragged them down to the river, then on scows towed them to the palace site where they were carved into colossal bulls and hauled to their destined position by hundreds of slaves. How many thousand Israelites were worked to death in this way we shall never know.

We may be sure that besides the manacled slaves, skilled artisans from Samaria and Judah worked on the palaces while others were time-keepers, overseers, stewards, minor officials of government; and the women became musicians and members of the royal and aristocratic harems. When, therefore, we look at the vast irrigation works, the royal cities, the palaces and the life depicted on the miles of reliefs, we must be reminded of the immense Israelitish contribution in treasure, labor and thought to the glory of Assyria. Furthermore all these deported thousands with their priests (2 Kgs. 17:26-28) became the nucleus of the community of Jews that later, increased by Nebuchadnezzar's

FIG. 80.   COLOSSI IN SARGON'S PALACE.

The palace walls of sundried brick, usually were finished with a dado of glazed tile or of alabaster slabs sculptured in low relief like the one toward the center of the picture. At the various entrances were huge blocks carved with guardian divinities called Cherubim. The two pictured above, show a crown with six bull's horns (emblems of divinity); human head (symbol of intelligence) with conventionally rendered hair and beard; a bull's body (symbol of strength and vitality) adorned with conventionalized masses of hair; an eagle's wings (symbol of swiftness: 2 Sam. 22:11); five feet—so that the proper number will appear if viewed from front or side. The cherub that was brought from this palace to Chicago by the Oriental Institute weighs 40 tons!

captives from Jerusalem, formed a permanent racial contribution to Mesopotamia and a focal point of Jewish religion.

BY THE RIVERS OF BABYLON

Under Nebuchadnezzar II (604–561 B.C.) Babylon became the political, commercial and religious center of the civilized world. When Egypt induced Jehoiachin to revolt against Nebu-

chadnezzar, the Chaldean armies came south in 597 B.C to pun-
ish the offender. After the siege and capture of Jerusalem, there
were plunder and the deportation of 7000 men of ability fit for
war; 1000 craftsmen and smiths; 2000 best citizens including all
the nobles and the royal family (2 Kgs. 24:10-16). The next
and last puppet king, Zedekiah, repeated his nephew's foolish-
ness: result, a two-year siege, the final destruction of Jerusalem
and the deportation of all the people of Judea except some of
the poorest who were left to act as vine dressers and plowmen
that the land might not relapse wholly into a wilderness (2 Kgs.
25:1-21). Thus in two stages the wealth, culture and religion
of Judea were transplanted to Babylonia, 586 B.C.

A Glimpse of Babylon

When these wretched hordes reached the land of the Two
Rivers they saw first of all Babylon now being rebuilt by their
ambitious conqueror. When it was finished the city was the most
magnificent in the ancient world. How weak the walls of Jerusalem looked in retrospect when compared with the eleven miles
of Babylon's fortifications, studded with towers and pierced by a
hundred gates of bronze! The walls, twenty-five feet thick, were
of fired brick laid in bitumen; how high we do not know. The
outside wall was reinforced by a walled moat; inside was wall
number two of similar thickness, built of sun-dried brick and
equipped with towers at regular intervals. Well might the city
seem impregnable. Within these walls again was a citadel en-
circled by a double rampart to protect the palace. As the line of
captives entered the city along the Sacred Way they would pass
under the Ishtar Gate from which tiers of bulls and dragons, 575
of them in enameled brick, looked down on them, while beside
them walked sixty enameled lions on the wall (Fig. 84). This
raised and beautifully paved way led straight to Esagil, the
Temple of Marduk in the heart of the city, nearly a mile and a
half from the outer wall; its huge ziggurat in seven stages in
honor of the sun, the moon and five planets, towered in dazzling

colors into the heaven. Near by, the new palace walls were rising, eighteen feet thick and painted white. Some of the exiles were destined to see its glorious courts and rooms in which were concentrated all the arts and decorations that this land of art had

FIG. 81.   TILED DADO FROM THE SIN TEMPLE, KHORSABAD.

A magnificent specimen of tile decoration in brilliant color, representing from left to right a lion, an eagle, a bull, a fig tree and a plow—which was probably also a seeder. These figures are in relief and are each composed of many tiles, not after the fashion of a mosaic but of equal-sized modelled bricks. The treatment is conventionalized, relative actual size is disregarded—as of the eagle, tree and plow—and the whole architectural panel is enclosed in a dainty border of rosettes. The meaning of this combination of objects is not evident.

developed through three millenniums. Well might Nebuchadnezzar exclaim as he walked on the roof of his palace, "Is not this great Babylon, which I have built as a royal residence, by my own mighty power, and for my own glorious majesty?" (Dan. 4:29-30).

Then the sacred way turned westward at right angles from the ziggurat and left the city by a long brick bridge over the Euphrates. On the further bank was a new city within which the king was erecting the "Hanging Gardens," famed as one of the Seven Wonders of the ancient world (Fig. 85). These were said to consist of a terraced tower with trees and flowers, which cun-

ning hydraulic engines turned into a veritable mountain for the
pleasure of Nebuchadnezzar's Iranian wife. As the way turned
south, the exiles were distributed to those parts of Babylonia
which the king had designated. Just where they were located we
do not at present know. Our only clue is derived from Ezekiel
1 : 1, where we hear of a "River Chebar"—probably the great
canal called Shatt en-Nil, 120 feet wide. As if to confirm this
chance reference, near this canal were discovered the archives of
the wealthy banking house of Murasu and Sons, dated 464-405
B.C., and containing many Jewish names.

LIFE IN THE LAND OF EXILE

Nebuchadnezzar was too able an administrator not to make
shrewd use of the human material brought from Judea. Certainly
it would be wasting valuable men to condemn good administra-
tors to dig ditches. Segregating the brainy aristocrats who had
formed the official class in the old home, he re-educated them to
serve in responsible government positions. We have a direct statement of this training in the "literature and language of the Chal-
deans," in the Book of Daniel (1 :3-5) which though a work of
fiction no doubt embodies a true tradition. Other able men would
be sent as staff members with the governors of provinces; still
others would go into business (*cf.* the reference to Murasu and
Sons above). In fact, it would seem that the Jewish genius for
government and international business which has characterized
the race for two thousand years, received its most promising start
during the Babylonian Exile. It was a wonderful revelation and
an intriguing opportunity to be transplanted from the edge to the
very center of empire.

We may be sure, next, that the thousand craftsmen and smiths
from Jerusalem would be utilized in the vast building enterprises
of the king. Happily, though the records of his numerous campaigns have not yet been recovered, we have voluminous testimony to his flair for building. Not only did he rebuild and enlarge
Babylon, but he restored the temples and ziggurats in most of

the cities of his realm—Borsippa, Sippar, Kutha, Erech, Larsa, Ur. Every Jewish artisan would be sure of a job.

We have striking confirmation of this in some tablets discovered in Babylon near the Ishtar Gate in the ruins of a large public

FIG. 82.   LION COMING FROM CAGE. PALACE OF ASHURBANIPAL
(7th CENT. B.C.).

The Assyrian artists were superb masters of animal sculpture. Observe the extraordinary size and strength of the beast, his cautious exit as if he distrusted his newfound liberty, his savage face and the suggestion of an incipient roar. These lions were caught in the mountains miles away, kept in dens where they could be always at hand, and when the king was ready for his sport, taken to the hunting ground and let out at the proper rate. That is why a den of lions to put Daniel in happened to be so handy.

building evidently used as a distribution center for royal doles and wages. These tablets show what tremendous gangs of men from all over the Near East were working for the king at all sorts of enterprises in Babylonia from 595 to 570 B.C. Payments were made in rations of oil, barley, and the like. Mentioned by name are king Jehoiachin of Jerusalem with five of his sons, who were no doubt pensioners of leisure. But among workers are listed mariners and musicians from Ascalon, mariners and craftsmen from the Phoenician cities; from Egypt, mariners, ship-builders, horse-trainers, monkey-trainers; from Asia Minor, carpenters, ship-builders. The tablets contain many Jewish names: one Jew is called a gardener, and rations for hundreds of craftsmen are recorded.[1]

Men of humbler skill would be put to a thousand tasks in the field (Is. 14:3). The irrigation system required constant attention, especially since recent wars had seriously damaged it. So extensive and intricate a job could properly be administered only by a strong central government. We have Nebuchadnezzar's statement that he repaired and extended these works, reclaimed waste lands, drained swamps and put them under cultivation. Engineering problems had to be solved in the construction of dams, sluices and reservoirs. Among the tens of thousands of canal diggers and the thousands of overseers, checkers and timekeepers, to say nothing of assistants to the Babylonian engineers, we would surely find many Jews. Of course thousands more would be put to supply the basic need of food. Farmers from rocky Judea would have to be re-trained in this land of irrigated abundance; but they would be apt pupils, just as today the anaemic ghetto-dwellers of Polish and Roumanian cities have become robust workers on the mechanized farms of Zionist Palestine. Babylonia had soil that was fabulously rich: Herodotus says that wheat returned two to three hundredfold. Other products were sesame, barley, ochrys, palms, apples and many kinds of shell fruits.

Plenty of tablets from this period throw light on living conditions. Land could be rented direct from the king or from officials of the various temples who controlled large tracts. Rent was paid in kind. If a man failed to attend diligently to his crops and so reaped a poor harvest, he was required to pay according to the yield of adjoining fields. The tablets give examples of leases of land for date cultivation, in which provisions specify the planting of trees, surrounding the property with a wall and supplying water. These are quite like present-day contracts.

Conditions in exile varied in different places and times. The first band deported was allowed to build houses and plant gardens, and was encouraged to "seek the welfare of the land—for in its

[1] See W. F. Albright, in *Biblical Archaeologist* for Dec. 1942.

FIG. 83.
ASSYRIAN KING
IN HIS CHARIOT.

The king's hat is
shaped like an Arab
fez, only a spike in-
stead of a tassel pro-
trudes from the top.
His beard is either
curly or is convention-
ally so represented. On
either arm he wears a
large bracelet like a
wrist watch. The chari-
oteer wears a fillet in-
stead of a cap. Behind
him rides a eunuch
with a puffy beardless
face. Behind the char-
iot walk two more
eunuchs wielding fly-
flappers, and by the
wheel a soldier with
short fringed skirt,
stockings or puttees,
and leather shoes held
on by garters. The
chariot is strong and
imposing; the umbrella
over the king is cov-
ered with heavy cloth
adorned with rosettes,
decorative bands and
tassels. Even the tail
of the horse is mar-
celled and neatly tied.

welfare shall you find your welfare" (Jer. 29:1–7). In spite of the crueties of war and the hardships incident to transplantation, the king's policy was to make his people happy and prosperous. The best proof that he succeeded is the fact that so few Jews felt it desirable to return to Palestine when the opportunity came under Cyrus. Most of them were absorbed in the imperial amalgam. They were allowed to live in communities of their own with the privileges of their religion under their chosen elders, priests and prophets (Ezra 8:17; Ezekiel 1:1; 8:1; 14:1; 20:1—unless these are late editorial additions). But the prophetic office was sometimes abused and the man of visions was sometimes hoodwinked by his own wishful thinking. Even before the deportation of 586 B.C. a lunatiç fringe developed among the Jewish diviners in Babylonia and stirred up sedition. Jeremiah had to send a stern warning from Jerusalem (Jer. 29:8–9) and proclaimed that two rascals whom Nebuchadnezzar had roasted in the fire for their subversive activities had perished by divine command (Jer. 29:15, 21–23).

From the Biblical references just given one gathers that the religious life of the Exile was its distinguishing feature. But because of their deportation the priests were out of a job, and both they and the prophets had to find some new channel of religious activity. They therefore took up teaching. They turned towards the past, to the stories of their national heroes and the incidents of their tumultuous history; they set themselves to interpret it all in the light of religion and to rewrite it as a series of lessons for the admonition and guidance of future generations. Thus they changed what had been story and history into a textbook of religious education, sagas and chronicles into a Bible. This new slant, with its underlying philosophy of history that whenever Israel was faithful to Yahweh the nation prospered but whenever it was unfaithful it was punished, can clearly be seen in such passages as Judges 2:11–17; 1 Kings 11:11–13; 2 Kings 17:7–23, and many others. The Books which they recast are Joshua, Judges, Samuel and Kings. This editing is called the

FIG. 84. THE ISHTAR GATE, BABYLON.

This massive gate spans the sacred way. It was decorated with animals in enameled tile, of which it is estimated there were 575 on the entire structure.

Deuteronomic Revision, because it was made in the spirit of the Book of Deuteronomy.

Among other literary works assigned to this period by modern scholars are the Book of Ezekiel, Lamentations (chaps. 1, 2 and 4), Isaiah (chaps. 40–55), parts of Leviticus (the Holiness Code, chaps. 17–26), the introduction to Deuteronomy (chaps. 1–4) and various additions to the original book, and a good many Psalms (possibly 22, 51, 69, etc.).

IN THE HEART OF PERSIA

With the conquest of Babylon by Cyrus in 539 B.C., Mesopotamia became part of the Persian Empire which before long dominated all lands from India to the Soudan, to the Aegean and Black seas. Attempts were made also to subdue Greece and the Danube country. The Persian kings ruled from four capitals, Babylon, Ecbatana, Persepolis and Susa. During all its existence therefore the Persian government had in its keeping the entire Jewish nation wherever its scattered fragments happened to be.

Daily life among the people of the Dispersion went on much as it had gone on in Babylonia and Assyria. Jews were still in places of influence under Persian kings. According to Herodotus, Zerubbabel was a personal friend of Darius I and by him was made governor of Jerusalem. Nehemiah was not only cup-bearer to Artaxerxes I (464-424 B.C.) but trusted friend; and while the Books of Daniel and Esther are not historical, we see between the lines the procession of talented Jews in the entourage of the kings: Daniel and his Three Friends (Dan. 1:18-20), Esther the Queen (Esther 2:16-18), and Mordecai (Esther 10:1-2); and there are hints that Jews by the thousand are to be found in all the provinces of the vast empire (Esther 3:8-9, 12-13; 8:9-10).

The kings under whom they lived and toiled have in recent years become vivid to us through the spade of the excavator. The "Shushan" of Esther is Susa, the old capital of the Elamites, rebuilt and glorified by Darius I and restored and enlarged by Artaxerxes I and II. It was uncovered nearly a century ago and

FIG. 85. BABYLON: THE HANGING GARDENS.

An imaginative reconstruction of the most famous of Nebuchadnezzar's works, classed by the Greeks as one of the seven wonders of the world. It was a pleasure garden for his Median wife Amytis, built to imitate the terraced hillside of her native Persis. Each terrace was supported on arches and flagged with stone, and enough earth was spread upon it to sustain not only grass and flowers but flowering shrubs and trees. Water was raised by an apparatus like a chain pump. Sheets of lead beneath the reeds and bitumen that underlay the loam kept the water from seeping through to the apartments below. Broad stairs led from the ground to all the terraces, even to the topmost which was 350 feet above the city.

Excavations in 1903 made north-east of Nebuchadnezzar's huge palace brought to light the foundations of a unique building and a vaulted crypt or cellar which certain inscriptions indicated to have been a sort of refrigerator for preserving perishable foods. It is supposed that these remains belong to this once splendid mountain of pleasure.

its relics are now in the Louvre. Chief among the finds was the building called "Apadana" or audience chamber. Its walls were adorned with friezes of enameled brick, and the roof of cedar was upheld by lofty pillars with capitals of kneeling bulls (See Figs. 86–87). This was the palace where Esther superceded Vashti as queen, and outwitted Haman. The wealth of the monarchs may be imagined from what Plutarch says in his Life of Alexander: "At the taking of Susa, Alexander found in the palace 40,000 talents in money already coined, besides an unspeakable quantity of other furniture and treasures, among which was 5,000 talents-worth of Hermionian purple." But more extensive and magnificent was the palace at Persepolis built by Darius I and Xerxes and excavated by the Oriental Institute of Chicago from 1931–35 (Fig. 88). The terrace on which the buildings stood, one thousand by sixteen hundred feet and fifty feet high, was reached by monumental stairways on which in bold reliefs still perfectly preserved are processions of troops, officials and ambassadors coming to a royal durbar and bringing gifts. There are nearly a thousand feet of them (Fig. 89). And as for treasure, Plutarch again says: "Nor was the money found here less than at Susa, besides other movables and treasure, as much as ten thousand pairs of mules and five thousand camels could carry away." All of the palaces that could be burned were burned by Alexander to get even with Xerxes for having burned Athens. When scholars have translated the twenty thousand cuneiform tablets found in the hall of archives, we may have the Persian version of their defeat by the Greeks at Marathon and Salamis and Platea, and perhaps something about the Jews of the Dispersion.

Under the Shadow of Hellenism

With the conquest of the East by Alexander (333–323 B.C.) a great change occurred in the life of all peoples. Alexander was not merely a conqueror, he was an apostle. With a boyish enthusiasm he resolved to make Greek culture dominant throughout the world. He built Greek cities at many Asiatic places, settled

FIG. 86. SUSA: THE APADANA OR WINTER PALACE.

In this age-old city of the Sumerians called in the Bible "Shushan," the late conqueror Darius I built a palace and his son Artaxerxes I—the Ahasuerus of Esther—extended and glorified it. Here reconstructed is the hypostyle hall of the palace. The pillars with their bull capitals are of gray marble, the beams are of cedar richly painted and adorned with metal and tile detail. The ceiling is coffered and painted. Embroidered hangings which though they have perished can be restored from contemporary sculptured representations keep out the glare of the sun. This is the scene of the trials and triumphs of queen Esther.

Greek veterans with their families here and there as colonists, encouraged the Greek organization of civic life, planted Greek ideas in all realms and on "barbarism" made a tremendous impact that grew in force as the years went by. Under his successors, from Antioch on the north and Alexandria on the south, both newly founded or refounded, came influences that accentuated in Judaism the difference between conservative and liberal. By the third century before Christ the children of the upper classes in Palestine had already been tainted with Hellenism. They assumed the Greek mantle and a broad-brimmed hat, and joined the semi-political and semi-social guild of the Epheboi—the Young Men's Greek Association—of which these were the insignia. They attended the gymnasium, which was not only a place for exercise but a social club; took part in sports, became enthusiastic about the theatre, tried their hands at writing Greek poetry and twanging a lyre; dabbled in politics, and in general cultivated that natural point of view that contrasts so markedly with the religious point of view of the Jews. They often changed their Hebrew name for a Greek one: Solomon became Alexander, Joseph became Menelaus. But the growth of this pagan liberalism stiffened the opposition of the faithful. The conservative party saw in it the decline of morals and religion, and therefore with all the greater zeal they hugged to their bosom the sacred Law and practiced its commands with even greater scruple.

Political events in the late fourth and succeeding centuries still further accentuated this divergence. Ptolemy I, who in the scramble for power on Alexander's death had won Egypt and Palestine, tried to bolster his kingdom by transporting thousands of Jews to people his capital, Alexandria. Those of the pious thus transplanted would take their religion with them, establish their synagogues in a strange land and try to bring up their children in the love of Yahweh and the fear of the Law. Those of the liberals would find in the Hellenic city far more to interest them than old Jerusalem on its barren rock could ever offer; they would enthusiastically say that life for them began in Alexandria.

FIG. 87.   SUSA: BULL CAPITAL FROM THE ROYAL PALACE.

These conventionalized bulls, ancient symbols of strength, top the tall fluted columns in the great hall that covered two and a half acres. No capitals like these have been found in other civilizations.

After this deportation, for a couple of hundred years Jews continued to flock thither. Liberals came chiefly to engage in trade, for the new city was fast attracting to itself the commerce of the world. Newly opened routes to the Red sea coasts, the rich lands of south Arabia, India and east Africa, seemed naturally to converge here. To Jews who were commercially minded or politically or culturally minded there was no place like Alexandria. On the other hand, after Antiochus of Syria had wrested Palestine from Ptolemy's grasp, the rulers of Syria became militantly active in pushing the Greek religion and therefore in persecuting Judaism. As a result, a tide of pious people set towards Egypt, in the hope that the liberal policy of the government towards religion would do them more good than the paganism of Alexandria would do them harm. So the number of Jews in Alexandria grew until by the end of the Greek period they were the largest Jewish community in the world. In numbers, wealth and influence, the Dispersion quite outweighed the home land.

THE OLD TESTAMENT IN GREEK

This fact had one fateful result. There grew up in Egypt generations of Jews who could not speak Hebrew or Aramaic. When the Law was read in the synagogue on the Sabbath it was heard in an unknown tongue, for only the rabbis knew any Hebrew. That was a disintegrating influence the "Pious" had not reckoned with. The best way to overcome it was to translate the Law into Greek. To be sure, the ultra-conservatives objected; they pointed out that the Hebrew scriptures were not understood even in Jerusalem and that when they were read in the synagogues the reader "targumed" verse by verse, that is, translated orally into Aramaic which since the Exile had been the popular speech. They contended that the Law was too sacred to be written down in any language but its original Hebrew. But the majority who looked at matters through the clear eyes of Greek common sense maintained three things: first, that it was a waste of good time to read the scriptures twice where once would do; second, that good scholars should fix in permanent form, once for all, the traditional "targum" that was now carried only in memory; and third, that if the blessings of the Law were to be extended to the Gentiles by way of proselyting, the surest means would be to give them the Law in a language they could understand. So the more liberal view prevailed; the Jewish community in Alexandria as a whole sanctioned the undertaking, and not far from the middle of the third century B.C. a group of scholars collaborated in reducing to

FIG. 88. PERSEPOLIS.

View from the cliffs showing the restored harem palace in the foreground, ruins of the palace of Xerxes to the left, and columns of the apadana in the background.

writing the books of the Law, in Greek. No doubt the reigning Ptolemy (Philadelphus) encouraged the work, for he was a liberal-minded as well as an enthusiastic Hellenist; besides, it is said, he wanted a copy of the Law for his famous library.

When it became the custom to read the Prophets as well as the Law in the synagogue on week-days—though not on the Sabbath—the community approved a translation of that body of scripture. Last of all, private and unauthorized translations of the third and least sacred division of scripture were made—the so-called "Writings," which included Proverbs and other "Wisdom" literature, the Psalms, Chronicles, and the like. This work continued into the Christian era. Philo (c. 40 A.D.) the famous Jewish scholar, was acquainted with all of our Old Testament in Greek except the books of Esther, Ecclesiastes, Song of Solomon and Daniel. Because it was said that all of the seventy races of the world could now read the Law in the universal Greek, this version was later called the Septuagint [2] (Greek for seventy is *septuaginta*) and present-day scholars refer to it as LXX.

This first translation ever to be made of so extensive a body of literature became the most influential book in the world. When Christianity appeared, the Septuagint was taken over bodily into the Church and became with the New Testament additions the Christian Bible. It was current in Greek all through the early missionary centuries, and from it were made the Versions that did for the backward races of the East and Europe what the Greek version of the Old Testament had done for the children of the Dispersion—gave them the Scripture in their own language: Egyptian (Coptic), Ethiopic, Gothic, Slavic, Armenian; and finally by way of Latin, all the local tongues of Western Europe including English.

A PUBLISHING HOUSE

The rabbis of Alexandria were the editors of the Greek editions of their scriptures, and the copying establishments—or as we say today, the publishing houses—were probably connected with their homes. If we should visit such a home we should first have to thread the narrow lanes of the Jewish quarter in the eastern end of the city. Approaching the door in a plain mud-brick wall

---

[2] The usual explanation given of the origin of the term "Septuagint" is that the translation from the original Hebrew into Greek was made by seventy scholars who were sent to Egypt for the purpose by the High Priest at Jerusalem. Even that explanation is faulty inasmuch as the legend on which the explanation is based distinctly says that six scholars from each of the twelve tribes of Israel were sent—a total of seventy-two. The explanation given in the present text came to the author from Prof. William A. Irwin of the University of Chicago Divinity School.

abutting on the street, we should see hanging by the doorpost a folded parchment on which is written the "Shema" or basic creed of Judaism—"Listen, O Israel; the LORD is our God, the LORD alone; so you must love the LORD your God with all your mind and all your heart and all your strength" (Deut. 6:4). Jews piously touch this parchment as they pass through the door-

Fig. 89.   PERSEPOLIS: DECORATIVE PANEL FROM THE APADANA STAIRWAY.

Lion and bull relief, used again and again on Persepolis stairways, sometimes called the "arms of ancient Persia." The soldiers are Persian and Median guards. Above is the symbol of the god Ahuramazda.

way. Within the house, all is cosy and refined like many a rabbi's home in Jerusalem. The family life is regulated by the hours of prayer and the other demands of the ritual. The language of conversation in the home is Aramaic, as in Jerusalem, though in intercourse outside it is Greek.

Passing through the rear of the home and crossing a small court with fountain and garden, we come to a separate building where the copying is done. A battery of five to ten transcribers, all professionals, sit at desks facing a reader. Each writer has his roll of papyrus, his pens and ink. As the chief scribe who is also a rabbi and a scholar reads slowly from his Septuagint roll, all the others write in concert swiftly but carefully lest they change one jot or tittle of the inspired word. All copies are afterward proofread to make sure every transcriber has both heard and written accurately. The results are marvels of exactness and of beauty.

From the chief rabbi we learn of the demand for the sacred books in different parts of the Diaspora. Naturally the most frequent call is for the Torah or five books of Moses, for that is required reading every Sabbath in every synagogue. Next come the Prophets, which are read on weekdays or on certain occasions only. Last of all, the Writings. This last named collection was still in process of creation in 132 B.C. and it was destined to continue many centuries after that time. Something of the urge that lay behind this literary activity is conveyed by the Preface to *The Wisdom of Jesus, the Son of Sirach* ("Ecclesiasticus," in the Apocrypha) :

"Whereas many and great things have been delivered unto us by the Law and the Prophets, and by the others that have followed in their steps . . . my grandfather Jesus, having much given himself to the reading of [the same], was drawn also himself to write somewhat pertaining to instruction and wisdom, in order that those who love learning . . . might make progress much more by living according to the Law. . . . Having come into Egypt in the eight and thirtieth year of Euergetes the king [*i.e.,* 132 B.C.] and having continued there some time, I found a copy affording no small instruction. I thought it therefore most necessary for me to apply some diligence . . . to interpret [*i.e.,* to translate] this book, and . . . set it forth for them also who in the land of their sojourning are desirous to learn, fashioning their manners beforehand so as to live according to the Law."

It came to pass therefore that in Egypt there was greater interest in multiplying the sacred writings and a greater liberality in admitting new works than was found in the home land. Jews in

Alexandria were for several generations exposed to Greek influences and unconsciously took on a point of view that seemed to many of the leaders in Jerusalem to be unorthodox. Then again, the constant criticism they were under at the hands of Gentiles of all sorts led some of the learned rabbis to attempt a defense of the faith such as perhaps would seem unnecessary at home. For example, a book that was in great demand was *The Wisdom of Solomon*. It was composed in Greek in Alexandria by an Egyptian Jew of high culture and broad spirit. He tried to show that the wisdom of the Hebrew sages and the Jewish morality were superior to anything Greek philosophy could produce. Such a point of view could have come only out of the Dispersion, and the Jews in Palestine would think such a work more like a human product than a revelation from on high. Such a book would sell in Egypt and in Greece and the cities of Asia Minor but almost not at all in Jerusalem. Other books that arose in the Dispersion were the *Book of Enoch,* that appealed especially to those who were earnestly expecting the Messiah (Jude 14–15) and who were curious about angels, the future life and the like; the *Testaments of the Twelve Patriarchs,* and the *Psalms of Solomon.*

So Alexandria was the center from which manuscripts in Greek were sent to synagogues all over the Greek-speaking East, the vital heart of the propaganda movement to extend to the Gentiles the knowledge of the true God and his moral claims upon men.

THE CITY AND ITS LIFE

We can hardly understand the impact made by Hellenism upon the Jews of the Dispersion without taking an intimate view of the great city in which lived the largest single body of Jews in the first century before Christ. Let us approach it by sea.

In the year 47 B.C., on the fourth morning out from Caesarea, we awake on the deck of our fifty-ton ship in time to see a blazing beacon climb above the south-western horizon. When the sun arises the fire sinks, and in its place a towering lighthouse rears its bulk to mark the entrance to the eastern harbor of Alexandria.

An hour later we enter the narrow mouth between the southern breakwater and the island on which stands the great Pharos. For two hundred and thirty-two years now it has been one of the Seven Wonders of the World; it is destined to last many hundred years longer. Its splendid white marble shaft rises in three stages, five hundred and ninety feet, and throws its light thirty-four miles. Sostratus, a master architect from Cnidos, made it (Fig. 90).

The azure bay is studded with galleys and triremes, their long pennons whipping in the breeze. We hear the shouts of the sailors and the chanty-songs of the slave longshoremen as they load and unload bales and sacks and boxes. Behind the quays and the broad stone stairs that lead up from the water-front, glow the most splendid buildings any living city can boast, chief of these the Royal Palace, rising tier on tier above a hilly promontory on the south. In that palace at the present hour lives Julius Caesar, protector and consort of Queen Cleopatra. A trireme that serves' Caesar for a yacht is moored in the little royal harbor by the palace stairs.

Now we land, pick out the least rascally-looking guide from among the many who offer their services, and make our way on foot through the jostling crowd towards the center of the town. Jason is the guide's name, a Hellenized Jew, a young fop with plenty of make-up on his face and surrounded with an aura of perfume. Soon we cross a paved street a hundred feet wide and bordered with marble colonnades. It runs east and west straight through the center of the city for three miles to the cemetery beyond the western gate. This is Canopus Street. Pushing across it we enter directly the precincts of the Paneum. Passing by the temple dedicated to the god Pan, we make for a huge conical mound that rises in the center of the enclosure. A special path leads up to a platform on the summit. No finer orientation point could be chosen, for below us now lies the whole city as on a map (Fig. 91).

"There in front of us," says guide Jason, "is the mighty Pharos and the harbor you entered this morning (Fig. 91, 1), with the

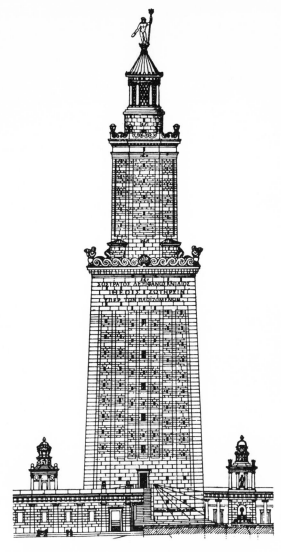

FIG. 90.   THE PHAROS OF ALEXANDRIA.

Built by Sostratus during the reign of Ptolemy Philadelphus (285-247 B.C.), the Pharos may well be called the father of lighthouses. It is said to have cost 800 talents—or $1,000,000, equivalent in purchasing power to much more than that today. The light came from a huge bonfire kept burning in a brazier. Donkeys brought up the wood on an incline within the building as far as the top of the second story; thence it was elevated by windlasses through a well to the upper landing.

royal palace and the Lochias quarter to the east of it (Fig. 91, 2). The rocky low-lying island of Pharos from which the lighthouse takes its name, extends westerly and forms a natural breakwater for the harbor (Fig. 91, 3). Over here to the northwest, cutting the harbor into two parts is a viaduct we call the Heptastadium, seven stadia long (1400 feet) that connects the island with the city (Fig. 91, 4). Perhaps you can see that near each end it is pierced for the passage of smaller craft from the eastern or Greek harbor to the smaller western one which we call the 'Harbor of Happy Returns' (Fig. ˙91, 5). The viaduct carries also an aqueduct.

"I know you are thrilled by the color of this sea. Like an aquamarine is the shallow harbor, and like an opal the gleams and glooms of the sunken ledges beyond, covered with many-colored seaweeds and sea anemones. Now and then the sea breaks white on them. Farther from shore in deep water the azure becomes cobalt.

"Now look due west. There inside the wall is the old town of Rhakotis (Fig. 91, 6), at present the quarter for the workmen, for warehouses and shipping. The inhabitants are all Egyptian. Most of the city's commerce is handled from the western harbor, and the docks for building, repairing and outfitting ships are in Rhakotis. On the little hill to the south, just outside the wall, do you see that huge building? That is the Serapeum (Fig. 91, 7) where Ptolemy I introduced the worship of the god Hades, lord of the under-world, and to attract the Egyptians claimed that Hades was in reality the Egyptian Osiris-Apis, the bull incarnation worshipped at Memphis where is the bull cemetery. This god is now the most important divinity in Alexandria.

"Now we come to the inland sea, vast lake Mareotis, that bounds the city along its entire south side and extends southward for miles (Fig. 91, 8). All those boats with pigeon-wing sails are coming from the Nile through a canal and they bring to this city not only all the food we need but whatever Egypt exports to foreign lands. The huge grain supplies for Roma all come in this

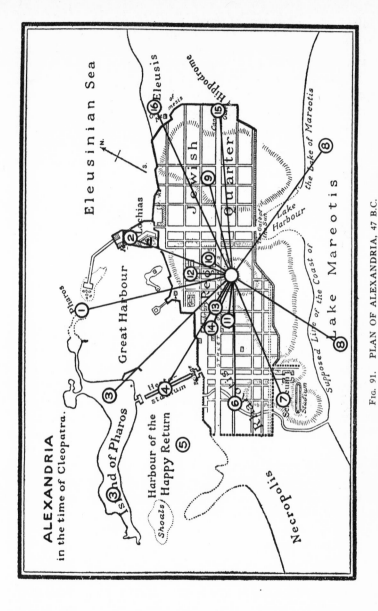

FIG. 91.   PLAN OF ALEXANDRIA, 47 B.C.

The focal point of the lines represents the position from which we view the city. The figures refer to places mentioned in the text.

way to Alexandria and their cargoes, transferred to barges, are taken by a canal that goes under Canopus Street to the Harbor of Happy Returns. There they are trans-shipped to those magnificent express boats you see lying at the quays. We must go picnicking on this lake this afternoon. The papyrus reeds make in places a veritable forest into which we shall push, and shaded by their leaves we shall eat our supper and drink our wine. All along the shore you can see the vineyards which supply the finest wine in Egypt.

"This brings us to the Jewish Quarter on the east (Fig. 91, 9). In spite of its size and wealth it is not a very safe place, for we Alexandrians are a turbulent lot and on the slightest provocation use the Jew for a scapegoat. We envy Jewish ability and wealth, and we resist the extension of the slightest privilege to them. So we spread the silliest reports about them: that in their Temple at Jerusalem is a golden ass's head to which Jews pay divine honors; that every year they catch a Greek boy, fatten him up on dainties, kill and sacrifice him according to their ritual, eat his heart and swear everlasting hostility to all Greeks.[3]

"To the north of us is the Royal Quarter (Fig. 91, 10). Here as well as in the section immediately below us most of the wealthy foreigners live. One glance at the magnificent buildings tells the story. On the near side of Canopus Street to our left is the Gymnasium (Fig. 91, 11) where I go for a little exercise every day, but mostly to meet my friends. The porticoes that surround its garden will hold all the elite of the city without crowding. That building just to the left of the Gymnasium is the Law Court. Most of the famous buildings of the city however are to the north of Canopus Street toward the sea. Let me name them for you, beginning on the right in line with Cleopatra's palace east of the harbor.

"First is the theatre overlooking the bay, where 'The Birds' of Aristophanes is now being given (Fig. 91, 12). It holds fifty thousand people. No need of scenery in that theatre with all the

[3] Josephus: *Against Apion* II, 7, 8.

harbor, the busy sails, the war triremes with their flashing oars, and the alabaster tower of Pharos for a backdrop. Next, the Forum where most of the financial deals are arranged and around which most of the better shops are clustered. Next the Caesarion, just now being built by Julius Caesar. They say he is going to marry our queen and rule the world from here! In line with this on Canopus Street is the Mausoleum (Fig. 91, 13) where Alexander the Great is buried. Ptolemy I had his body brought to this city from Babylon and now it lies there in a coffin of solid gold which encloses, they say, a leaden one filled with honey in which the remains are preserved. All of the past Ptolemy-Pharaohs are also buried there in magnificent tombs. The great block of buildings directly to the west is the world-famed Museum and Library (Fig. 91, 14). That we must visit, and the best time is now."

Having thus surveyed the city from this unobstructed vantage-point, we descend the spiral stairs and in ten minutes are at the Museum entrance. Jason is evidently a frequenter, for the door-man lets him through without question. We find ourselves in the midst of a spacious garden surrounded by colonnades beneath which well-dressed people are slowly walking or sitting in groups for discussion. Fountains are playing and in the middle as center-piece to a large circular basin is the sculptured group representing Father Nile and his children, finest example of the Alexandrian school of Greek art. As we stroll about in the Museum grounds which cover nearly a third of the city Jason tells something of the institution:

"It was founded, they say, by Alexander himself and endowed with lands for support; but more likely Ptolemy I was the founder It is really a Greek university. Those dignified men who seem to be the centers of attention are 'members' or professors. They live outside but have their chief meal here in the refectory build-ing yonder. Any subject is taught for which there is popular inter-est, whether science or literature or mathematics or astronomy or philosophy of any brand. If there were time we would listen in when a lecture is scheduled in one of the many lecture-halls scattered through the grounds."

Just then Jason catches sight of a bearded philosopher whom he evidently knows, and hastens to introduce us to him. He proves to be the chief librarian, who at once generously invites us to see his treasures housed in a magnificent building overlooking the harbor.

"I apologize for the condition of the northern part of the library," he said, "for we have recently had an accident. Six months ago while Caesar was trying to get control of the city at the same time trying to outwit the army which our young Ptolemy was bringing against him, his men made a night raid and set fire to the entire Egyptian fleet anchored at the rear of our building. There were fifty men-of-war, twenty-two guard ships and thirty-eight other craft. Some of the buildings near the quay caught fire and then the flames leaped to our library. Before we could put out the fire we had lost fifty thousand rolls, among them some of our most precious ones. But we have nearly eight hundred thousand left, the largest collection of books in the world."

Then opening a door he leads us into the stacks—streets of stacks, one might say—in the pigeon-holes of which we see the ends of the rolls all neatly labeled. At intervals, an open space with tables and chairs where privileged ones can sit and read or copy at leisure.

"We think we have a copy of the works of every Greek writer of note who ever lived," the librarian went on. "Here, for example, is a first edition of Homer made during the tyranny of Peisistratus of Athens."

". . . And here is a complete copy of Sappho's poems written evidently by a feminine hand on purple vellum. . . . This well-worn series of parchments are a complete set of Euclid, who was one of the first teachers in the Museum in the days of Ptolemy I. These thirteen rolls are his *Elements of Geometry.* You doubtless know the story, how the king, seeing the magnitude and difficulty of this subject, asked the philosopher whether there was not a

FIG. 92. A CHARIOT RACE IN THE CIRCUS MAXIMUS, ROME, FROM A PAINTING BY GÉROME.

The straight portions were at least 600 feet long. Down the center was a "backbone" (spina) adorned with statues and showing the devices by which the races were directed. This race was for quadrigas or four-horsed chariots. The capacity of the Circus Maximus at Rome was 200,000.

short cut to knowing it; whereto Euclid replied, 'Your Majesty, there is no royal road to geometry'; and there is another story about the boy who learned the first proposition in the *Elements* and then asked, 'What do I get by learning these things?' Then Euclid called his slave and said, 'Here, give this boy threepence, since he has to make something out of what he learns'."

Here for an hour we wander, wide-eyed at the books and the librarian's comments. This is a new world that makes the schools and the pious learning and hair-splitting of Jerusalem seem mean enough by comparison.

Bidding goodbye to our learned host we find some litters and ride to a stylish restaurant for lunch. On emerging we discover that the drift of the crowds in the streets is setting strongly eastward. Then Jason remembers that there are races at the Hippodrome this afternoon. Everybody is excited. All the talk is about the favorite charioteers and their fours; of the fabulous pay they get—more than the salary of a Roman senator; of the tricks they will play to win; of the bets that are up and how the winners will spend their cash. We follow the crowd as it streams out the Canopic gate, through the Grove of Nemesis, where the head of unlucky Pompey was buried after his murder at Pelusium, and after a mile or so we come to the Circus (Fig. 91, 15). The excitement increases as fifty thousand men crowd the seats, and it becomes a frenzy when the chariots appear and the big-shot charioteer, who in his twenty-four years of professional racing has won 1462 times and cleaned up 36,000,000 sesterces (£280,000 or $1,400,000), leans over his dashboard and gives his four the lash. When the victor is announced, pandemonium breaks loose and the homecoming of the crowd is a riot that calls out the police (Fig. 92).

That evening Jason wants to take us to a night club in the notorious suburb of Eleusis to the east of the Grove. (Fig. 91, 16)— about which the less said the better. We decline with thanks, and making the best of the moonlight, we ride out to the suburb of Nicopolis about two miles farther east. There the wealthy Alexandrians own sumptuous villas in the midst of gardens. The beach, thronged with bathers and edged with tumbling breakers, gleams white against the golden background of the moonlit sea.

We happen to learn by chance that on the next day, the Sabbath, special prayers will be offered in all the synagogues for Julius Caesar, and a special week of thanksgiving will begin. It seems that during the "late unpleasantness," when Caesar had been virtually besieged in his palace by the angry rabble and threatened by the army of young Ptolemy XII who was trying to put his sister Cleopatra off the throne, an army of Jews and Nabateans under Antipater, political ruler for the Jewish High Priest Hyrcanus, had marched to Egypt, utterly defeated Ptolemy, and so made Caesar's mastery of the situation complete. As a sign of his appreciation, Caesar made Antipater a Roman citizen and Procurator of Judea, Samaria and Galilee under Hyrcanus, while he confirmed Hyrcanus as High Priest and made him hereditary Ethnarch and a Roman senator. And now Caesar has just issued a proclamation from the palace in Lochias by which all the Jews in Alexandria shall be given henceforth equal rights with Greeks before the courts. This was a tremendous gift which set the house of Israel trembling with joy.

On Sabbath morning therefore at the time of prayer the streets of the Jewish quarter are thronged with people and every synagogue is filled to the doors. We go to the chief synagogue which is the pride of every Jew, a building plain without but within a glorious five-aisled sanctuary in which gold lamps shed their perpetual light before the Ark and all the accessories are of precious metals and costly woods; in which there are seventy-one chairs of gold for the members of the Great Council. There from the tribune we hear the Torah intoned and with the great congregation we utter the "Amens" whenever the ruler of the synagogue waves his handkerchief as signal. When the time for the prayer arrives, the layman chosen for the occasion is summoned by the ruler to the front of the Ark where the sacred rolls are kept. He begins in a clear voice with the reciting of the "Shema" and the

blessings connected with it; and then he continues with an elaborate petition that Jehovah will bring eternal blessings on the head
of the great Roman who had so signally honored the Chosen
People.

Before the service is over, the congregation is aware of a tumult
outside the synagogue, and as they emerge into the street they
encounter a crowd of hoodlums who pelt them with bricks, rotten
fruit and whatever they can lay hands on. Many of the Jews are
afraid to leave the house and those who venture to go home are
insulted, knocked down with missiles and in general badly man-
handled. This is the gentle way the Greek and Levantine citizens
take to show their resentment at having Jews raised to an equality
with themselves by this foreign Caesar whose plans they have
recently so nearly wrecked.

Such was life in this turbulent town. The Jews were foreigners
in a city of foreigners. Many of the Jews were wealthy, but life
and property were insecure; some of them were learned, but the
Greeks regarded them as intellectual climbers who had no native
right to Greek culture; some of them were bigoted, and answered
insult by a kind of cringing defiance against their Gentile persecutors who they knew were beyond the pale of Yahweh's grace;
some of them were sincere and intelligent in their religion, and
endeavored by a blameless life and a diligence in the study and
promulgation of their sacred books to hasten the day when "Gentiles shall come to Thy light, and kings to the brightness of Thy
rising." Little they knew that some day in that very city a new
faith, an offshoot of Judaism, would destroy the splendid temples
of the Gentile gods and drive with a scourge the Jews themselves
from their burning synagogues. But that revolution broke after
Bible days were done.

CHAPTER XI

IN THE TIME OF JAMES, SON OF ZEBEDEE

(An Imaginative Reconstruction)

JAMES SAW the light of day in a well-to-do home in the town of Capernaum, not far from the year 6 B.C. We suspect that his family could not be classed as poor, because his father Zebedee used in his business at least two hired servants (Mk. 1:20); and later when James and his younger brother John became interested in a cousin from Nazareth who they thought was the Messiah, their mother Salome tried to see that neither they nor their Messiah had too hard a time (Mt. 27:55–56; Mk. 15:40–41; cf. Lk. 8:1–3). The lake furnished father Zebedee with a good business, that of supplying fish to the Greek fish-pickling factory at Tarichiae at the southern end. One could see a barrel of Galilee pickled fish in any bazaar in the Roman world. As Zebedee's business grew he took in his two sons as partners, and when he retired the boys took in two other partners who owned a boat, a certain Andrew and a Simon originally from Bethsaida (Mt. 5:18; Lk. 5:3). So fortune was good to that household.

Capernaum was a good place in which to be born. It was a town of perhaps 50,000 inhabitants, situated on the north shore of the Sea of Galilee where one branch of the great trunk line from Egypt to Babylon passed tangent to its north-west corner. King Herod Antipas maintained a personal representative there (Jn. 4:46–47); the Romans thought it of enough consequence to station a body of troops there under a centurion (Mt. 8:5) and to keep open a custom-house (Mt. 9:9). James and his brother therefore were not brought up in a corner but in the stream of whatever events were flowing.

The houses were built of black lava blocks which any one might quarry on the surface of the hill; for Galilee is a volcanic region and the lake is merely the result of a lava flow that dammed up Jordan. This gave to the town a somber appearance as it stretched its narrow length along most of the north shore; but the sparkling blue of the lake in its amphitheatre of hills more than compensated. Zebedee lived close to the water where he could hear his boats booming against the float when he couldn't keep his eye on them.

Galilee once had a reputation for being a heathen province. Whatever Hebrews lived here had formerly been wiped out, so that about 120 B.C. John Hyrcanus had to re-populate it with Jews. By James' time, while there were so many foreigners that a Galilean talked with a "Scottish burr" the Jews were enthusiastically Jewish (Mt. 26:73). The boys were trained in piety from their earliest days.

This would mean that the boys had a knowledge of the Law, which they showed by being able to read it, write it and explain its obvious meaning. If there had been daughters their mother, Salome, would have made herself responsible for their education at least as far as learning to read and perhaps to write were concerned, and she certainly would have taught them to "fear God and keep his commandments." But theoretically Zebedee was responsible for the education of his sons. Practically all he did, however, was to teach them the *Shema* or Creed (Deut. 6:4–5) and turn the more technical subjects over to the elementary school which every community of this size maintained in connection with its synagogue. This school was taught by a schoolmaster who, however humble, was socially respectable and was entitled to be addressed as "Rabbi" by his pupils. James was sent to him when he was six years old.

Little James was duly impressed on that first day when his father took him by the hand and led him to the schoolhouse. He found the rabbi seated cross-legged on a little platform a foot high. Before him on a low rack was a scroll of the Law, which with other selected Old Testament writings was the sole textbook.

The boys sat on the ground in a half-circle facing the teacher. There James was taught to read the Law in Hebrew beginning with the Book of Leviticus, the contents of which it was necessary for every Jew to know if he was to regulate his life acceptably to God; and he must pronounce the words correctly and reverently. Hebrew was a strange language to him, for at home and at play he spoke Aramaic, and later when he began to do business he would have to speak Greek. Hebrew was only for the synagogue. The first lesson was the letters of the Hebrew alphabet, *Aleph, Beth, Gimmel,* etc.; after that was mastered and recited, the teacher copied a verse which James had already learned by heart at home, and taught him to identify the individual words. The noise bothered little James at first: every small boy did his studying and reciting out loud, so that the schoolroom was a perfect babel. But the rabbi said that no one would long remember what he learned if he did not repeat his lessons orally.

After learning to read came writing, probably in Hebrew and certainly in Aramaic; and after writing, the art of figuring. Whatever the subject, the rabbi told James that to be a good pupil he should be like a cemented cistern which loses not a drop. Ancient pedagogy might not spare the rod, but it never heard of such things as interest, initiative, resourcefulness, originality or self-expression.

James never went beyond the elementary school. He was not going to be a scribe or a physician but just a fisherman; consequently the rabbi never suggested his going to the high school or the scribal college in Jerusalem. And since James was to be a pious Jew, he did not suggest his going to a Greek school, the nearest one being at Scythopolis or Gadara, cities of the Greek "Decapolis"; there he would have learned music and geometry and poetry and athletics.[1] The only athletics James needed was swimming, and the boys would teach him that.

The Sabbath was respected in James' home. Since it began

[1] On the Greek teachers from Gadara see *Cambridge Ancient History* XI:640–642.

Friday evening at sundown, Friday was called Preparation Day. No business might be begun on that day unless it could be completed the same day. On Friday Salome prepared all the Sabbath meals so that the Fourth Commandmen might not be broken; and since the Sabbath was not in any sense a fast day but a day of joy, James and John looked forward to the best meals of the week. Elaborate preparations were made for keeping the food warm, for no fire might be kindled on the holy day (Ex. 35:3). The Sabbath lamp was now lighted, family prayers said and on many a Sabbath eve Zebedee would tell his boys the stories from the sacred book or recite for them the ballads and other poems that express the piety and the patriotism of the Israelites. Thus the atmosphere of the home contributed to the formation of a character which the God of Israel might approve (2 Tim. 1:5; 3:14-15).

On Sabbath morning the entire family went to the synagogue. In Capernaum the building was not large enough to hold all the House of Israel at once and it was not in very good repair. Many were saying that they needed a new one.[2] However it was larger and higher than any private house, for no structure was permitted to "look down on" the synagogues. Its main doors on the south faced the lake which was only a hundred yards away, and consequently when the reader stood to read the lesson he faced Jerusalem, as he properly should. When Zebedee and his family approached, the father passed through the court in front of the edifice, where he washed his hands in preparation for the service, then entered the central door with the other men of the congregation, but Salome and the boys who at this time were under the legal age of twelve went round the west side of the building tc the rear where they found a flight of stone steps that led to the second story. Here they entered a gallery supported on pillars

[2] The new building was erected a few years later by a Roman centurion stationed at Capernaum, who was sympathetic with the Jewish faith if not an actual proselyte (Lk. 7:6). We have a fair understanding of what it was like, for an enlarged synagogue, built on the same site in the second century, has been unearthed by Italian excavators and partly restored. Fig. 93.

Fig. 93.   CAPERNAUM SYNAGOGUE (RESTORED).

The synagogue proper was in basilica form, with nave and aisles. Chief entrances were on the lake side (south), and the lunette window opened "toward Jerusalem." Below it (probably erroneous in this reconstruction) stood the "ark" where the scriptures were kept. The galleries for women and children extended around three sides. Adjoining on the east was a colonnaded court.

This is a rebuilding (c. 200 A.D.) of an earlier synagogue that may have been the one presented to the town by the Roman centurion (Lk. 7:5), in which Jesus wrought cures. (Mk. 1:21; 3:1) that ran around three sides of the building and was fitted with a wooden grill so that the occupants could look down through it on the congregation and could see and hear the reader and preacher though they themselves could be but dimly discerned. This was the women's gallery (see Fig. 93).

James and John of course made for the front row of seats. Looking below they saw near the middle of the main floor a structure about twice the height of a man. It was called the "press" or the "ark"; for conspicuously arranged along its front on an upper level were the rolls of scripture. As the service was about to begin they saw the Ruler of the Synagogue climb the ladder-like stairs and take his seat behind the rolls. He was not a teacher but he was honored next to the teacher and was somewhat held in awe by the boys because he had charge of discipline; if any thrashings were to be administered, he was the administrator (Lk. 13:14). His religious duties were to keep the sacred rolls in good condition and to appoint the reader and speaker of the day. Just now he arose officially to count the congregation to see if the necessary ten men were present, without whom there could be no service.[3] Having decided that a quorum was present, he signaled to a distinguished looking gentleman who occupied one of the "chief seats" arranged just below the "ark" and near the reader's desk.

Every one knew that the guest of honor today was an itinerant rabbi belonging to the congregation of Jerusalem but assigned to the task of visiting and instructing the congregations in the provinces. All eyes turned therefore to Rabbi Levi ben Sisi. The rabbi arose, stepped to the reader's desk in front of him and led the congregation in reciting the *Shema*, the Creed of Israel, as recorded in Deuteronomy 6:4-9: "Listen, O Israel, the LORD is our God, the LORD alone," etc. To the boys in the gallery this

---

[3] It is told of one Eliezar, son of Hyrcanus, that coming to the synagogue one day accompanied by his slave, he found that only nine men were present. He therefore gave his slave his freedom so that the requisite number might be counted.

Fig. 94.
A ROLL OF
THE LAW.

Parchment is the material: the rectangles of skin were sewed together at the lateral edges to make a strip from 10 to 30 feet or more long depending upon the amount of text to be written. The lines were arranged in narrow vertical columns, as in our newspapers. The book was written from right to left, the reverse of our custom. The long manuscript was wound on two spindles attached to each end. By rolling up one and unrolling the other the columns would pass in front of the reader as he needed. The spindles had ornamental knobs on the top. The whole row was carefully protected by a cloth, a metal case, or both.

was a solemn moment when they heard the deep tones of the men chanting the sacred words in unison. This completed, the Ruler took from its place in the ark a roll of the Law, handed it down to his attendant on the floor, who in turn placed it upon the reader's desk. The rabbi opened the cylindrical silver case, adorned with an inlay of the Creed and with designs in which the Star of David was prominent, reverently kissed the silken cloth with which the roll was covered, spread out the cloth on the sloping bookrack, separated the two spindles on which the parchment was wound, one at the front end of the manuscript and one at the rear; then turning the spindles by grasping the silver knobs on the top of each, he unwound one and wound the other, while delicate music arose from the row of bells that dangled from the knobs. In this way he made the long strip of parchment travel from one spindle to the other until his eye caught the particular passage which was thè lesson of the day as it fell in the three-year cycle of readings from the Law (Fig. 94). It was Exodus 20, the Ten Commandments. He read the passage beautifully, with a voice that reflected not only training in the art of speech but a cultured and reverent spirit. Having read a verse in the Hebrew he translated ("targum-ed") it into Aramaic, so that all who had forgotten the Hebrew learned in school might understand. When he had finished, he rolled up the scroll, gave it back to the attendant and sat down in the chair set beside the desk for the reader when he should deliver his sermon; and the eyes of every one in the synagogue were fastened upon him (Lk. 4:16-17, 20).

Then from his seat he began his sermon of instruction, based upon the Fourth Commandment (Ex. 20:8-11), which prohibited work on the Sabbath. He told the people that the commandment was clear enough but that trouble began when one tried to define "work." According to the great rabbis of Jerusalem, the work meant by the Law was divided into thirty-nine classes, such as sowing, plowing, reaping, baking, spinning, etc. But under each of these heads there were many special cases that must be considered. For example, what is reaping? Not only gathering grain in large quantities with a sickle; but plucking a few heads of grain as one passes along a path through a wheat-field; likewise, rubbing the heads in one's palms to break off the chaff, and chewing the kernels, is in reality threshing and grind-ing, and therefore prohibited (Mt. 12:1–2). One must learn to discriminate also between different types of labor like tying a knot, for example. Tying a camel-driver's knot or a boatman's knot renders a man guilty; but if a man can tie or untie any knot with one hand, it is not work and the man is not guilty; and a woman may tie on an article of dress, or may tie up a skin of oil or bundles of food without becoming guilty. There was also the question whether one might with impunity eat an egg laid on the Sabbath by a hen which did not know the Law. Rabbi Hillel permitted it, Rabbi Shammai did not. Personally the speaker agreed with the great Shammai.[4]

The learned rabbi went on refining for an hour, but since both John and James were fast asleep after the first five minutes, we need not recount what they didn't hear.

We must confess also that Zebedee was little impressed by all this hair-splitting. In talking over the sermon with Salome at home he observed that if the rabbi was right, a plain man like himself who had work to do and a family to support couldn't be a good Jew; it took too much valuable time. That afternoon sev-eral of his friends dropped in, men who he knew were very much interested in religion. They confessed that the learned discussion of the morning was mostly poppycock. There were a good many in Israel who were like these men, and though they were not a party in any sense, they had been given a name or names, "the poor," "the quiet of the land." They were simple folk, steeped in the teachings of the Psalms and the Prophets and the Apocalyp-tical writings, interested in the moral rather than the political aspects of the coming Messiah, and "living in the expectation of the comforting of Israel" (Lk. 2:25). They were particularly

---

[4] For further illustrations of this hair-splitting, see J. Hastings: *Dict. of the Bible,* sub "Sabbath."

open to any new teaching that laid emphasis on piety and patience (Mt. 5:3, 5-9).

James was now twelve years old, time to become a "son of the Law"; that is, he was now regarded as an adult who was responsible for keeping the precepts of the Pentateuch. Zebedee had long promised James that for the Passover celebrated the spring after he was twelve, he would take him on the annual pilgrimage to Jerusalem. Zebedee knew that the Law required three pilgrimages (Deut. 16:16), but a man who has a family to support cannot afford to go but once a year. That once would be to the greatest of the feasts, the Passover, held on the 14th Nisan. Accordingly a week before the great day, Zebedee, Salome and James left home, father and son on foot, the mother on a donkey. The journey was one hundred miles. Many another family from Capernaum left with them, following the road that skirted the lake on the west. Tiberias had not yet been built, but they avoided the cemetery where it was to arise 20 years later and came to Tarichiae at the end of the lake. Then they began the long descent of the valley where the Jordan river twisted and turned in its serpentine bed to the east of their road. Soon they came upon the huge Greek city of Scythopolis (Beth-shan) which was larger than Jerusalem and given over to the manufacture of flax that grew in the irrigated fields surrounding the town. James could see the tall mound rising from the middle of it, which his father told him was the ancient city upon whose walls the bodies of Saul and Jonathan had been exposed by the Philistines (1 Sam. 31:10) (Fig. 95).

In the outskirts, the little caravan was joined by another of smaller size that had come down by En-dor (1 Sam. 28:7-25) from Nazareth. In the company James found his cousin Jesus, a boy of his own age, and his parents, who took this journey faithfully every year. Pilgrimages like these were about the only time Salome ever saw her sister Mary.

The climate grew hotter as the valley dropped deeper and deeper below sea-level, so that sleeping in the open was very com-

FIG. 95.   THE MOUND OF BETH-SHAN.

This fortress was occupied from prehistoric times until in the seventh century its Byzantine defenders against the Arabs cut the irrigation system and flooded the surrounding plain. The malarial mosquito thus introduced made the site impossible for living. The excavations here shown have cut down through forty-five feet of rubbish and unearthed the history of Beth-shan back to about 1700 B.C.

fortable. There were no large towns but everywhere the evidence
of intensive cultivation by irrigation, especially of wheat, flax,
figs and dates. Zebedee explained that the land belonged to the
Herod family and was worked by slaves. He said also that to
avoid passing through even the edge of the Samaritan country
which they were now traversing, some members of the pilgrimage often crossed the Jordan opposite Scythopolis and took the
road that ran through the town of Pella in Perea, the domain
of Herod Antipas; then they recrossed at Jericho where they
picked up the regular route.

The climb from Jericho up the twenty miles of the treeless and
waterless wilderness of Judea to Jerusalem was almost terrifying
to young James who had never seen any country but the kindly
and fruitful Galilee (Fig. 96). But he was repaid for the heat and
the dust, the thirst and the weariness, when climbing the last
steep ladder of Olivet he turned the crest and saw the Holy City
so near he could almost touch it. How golden it lay in the afternoon light; the Temple, goal of his hopes, shone like the sun,
while from its courts rose the first black smoke of the evening
sacrifice. Every one gave an involuntary shout at the sight, and
Zebedee raised a song that was caught up by those nearest and
soon spread to the whole pilgrimage (Ps. 122):

> I was glad when they said unto me,
> 'Let us go to the house of the Lord'
>
> .   .   .   .
>
> Pray for the peace of Jerusalem;
> They will prosper who love you.

James had never before seen so many people. The temple
courts into which he could look from this elevation were swarm-
ing, groups were on nearly every housetop pointing and gesticu-
lating, lines of men and animals were passing through the two
city gates he could see, while the western slope of Olivet was
densely populated with the little camps of pilgrims who had
thronged hither from all the lands of the Dispersion.

FIG. 96. WILDERNESS OF JUDEA AND THE JORDAN RIVER
FROM THE AIR.

Since the soil is heavily impregnated with chemicals, vegetation grows only **where the** river washes it clean. The north-south caravan trail can be seen at the foot of **the hills** beyond the river.

They found an unoccupied spot on the more northerly slope and there pitched their tiny tent with the city in full view, the narrowing valley of the Kedron with Herod's stadium in front, and the gently undulating hills of the watershed to the west and south for a skyline. . . . "As the mountains are round about Jerusalem" (Ps. 125:2). And how silver and ethereal it all looked when daylight faded and the great round Paschal moon peered over the crest of Olivet, and the camp-fires on the hillsides twinkled back the welcome of the myriad stars.

*   *   *

Passover morning dawned or rather the morning that ushered in the Passover which began at sunset. The passover meal was the first incident in the "Week of Unleavened Bread." Every one was early up and many thousands crowded into the city in the vain hope of attending a synagogue within the walls. Zebedee more wisely decided to say prayers at home and then take James straight to the temple courts in order that he might miss nothing of his first memorable Passover. Salome spent the morning visiting with her sister Mary; the women planned to go up to the temple only in the afternoon at the time of the Passover sacrifice.

Before ten o'clock Zebedee and James entered the "Gate of Samaria (Map III, A, p. 277) in the northern wall and followed the street down the gradually sinking Tyropean valley that cuts the city in two, till they passed under a magnificent viaduct that led high over the bazaars from the palace of the Hasmoneans on the western hill direct to the Sanctuary courts. Then immediately they found a staircase (Fig. 97, D) that ascended through the west retaining wall of the temple area, and landed them in a dense crowd in the outer court (Fig. 97, E). Zebedee explained that this great space between the enclosing walls and the raised platform in the center was open to any one, Jew or Gentile, except to such Jews as happened to be ceremonially unclean—having touched a corpse, for example. All around this court was a magnificent colonnade of white marble pillars, each made of a single

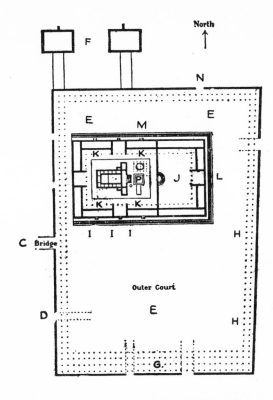

FIG. 97.   PLAN OF THE TEMPLE AREA.

C. The viaduct from the western hill over the Tyropean valley to the Temple courts
D. The stair from the Tyropean valley to the Temple courts
E. The court of the Gentiles
F   The Fortress of Antonia
G. The Royal Porch
H. Solomon's Porch
I. Stairs to the upper terrace, by which were the warning inscriptions
J. Court of Women
K. Court of the Men (or of Israel)
L. The Beautiful Gate
M. Gate of the Sheep Fold
N. Tadi Gate in the city wall
O. Place of Slaughter
P. Altar of Burnt Offering

piece, which formed against the outer walls a shaded cloister, two pillars deep on three sides, but on the south four deep. Above the timbered ceiling of the cloisters, on the roof, James saw scores of Roman soldiers pacing to and fro.

"How do the soldiers get up there, and what are they doing?" he asked.

"They came from the fortress yonder with its four towers (Fig. 97, F); 'Antonia,' they call it, from King Herod's Roman friend, Mark Antony. The garrison of Jerusalem stays there, and at Passover time the number is doubled by a regiment from Caesarea. There is a run-way from the fortress straight down to the roof of the cloisters, and there are other stairs from the fortress direct to the temple court. In case of a riot they can empty the fortress into the Temple in no time. Those sentinels yonder are just to keep order and watch for trouble."

Under the southern portico, or the "Royal Porch" (Fig. 97, G) was the temple market.[5] The splendid pillars were arranged like a Roman basilica, a lofty central nave flanked on each side by a lower aisle, which in all Hellenic cities served as a law court and a place of trade. It ran the full length of the southern wall of the Sanctuary area. Between some of the pillars there were permanent booths; other spaces were occupied temporarily. As the two approached this great hall, James asked, "Don't they sell the lambs here? I see plenty of crates full of pigeons, but no animals."

"No, it would be too messy," answered Zebedee. "You just buy a ticket here and the animal will be delivered to you at the north entrance of the temple, right opposite the altar of sacrifice. See what a tremendous business the merchants are doing today!"

"What are you going to do about our own lamb, father?"

In reply his father produced his parchment receipt that entitled him to a lamb, one year old and without spot or blemish (Ex. 12:5) to be claimed that afternoon at or after one-thirty o'clock.

"Twenty of us men from Capernaum have arranged to share a lamb, pro rating the cost according to the size of the families

[5] Some scholars think that this market was held in the north portico.

FIG. 98. MODERN MONEY-CHANGERS IN JERUSALEM.

The "bank" consists of a wooden chest, two legs of which rest on the narrow stone ledge that flanks the street and two on a wooden box in the street itself. To "overthrow the tables of the money-changers" it would be necessary only to kick the the box from under. The key to the bank hangs on a nail by the window.

(Ex. 12:4). The lamb was paid for yesterday, and I have been chosen to make the offering for the group this afternoon. Uncle Joseph has been appointed to do the same for the Nazareth group."

"What are those big chests on stout legs for?" asked James, pointing to a row of them down the whole length of the inner aisle. A long line of customers waited in front (Fig. 98).

"Those belong to the money-changers. You see, every Israelite has to pay an annual Temple tax of half a shekel. It must be paid in a special Temple coin of silver and any other money spent or given in the Temple must also be in Temple coinage. Consequently when people of the Dispersion come up to the Feast—or when I, for that matter—with Roman denarii or Persian darics, we must all change our money for temple coinage—and pay well for the privilege (Fig. 99). A den of thieves, I call them!"

They now drifted over to the east portico or "Solomon's Porch" (Fig. 97, H) where the teachers were wont to hold forth. When inside the cool shadows they saw at various places a rabbi seated cross-legged on a tiny platform with his back to a pillar, and seated in front of him a circle of people. It looked for all the world like James' school at home. In some cases there were groups of rabbis engaged in discussion for the benefit of the Passover crowds, or in answering questions. It was good publicity and brought in considerable cash. Payment however was not obligatory, and not only the sitting group but the fringe of standing listeners were quite free to ask whatever questions they liked. As James and his father approached one such group they were surprised to see cousin Jesus standing near the rabbis, so interested in the discussion that he was unaware of their approach. Jesus tried one or twice to ask a question, but some one with a louder voice got the right-of-way. At length he managed to catch the attention of one of the rabbis, who was struck by his eager face:

"Have you a question, my son?"

"Yes, sir, I have, if you please. I want to know if the Messiah when he comes will have to kill all the wicked, as the prophet Elijah killed the priests of Baal?"

"Well, son, that is a rather hard question which I would better refer to Doctor Saul who specializes in the Prophets, as I specialize in the Torah. What do you say to this question, Doctor Saul?"

The question was repeated for the learned Doctor's benefit.

"The great Rabbi Shammai has passed upon that point," replied Doctor Saul. "In his comment upon Psalm 2:9, which reads,

> "You shall break them with an iron rod;
> You shall crush them like a potter's vessel!"

Rabbi Shammai decides that the reference is clearly to the function of the Messiah. I therefore answer your question in the affirmative."

"But my mother says that she can't believe the Messiah will act that way. She quotes from the prophet Isaiah,

> "The bruised reed he will not break
> And the smoking flax he will not quench.
>
> .   .   .   .
>
> He shall lead his flock like a shepherd."

"Where did your mother take her degree?" sneered Doctor Saul; and the crowd laughed uproariously while the discomfited Jesus blushed and tried to hide in the crowd. James felt sorry for him and went away. But he noticed that Jesus still stayed.

As they were going Uncle Joseph came up in a somewhat excited and angry mood.

"Zebedee, can you lend me five shekels?" he whispered.

"What is the trouble, Joseph?"

"The Nazareth group asked me to buy the lamb for them and offer it this afternoon on their behalf. They gave me enough money to pay for it, as we thought. But when I came to buy, those rascally priests had raised the price even beyond last year's, which was high enough in all conscience. I just didn't have the money. I told them that next year I would bring my own lamb; but they laughed. 'All right, old man, try it on!' I knew they had me, for the lamb would have to be inspected, and their fee for inspection is high enough to make up the difference. It is an intolerable situation—and all in the name of religion!"

Zebedee loaned him the five shekels and Joseph returned to the merchants.

Zebedee and James now worked their way across the Court of the Gentiles towards the central platform that rose some fourteen

FIG. 99.   A TEMPLE SHEKEL.

A silver coin issued by the Jewish rebels against Rome, 70 A.D. Obverse (*left*): "The shekel of Israel," in old-Hebrew characters; a jewelled chalice, above which "Year Five." Reverse (*right*): "Jerusalem the Holy," in old-Hebrew characters. A flowering lily.

steps above them. Mounting, they found a narrow terrace and then at intervals flights of four steps that led to the gates of the inner courts which only Israelites could enter (Fig. 97, I). By these steps, were some blocks of stone on the low wall that marked the sacred boundary. On them were notices engraved in the Greek language. Zebedee pointed with his finger as he translated to James: "Let no stranger [Gentile] enter within the limit and enclosure of the Sanctuary. He who is caught will carry the guilt on himself, because death will follow."

"Who puts him to death?" asked James.

"This crowd would lynch him," replied Zebedee (Acts 21:27-36). "That is why those soldiers are on the watch."

From this vantage point they could look over the vast assembly, and also get a close-up of the various types of people who were coming and going through the boundary gates. Presently passed two young men evidently from the wealthy class, for their robes were of silk trimmed with fur, their turbans spotless white, gold chains were about their necks and jeweled rings on their fingers. Two black slaves were clearing the way, but the crowd parted deferentially of its own accord. Zebedee looked closely but did not recognize them. As they passed to enter the Temple he learned from their followers that one was a Sadduccee, member of the Sanhedrin; [6] the other was Joseph of Arimathea, a very wealthy Pharisee and a member of the Council but also a very good man.

"What are Sadduccees?" inquired James. "We never see them in Capernaum."

"No, they are members of the aristocracy and belong to what we call the 'liberal' party. In the old days of Jonathan Maccabeus, some of our leaders favored the worldly political schemes of Jonathan and the introduction of Greek ways into our simple Jewish life. Unfortunately because they were wealthy they had more influence than the Pharisees who opposed them, and our state became more and more secular. When the Romans came, the Sadduccees sided with them because the Romans allowed them to manage the temple. From their number Pompey chose the high priest, as the Romans have done ever since. All the priests belong to the Sadduccees, for of course they are dependent for their living on the sacrificial system over which stands the high priest, backed by Rome. They are not very religious, as a matter of fact. They stand by the Law of Moses but do not care a fig for all the hair-splitting such as we hear from the scribes in our synagogue. They frown on all the ideas about the Messiah, for they do not want any overturning of things as they are. No wonder! for they are now on top. And their young sons like those

[6] The supreme council of the Jews, made up largely of members of the aristocracy.

who have just passed by, are more Roman than Jewish. They practice in the gymnasium, they take part in the sports in the stadium, they go to shows on the theatre, and as for the Sabbath— well, they do about as they please."

"Yes, and if we left it to them and the Romans we would have no religion left—except the right to keep up the monopoly on lambs!" said a harsh voice behind them.

Zebedee turned and recognized the speaker, a young man about twenty years old, from Capernaum.

"Hello, Simon," he said in surprise, "I didn't expect to see you here."

"Why shouldn't I be here? Am I not a good Jew, in spite of my hatred of these Sadduccees and their Roman friends? There is a big crowd of us here (in a whisper) every one of us with a sword under his tunic. You can count on us Zealots to be ready for any emergency—if not to create one!

"There are five thousand of us in Galilee alone, and we are enrolling new members every day all through the country. We are tired of waiting; we want action. The Pharisees are teaching everybody to keep the law in all its details, and then, they say, God will send his Messiah. We say, Get something started, make a crisis, and *God will have to send his Messiah to back us up*. If he doesn't, we will do the job ourselves, Messiah or no Messiah! Look at those soldiers up there! Doesn't it make your blood boil?"

Noticing a priest listening in, Simon suddenly thought it best to disappear in the crowd.

"What did he mean?" asked James.

"Oh, he belongs to a party that is trying to get up a revolution. But he would better think twice! Don't you remember how last year at Sepphoris a couple of these fanatics named Judas and Zadduk thought that the census taken by Quirinus was excuse enough to throw off the yoke of Rome? Result? Two thousand Galileans crucified."

They started to enter the gate to the Court of the Women

Fig. 100.   RABBI WITH PRAYER SHAWL.

The shawl has alternate bands of black and white; on its edges are tassels. In addition the rabbi wears a phylactery, the small black box on his forehead. It contains the "Shema" or Creed (Deut. 6:4-5). The prayer is being read from a hand scroll, in principle like the larger one described in Fig. 94, but having only one spindle.

(Fig. 97, J), but James caught sight of a poorly-dressed man who stood by the door-post in the attitude of prayer. On his head he wore the black and white prayer-shawl, on his forehead was a large phylactery and as he raised his palms aloft in supplication, James saw that he wore a second phylactery on his upper left arm (Fig. 100).

"What is he praying here for?" asked the boy.

"He is one of those Pharisees who enjoy letting people know how pious they are. They like to pray standing in the synagogue and in the corners of the squares, and they keep it up all the morning! They imagine that their prayers will be heard if they use words enough" (Mt. 6:7).

"What is a Pharisee, father?"

"There are all kinds, good and bad; but in general I would say that they are the religious party as opposed to the Sadduccees who are the worldly party. While both these parties believe in keeping the Law and maintaining the temple services, the Pharisees mean by the Law not only the written word but all the interpretations that the scribes have placed upon it to bring it up to date, and they give the same weight to both. Their aim is good, but by multiplying the number of our religious duties they really make it impossible for us common folks to please God."

"How does one become a Pharisee, father?"

"Well, first you have to be a Scribe, that is, one who has been to the scribal college and learned all about the written and the oral Law. Then you have to be voted in,—for it is a kind of inner circle, and only those are admitted who take a pledge in the presence of three members to keep the whole Law. The three then lay their hands on the candidate and he becomes a full-fledged Pharisee. They say there are not over six thousand of them, but they are very influential. Because they are so religious they have the support of the common people, and always win against the Sadduccees whenever it comes to a show-down on any religious, that is, legal decision. We do not like them, however; they are so snobbish and self-righteous, and they look down on us ordinary people. They have a saying 'These common people who know not the Law be damned!' " (Jn. 7:49)

They merely looked inside the Court of the Women, for it was time to return to camp for the noonday meal. But James noticed inside the gate a series of chests, thirteen of them, with big funnels coming out of their tops. Most of the people who went in to worship threw money into the gaping mouths. James was interested to see their manner of doing it. Poor people went up modestly and dropped in a small coin so softly he could hardly hear it; but one pompous Sadduccee approached and motioned to his slave to make a contribution; whereat the slave took out a bag and holding it high emptied its contents in a silver shower of shekels that clattered down into the hold like a drummer's tattoo (Lk. 21:1–7). Many spectators applauded, but James was disgusted.

The cloud of smoke that arose from the altar behind the temple barrier seemed to be getting denser, and the lambs were passing through the gate to the place of slaughter in a continuous throng.

"What is it all about?" asked James.

"There are morning and evening sacrifices every day," replied Zebedee. "First the burning of incense; then the burnt offering for the sin of the nation as a whole, the animals and the drink offerings being supplied out of the Temple funds; next the offering for the Emperor Augustus, likewise paid for by the tax; and when these are done, private individuals and groups make their trespass-offerings, sin- or thank-offerings and the like. That is what is going on now. Today these have to be curtailed to make room for the thousands of passover lambs that will be offered beginning at half past one o'clock. Everything goes on schedule. Joseph and I are due at two o'clock. Your mother and you can watch us at close range from the Court of the Women which is next to the Court of Israel" (Fig. 97, K).

Sounds of trumpets and the chanting of men rose fitfully above the babel of voices.

"Those are the Levites. Their singing began before the first pouring of the drink offering this morning, and will continue until the morning sacrifices are complete. They are singing the Psalms appointed for the day. When each Psalm is finished, two priests blow on silver trumpets as a sign that private prayers may now be said. There are many such choirs that chant in turn, relieving each other at intervals."

"I suppose that these hundreds of people we see all going and coming in white are the priests? They seem to be very busy about something."

"They certainly are busy. They have to assist at all the slaughtering of the lambs, as you shall see; and each group has to be relieved every half-hour or so."

Promptly at one-thirty the family of Zebedee was again in the temple. Salome, taking James with her, found her way to the Court of the Women, through the eastern or "Beautiful Gate" (Fig. 97, L) (Acts 3:2) with its valves of Corinthian brass so heavy that it takes twenty men to move them, and she took her stand in one of the porticos from which they could look through the lofty "Gate of Nikanor" into the inner Court of Israel and see the altar, the smoke of whose burning rose perpetually. Here they would wait until they saw Zebedee appear with their lamb at the Place of Slaughtering on the north of the altar.

Meanwhile Zebedee had gone round to the north gate of the temple terrace called the "Gate of the Sheep Fold" (Fig. 97, M) there to claim his sacrifice. Here was assembled the immense flock of lambs brought for the slaughter. They filled the western half of this northern court of the sanctuary, and through the "Tadi Gate" (Fig. 97, N) they extended quite outside the city wall to the north, bleating piteously as if dimly conscious of impending doom.[7] When it was Zebedee's turn, a priest examined his coupon,

---

[7] If we cut in half the figures given by Josephus for the attendance at Passover (2,500,000), we arrive at the number of families represented by dividing the result by 5 (250,000); then dividing again by 20—the maximum number who could share the expense of a single lamb, it gives us the astonishing number of 12,500 lambs required for this feast.

checked it and gave in its place the lamb he had bought; with it he and a group of similar sacrificers totaling twenty, passed through the Gate of the Sheep Fold into the Court of Israel (Fig. 97, K) and to the Place of Slaughter (Fig. 97, O). Upon their entering, the priests blew a blast three times on silver trumpets; whereat Zebedee and each of the others first placed their hand on the head of the lamb, in token that the sins of the offerer were laid upon the victims; then they threw the lamb on the pavement, the body pointing north and south, but the head twisted to look at the temple; drew a knife from their belt and cut the lamb's throat. Two rows of priests with silver and golden bowls stood ready to catch the blood of the twenty victims; then passing the bowls from hand to hand, the priest nearest the altar dashed the contents upon the altar's base (Fig. 97, P). The dead lamb was now hung on a nail and dressed. The fat was removed and burned by priests on the great Altar of Sacrifice, and the refuse was sluiced off with water drawn by a wheel with ropes and buckets from the immense cisterns constructed under the whole Temple platform. The largest of these, called the Great Sea, would hold two million gallons (Fig. 97, E). Meantime a chorus of Levites were singing the "Hallel" (Ps. 113–118), repeating the text till all the lambs of that group were disposed of. Zebedee now took the pelt and the carcass of his lamb and joined his family in the outer court.

Just as they came together, a blast of bugles issued without warning from the Fortress of Antonia. Looking up they saw that every Roman soldier was standing at salute, and high on the corner tower new soldiers swarmed into view, carrying aloft the bronze standards of their regiments, though out of deference to the Jewish second commandment they had covered from sight the "eagle" portion. An officer in resplendent armor advanced to the parapet and looked down with curious interest upon the throngs in the temple courts, upon the bleating lambs, the sacrifice and the smoking altar. No one in the crowd below made the slightest sign of recognition.

"Who is he?" asked James.

"That is Coponius, the Roman procurator or governor of Judea, the first procurator we have ever had; and this is his first Passover. He lives at Caesarea on the coast, but fearing that there might be trouble when so many thousands have gathered at the Feast, he no doubt thought it wise to be present. He lives in Herod's great palace over by the western citadel.[8] I hope he enjoys his reception!"

But there was work to do in camp. The men who had combined to buy Zebedee's lamb got together, dug a hole in the earth like a small well, and as the evening shadows lengthened, they spitted the lamb on a wooden stake and roasted it whole. No bone was allowed to be broken. Then the families clad in their best garments assembled after sunset, each in its own tent, and the ceremony of the evening meal was begun. First each took a cup of wine and drank it after Zebedee had invoked a blessing; then a hand-washing accompanied by prayer; then the bitter herbs dipped in the juice of dates and raisins mingled with vinegar—a symbol of the clay from which bricks had been made in Egypt; a second cup of wine was now drunk, and James, who had been coached for his part, asked,

"What do you mean by this service?"

To which Zebedee replied, "It is the passover-sacrifice to the Lord, who passed by the houses of the Israelites in Egypt when he struck down the Egyptians, but spared our houses" (Ex. 12 : 26–27).

After this in turn came the third cup of wine with its grace, the unleavened cakes, the free-will festival offering and the Passover lamb, which last had to be wholly eaten before midnight, a final cup of wine and the singing of the Hallel. (Ps. 113–118).

It was a beautiful sight—the thousands of ruddy fires dotting the great amphitheatre of hills, the moving groups casting shadows

[8] All Catholic scholars and some Protestant are of opinion that when the Procurator was in residence at Jerusalem he made only the Tower of Antonia his headquarters.

upon one another and upon the tents, the Holy City ghostly in the moonlight, black Antonia glowering with its four towers above the sacred House that flashed from its golden façade the brilliance of the moon. From a thousand tents the solemn music of the Hallel bade the world good-night.

As the strains gradually ceased and the families were preparing to sleep, Simon the Zealot approach the tent of Zebedee and asked if he might have a talk with him. The two men withdrew to a little olive grove beyond the tents and there, sitting with their backs against the same tree, Simon opened his heart on the subject dearest to it. He knew that Zebedee was an intelligent and influential citizen whose sympathetic understanding and good will would be worth much to the Zealot cause. They talked far into the morning. Simon used every argument he could summon to prove that Rome ought to be ousted: the impoverishment of the Jewish people systematically carried out over many years; the absorption of vast tracts of land by the aristocracy and their use of slave labor with which free men could not compete; the enormous wealth taken away by Roman conquerors and governors in twenty years—more than 40,000 talents of gold ($45,-000,000 or £9,104,000)[9] besides the annual taxes of 12,000,000 denarii ($2,000,000 or £500,000); the "improvements" made by Herod I in the way of new cities like Sebaste and Caesarea or the architectural adornment of old ones, all paid for ultimately by the peasant. He pooh-poohed the idea of deliverance by a Messiah and urged Zebedee to join the rapidly growing band of brave men who were willing to risk all in a military uprising.

But Zebedee was not convinced:

"Well, Simon, I agree with all your facts but I disagree with your interpretation and your methods. You will never get me to join your crowd. I still have faith that in God's good time some way of escape will be found that will enable us not only to be free politically but to be a blessing to all the world. You ought to read

---

[9] These figures are from Jacob de Haas: *Palestine the Last Two Thousand Years,* Chap. I.

more frequently Isaiah's grand prophecy about the Suffering Servant of Yahweh (Is. 52 : 13–53 : 12) and realize that our role in world affairs is not political or economic but spiritual."

"Bah!"

So they agreed to disagree.

Walk About Zion

Next day James was eager to see in the city some of the things of which he had heard. Before the sun was hot he and his father took the path that led down the Kedron valley. On the left in the cool morning shadows lay the olive groves from which the Mount of Olives got its name. As they started from the camp, James called his father's attention to the huge low-lying building that occupied the north-eastern basin of the Kedron valley, only four hundred yards away. The outside was oval in form, the center an unobstructed oval, and tiers of seats occupied all the space between. They could look down into it from their higher elevation on Olivet (Map III, 2).

"That is Herod's amphitheatre," explained Zebedee. "Sometimes they call it the hippodrome because horse races are held in it. The king built it about thirty years ago and in it held athletic games every five years in imitation of the Olympic games in Greece and in honor of the emperor Augustus. For the games he brought athletes from all nations, wild beasts from all countries, musicians and choral actors, hoping to rival the great spectacles at Rome. We Jews were horror-struck that our own king would establish such a heathen institution at our Holy City; but all we could do about it was to make trouble in general: Herod had his hands full from that time till his death."

As they walked southward, high above on the right towered the walls of the temple area, the corner pinnacle of which must have been three hundred feet above their path (Lk. 4 :9) (Map III, 3).

"What tremendous stones!" exclaimed James as he pointed to the foundation courses set into the solid rock of Mount Moriah.

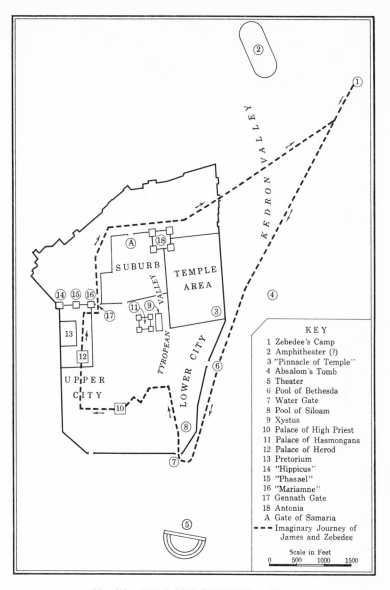

KEY

1 Zebedee's Camp
2 Amphitheater (?)
3 "Pinnacle of Temple"
4 Absalom's Tomb
5 Theater
6 Pool of Bethesda
7 Water Gate
8 Pool of Siloam
9 Xystus
10 Palace of High Priest
11 Palace of Hasmongans
12 Palace of Herod
13 Pretorium
14 "Hippicus"
15 "Phasael"
16 "Mariamne"
17 Gennath Gate
18 Antonia
A Gate of Samaria
- - - Imaginary Journey of
        James and Zebedee

Scale in Feet
0   500   1000   1500

MAP III.   PLAN OF JERUSALEM, 6 A.D.

"Old Herod knew how to build," said Zebedee. "Roman engineers handled those blocks, some of which are thirty feet long. This queer building here on our left with the peaked top is somebody's tomb. People think that Absalom is buried there, and they show what they think of him by stoning his monument as they go by (Map III, 4).

"That strange building down the valley, that looks like a lot of semi-circles built into the hillside, is a theatre like the one in Scythopolis. Herod was eager to introduce all the Greek and Roman customs he could, so he built this and several other structures I shall show you. We Jews who try to keep God's law strictly never go into them" (Map III, 5).

They had now reached the place where the wall on the hill above them made a sharp turn. Below the angle at the bottom of the hill was a lovely building with five colonnades in the Greek style, and steps leading down to something below.

"You will be interested in this Pool of Bethesda," said Zebedee. "It is the old spring of Gihon where Solomon was crowned, only now it has been beautified and made convenient" (Map III, 6).

They looked down the steps about ten feet to a marble pavement, and there, lying or sitting as near as possible to the spring which was half a dozen steps lower still in a natural cave, were fifteen or twenty beggars and sick folk. Women from the villages of Siloam on the eastern side of the valley were ascending and descending with water jars on their heads.

"Why are all those wretched people down there?"

"This is a miraculous pool," said Zebedee. "An angel comes down two or three times a day and troubles the pool, and—look, look!"

James looked intently. The water in the pool was bubbling and boiling; it rose a couple of feet in its marble basin.[10] Instantly all

---

[10] This is a natural phenomenon. The pool is fed by a reservoir in the hill, which has a siphon outlet. When the reservoir is filled by the water that gradually percolates in, it suddenly empties itself all at once and causes the rapid rise and commotion in the pool below. Lacking a scientific explanation, the Jews ascribed the cause to an angel; and faith did the curing. The spring still rises intermittently as it always has done.

was commotion among the sick; a great scurrying to get on their feet and scramble down the steps, or haste on the part of helpers to get their decrepit relative into the water. Splash! One bright-witted fellow rolled over and dropped off the pavement flat into the pool, sending up a shower of spray into the faces of the agitated crowd. A moment he lay sprawled out in the water, then a shout.

"Glory Hallelujah! Cured! God be praised! Hallelujah!"

His feet found the bottom, and slowly but with radiant eyes he climbed dripping up the steps.

"No more crutches for me!" he shouted; and picking them up where they lay, he flung them as far as possible between the marble pillars, while a lame man crawled as fast as he could to retrieve them for himself.

"You have seen a miracle!" said Zebedee in awed voice. "Who-ever first after the troubling of the water steps in, is made whole of whatever disease he has (Jn. 5:4, King James Version). That cripple was the fortunate one this time."

"Do they always get cured?" asked James, equally awed.

"Not always, I am afraid; but this one has been cured. See him climbing these steps to tell the world about it."

The healed cripple passed within a yard of them, laughing and crying, while all the others who could do so clattered at his heels.

Zebedee and James now descended the Kedron valley to the point where the eastern wall of the city turned at right angles west. There they found a strongly fortified gate in a heavily buttressed wall (Map III, 7).

"This is the gate from which King Zedekiah escaped when Nebuchadnezzar was besieging the city (II Kgs. 25:4) but of course what you now see is more recent than his day. We shall enter the city here."

A short walk brought them to another pool much larger than Bethesda (Map III, 8).

"This beautiful 'Pool of Siloam' was dug by King Hezekiah. You can see at the upper right end the mouth of the tunnel he excavated under David's city, to bring the waters of Gihon to this more convenient spot within the new walls. The colonnaded building which you see was built by King Herod a few years ago. It forms a hollow square about the pool and makes a grateful shade where people may sit and talk and the water-carriers may rest. See what a continuous procession of women come here from all parts of the town."

Straight ahead of them ran a street along the axis of the Tyropean valley. In places it sloped gently up, and in places it became stairs. On both sides were bazaars and houses of the poorer sort. Above these they could see the southwest corner of the temple retaining-wall, and opposite that, the level top of a large stone building (Map III, 9).

"That building is another of those with which Herod has desecrated our city. The name is 'Xystus'. It is a gymnasium with an open space for sports—quite heathen. The sons of the Sadduccees and other wealthy families go there to learn wrestling, boxing and disc-throwing, but pious Jews shun the place. The shame of it is that when the games are on, the priests sometimes leave their sacrifices and climb up to the top of the portico yonder, from which place they can look right into the arena."

James wished that it were not so wicked to look upon sports, for he would very much like to see them himself.

Instead of following the street to the north after a few yards they turned west into a narrow street that almost immediately started to climb the great western hill. The street became stairs; as far as they could see because of the twisting, the stairs continued, and every fresh turn brought more stairs into view (Fig. 101). Crowds of people clambered up and trotted down, women with water jars on their heads, marketing women who also carried everything on their heads from a cake of soap to a haystack. Donkeys with panniers full of charcoal or meat or refuse or bread-loaves or building-stone clattered downstairs or up, upsetting a child now and then or pushing pedestrians against the counters of the merchants. A camel loaded with grain in two huge sacks and led by a man on donkey-back loomed in sight. People ducked as he approached; and once while he endeavored

FIG. 101.   A STREET IN JERUSALEM.

No provision for wheels was ever made until in the late 19th century, and then for only a short distance beyond a few gates. Shops are small cubicles opening on the street and dimly lighted from the street which in many places is vaulted over. On the slats overhead, gunny-sacking is spread in summer as an awning. In early morning, hucksters from the country line both sides of the lane while donkeys with heavily-laden panniers trot merrily between.

to pass a string of donkeys coming the other way, his load swept down a bushel of bread loaves that were dangling on strings in front of a bake-shop. The camel never stopped, but the proprietor came out, erupting lurid oaths, picked up the bread from the street, dusted off from each loaf whatever his sleeve could remove, and hung them again for sale. A fascinating moving-picture as colorful as a Galilee vale in spring, only here the sun slanted down in streaks through gunny-sack awnings which the merchants had stretched across the street partly for comfort and partly to keep buyers from being too critical of their goods.

After a ten-minute climb Zebedee and James reached an easier gradient. The bazaars ceased; larger streets intersected their lane; houses became more imposing. They could see the low domes of several synagogues. Soon they stood in the presence of a palace of large dimensions. Zebedee knew it for the residence of the High Priest (Map III, 10). Naturally they could not enter, but they stood in the open square in front long enough to enjoy the view: the close-compacted city below them, little Davidsburg on its spur of rock which was the eastern hill, the glorious mass of the temple to the north-east, and in the distant south-east the deep gulf wherein lies the Dead Sea, bounded by the purple wall and horizon-line of Moab.

Two other palaces demanded their attention. Just north of where they stood rose the palace of the Hasmoneans (Map III, 11).

"What do you mean—Hasmoneans?" asked James.

"That was the name of our Jewish royal family from Hasmon, the father of the Judas who won our independence for us a hundred and seventy years ago. The last member of it was the beautiful Mariamne, whom Herod married for reasons of state and later murdered. Her tomb is just west of us on the next hill. All the ruling members of the Hasmonean family have lived here. But Herod built for himself a larger and finer palace here in the north-west. The memories of the old house were too much for him. We can pass through the grounds."

Taking a westerly and then a northerly street they soon stood before the frowning wall that enclosed a space perhaps half the size of the temple area. Its north and west walls were the city walls; on the south and east Herod had built new walls to match the others, and studded the whole with towers. It was in reality another citadel, strong as the Tower of Antonia (Map III, 12).

Zebedee and James entered the massive gate without challenge, for many strangers from far-away lands were also seeing the town, and the guards had been instructed to throw the grounds open. Both were astonished at the magnificence.

"Who lives here?" asked James, "now that old Herod is dead and his son banished?"

"Usually no one," said Zebedee. "But just now the Roman governor whom we saw yesterday afternoon is living here during his stay. Antonia where you saw him is only a fortified barracks but this is a palace worthy of Rome. Look at these gardens and the marble colonnades all round the inner face of the walls!"

While one straight way led from the gate past the front of the palace building, smaller winding paths invited the visitor to wander among the trees and the shrubbery. The two followed a stream of people and found behind the hedges the loveliest formal gardens, some in sunken squares or circles. Beautiful marble statues gleamed white through the foliage or were part of the fountains that gushed in the center of the designs. Zebedee, astonished at all the water, asked a friendly-looking guard how it was possible. He replied:

"King Herod who built this citadel used Roman engineers, and they had discovered how to make water run up-hill by enclosing it in a stone pipe. They say it comes from springs on the hills to the west." As proof he told them to look at certain blocks of stone behind the guard house at the northern gate, left there for purposes of repair. Later they did so, and found that a hole was bored through the center of square stone blocks and the blocks were set side by side. This made a continuous pipe. Of course the blocks had to be flanged and grouted with lead to be tight and capable of standing pressure.

FIG. 102. TOWER OF PHASAEL.

The Turks rebuilt the Tower, the ancient stones having been re-used many times. There is a solid stone platform below which is the foundation for Herod's Tower of Phasael as proved by excavations made in 1940. It consists of cubes over four feet on a side, the outer faces bossed and the margins drafted. The base measured 68 feet on a side, and the Tower rose in two or more stages to a height of 155 feet. The present tower is part of the citadel of the Crusaders and Mameluke sultans. It is wholly surrounded by a moat. The Jaffa gate is around the corner.

Besides the gardens there were within the citadel a barrack, several service houses and the great palace. A guard at the palace door took delight in telling the wide-mouthed crowd how many rooms the palace contained and how there were two dining rooms in which one hundred guests could recline at one time for dinner. He also pointed out a square court in the next bay, called the "Pavement," where the Procurator tried cases in the presence of the public (Jn. 19:13). If they looked carefully they would see the raised platform at the back side, next the colonnade, where the throne-chair or "Bema" was set and the Procurator made his decisions. The crowd gaped curiously as they moved past.

At the northern end of the enclosure were the soldiers' quarters and the stout northwestern gate of the city. Dominating the whole were three magnificent towers. Another guard told the sight-seers that the towers had names—which is what soldiers like: "Hippicus" in the corner was named for one of Herod's friends (Fig. 102); "Phasaël" the tallest, was Herod's brother; the third, "Mariamne," was his Jewish wife, the only person Herod ever loved, whose death by his own orders nearly drove him crazy (Map III, 14, 15, 16).

Zebedee and James now left the city by the Gate Gennath in the north wall just east of the three towers (Map III, 17), skirted the wall that Hezekiah had built around the northern suburb, and so past Antonia (Map III, 18), towards the camp.

CHAPTER XII

IN THE FIRST CHRISTIAN CENTURY

THERE are books aplenty in which one may read about daily life in Greece and Rome—what people ate, what they wore, how children were brought up, how business was conducted and how the government was carried on. All of this, while interesting and valuable, need not be repeated here, for our concern is with those phases of life which illuminate the Bible.

Christianity fell heir to many an inheritance. It took over intact the Jewish scriptures, and with it the Jewish tradition of morality, highest in the world; the Jewish synagogue with the general pattern of its ritual; the Jewish Sabbath, soon to be transferred to Sunday. From Hellenic civilization it inherited the Greek language which was the speech of cultured people everywhere; many of its forms of thought; its habit of letter writing not only for correspondence but as a form of literary expression. That is why we now have a New Testament with its epistles, its sermons and its histories. From Rome it received the blessings of the *Pax Romana*, without which the gospel could never have been so successfully propagated. In the first Christian century the world was at peace. Piracy had been stamped out of the Mediterranean by Pompey a hundred years earlier, and now the messengers of Christianity could traverse the seas without danger of capture and sale. Brigandage was in process of being suppressed not only along the major highways of commerce but in the more remote mountainous districts. Travel was easier and safer in the first century than at any other time until the twentieth. While Paul recounts storms and shipwrecks at sea, he makes no mention of pirates; but on land he speaks of his perils among robbers. The process of eradication was still going on in his day. However, robbers were not numerous enough to interfere with the spread of the gospel.

Then there was the *Lex Romana* which guaranteed some measure of legal security to all members of the empire, even to slaves; but to those who were fortunate enough to be Roman citizens, it guaranteed certain valuable privileges which protected from undue disturbance the messengers of the new faith.

Rome granted the right to assemble peaceably for religious and other purposes, the only requirement being a proper registration with the authorities. Before its law all the multitudinous faiths of the world had equal standing. When the Christian ambassador Paul got into serious trouble with Jewish or Gentile mobs, he had only to say, "I am a Roman citizen," to bring before him on their knees, as at Philippi, the magistrates of the town (Acts 16:37-39); or as in Jerusalem, to win from the commander of the garrison of Antonia protection, respectful treatment, and an escort of horsemen for his journey to Caesarea (Acts 22:23-29; 23:23-24).

Life in New Testament times was mobile. The impression one gets in reading the Epistles is that of incessant travel. Look at these phrases: "This will be my third visit to you" (2 Cor. 13:1); "Demas has gone to Thessalonika, Crescens has gone to Galatia, Titus to Dalmatia" (2 Tim. 4:10); "I have sent Tychicus to Ephesus" (2 Tim. 4:12); "Bring the cloak I left at Troas" (2 Tim. 4:13); "Erastus stayed at Corinth, I left Trophimus sick at Miletus" (2 Tim. 4:20); "I left you behind in Crete" (Titus 1:5); "Do your best to come to me at Nicopolis for I have decided to settle there for the winter" (Titus 3:12).

All this constant activity was made possible by the Empire's interest in transportation. Roman roads are of course famous. They were built largely by the soldiers of the legion who thus utilized the time not spent in fighting or guard duty. While the roads were constructed primarily to expedite government business and the transfer of troops, they were also the highways of trade, which was the life-blood of the Roman Empire. The grades were modified to facilitate the use of wheeled vehicles as well as mule-borne litters. Roads were built to endure; hundreds of miles of them are in use today.

The early Christian missionaries used these roads, for they connected the great strategic cities of the Empire. Christianity first struck root in these cities. That is why a dweller in the country, a *paganus* or peasant, speedily came to be called a pagan, one who did not know Christianity. Paul showed his generalship by thus planting his gospel at the crossroads of traffic. One great road began at the Cilician Gates and was really the western continuation of that almost prehistoric road from Mesopotamia traced in Chapter IV (Maps II, IV, see pp. 151 and 289). Paul was born in a city that lay on that route and he used the road himself more than once in his missionary journeys. It can be followed and its chief towns located on Map IV. From one of its two major terminals on the Aegean, Paul passed by sea to Neapolis (port of Philippi) in Macedonia where he made use of a second section of the trunk line from the East to Rome, called the *Via Egnatia*. This led to two western terminals at Dyrrhachium or Apollonia, whence one crossed the narrow Adriatic and picked up the third section called the *Via Appia* that ran straight as a bowstring from Brundisium to Rome. Paul used the final stage of this section from Capua to Rome, coming up from his ship that docked at Puteoli on the bay of Naples.

This composite of land and sea sections from Rome to Cilicia and then to Syria was one of the life-lines of the Empire and was kept open summer and winter. Along it Cicero had made his way into exile, and Antony and Octavius had marched to avenge Caesar's death at Philippi. Over it went all the proconsuls, generals, troops and civil officials to their stations in the East. Travel was systematized, divided into stages, supplied with hotels and relays of animals, so that it became one of the speediest roads in the world. One could go from Rome to Byzantium (modern Istanbul) via Neapolis in twenty-four days, and to Alexandria in thirty days. Before such speed (!) had been attained, Cicero

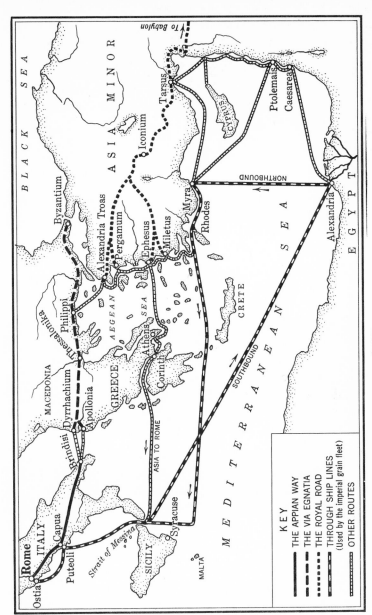

Map IV. ROMAN LAND AND SEA ROUTES.

tells us that it took forty-seven days for his mail from Rome to reach him in Cilicia. An airplane covers it today in a few hours.

Sea routes were naturally more numerous. The Mediterranean and Aegean seas were full of shipping during the open season which lasted from March to November; in the winter months captains rarely ventured out of the harbor. There were what we might call express and accommodation services. Paul used both. When he was going from Troas to Caesarea, for example (Acts 20–21), he was "accommodated" almost too exasperatingly. When however Paul was sent as a prisoner from Caesarea to Rome, he made use of the local service along the Syrian coast as far as Myra and there transferred to an express grain ship from Alexandria, and but for the storm he would have made hardly a change of sail and very likely only one or two stops to the port of Rome.

All these immunities and facilities lay back of the phenomenal spread of Christianity by which in less than a century the gospel was carried from Babylon to Spain.

Perhaps we can understand the vivid Christian life of the first century by taking samples of it in three different cities.

CORINTH

This city was located most strategically for the purpose of Christian propaganda. It lay at the western end of the isthmus of Corinth which offered the only land route between Europe and southern Greece. Corinth lay on a far more important route by sea from Ephesus and all points east to the Adriatic and all points west. While the grain ships passed it by, using a more southerly route, all of the smaller merchant craft put in there because they were afraid of the risky passage around cape Malea, the southern prong of Greece. They preferred to unload at Cenchreae at the eastern end of the isthmus, transfer their goods overland four miles and reload on another ship at Corinth for the voyage west. Smaller boats could even use a railway 3¾

FIG. 103. CORINTH AND ACRO-CORINTH

Beneath your feet is the still unexcavated part of Corinth; in the foreground is the temple of Apollo, 600 B. C. Against the sky is the huge citadel, 1500 feet above the city. Behind the temple and off the picture to the left (east) lie the market place and the fountain of Pirene. If you turn squarely round, you will see one of the most famous views in Greece: the flaming blue gulf of Corinth and the mountain masses to the north in which both Parnassus and Helicon can be distinguished.

miles long by which the entire ship and cargo were pulled across the isthmus. In either case there was employment for thousands of longshoremen, mostly slaves of course, and Corinth was the city where all the business was centered.

One has to see Corinth to appreciate the wonderful situation of the ancient town (Fig. 103). It lay on terraces two miles south of the Corinthian gulf, and behind it rose the Acropolis, a round knob 1800 feet high. From the top of this citadel one could see Athens forty-five miles away, the mountainous islands of the Aegean, the mountains and valleys of Argos and Sparta to the south and west. At its feet lay the azure gulf of Corinth to the north, with the cloud-gathering peak of Parnassus beyond it. Both Parnassus and the gulf were also visible from the city itself, a gorgeous backdrop for the spectators in the theatre.

While old Corinth had been destroyed by Mummius in 146 B.C., Julius Caesar saw the necessity of rebuilding it. He colonized it with some Italian veterans, chiefly freedmen, and encouraged merchants of all races to resume their operations that had been temporarily interrupted. Consequently the population of this city, numbering probably 700,000, was mixed. In Paul's day there were descendants of the original Latin colony as betrayed by the names of Corinthian Christians found in the New Testament— Gaius, Quartus, Fortunatus, Achaicus, Crispus, Justus; there were Greeks, who were the most active traders of the Roman world; slaves numbering 500,000 from all the races of the earth; and plenty of Jews who were both manufacturers and traders. When Paul was in Corinth there were more Jews than usual in town. The Emperor Claudius had just banished all Jews from Rome (Acts 18:2) because, as Suetonius tells us, "They were incessantly raising tumults at the instigation of a certain Chrestus." Among these newly expelled Jews were Aquila and Priscilla, whose history well illustrates the mobility of Jews in that epoch. They were natives of Pontus in Asia Minor, had lived in Rome, were now in Corinth (Acts 18:2), later went to Ephesus (Acts 18:18–19). They were evidently people of some wealth. Their business was tent manufacturing, no doubt as employers of labor; and their house was large enough to serve as a meeting place for the church in Ephesus (1 Cor. 16:19). Paul lived in their house while they were at Corinth (Acts 18:3). It is important to state that the Jews as a race were generally despised and hated throughout the Roman world. This is no doubt one reason why the Christian Church so rapidly dissociated itself from the synagogue and within two generations became predominantly Gentile.

On the whole, Corinth was a very plebeian city, lacking the culture of Athens and possessing all the vices one would expect from a completely commercialized town with its tens of thousands of slaves and its huge floating population of sailors bent on having a spree while their cargoes were being shifted. Out of this heterogeneous population Paul was able to build a Christian Church.

One other factor periodically augmented the populace of Corinth, stimulated its trade, and brought Paul an extension of opportunity. That was the biennial celebration of the Isthmian games at the eastern end of the isthmus just south of the port of Cenchreae. There today among the pine trees on the high terrace that overlooks the Saronic gulf one can trace the outline of the stadium, the theatre, the training ground, the temple of Neptune to whom the games were sacred, and the boundary wall of the enclosure. All the sports which the Greeks loved were practiced here—foot-racing, boxing, jumping, wrestling, javelin and discus throwing and chariot racing. The prize was a wreath of pine twigs from the nearby grove. Though Paul perhaps never attended these games, most of his hearers must have done so and the language of sport would be perfectly familiar to their ears. That is doubtless why Paul makes frequent use of the vocabulary of the athlete. He speaks of boxers, runners and the crown of leaves (1 Cor. 9:24-27); of gladiators fighting wild beasts (1 Cor. 15:32); of the goal and the prize (Phil. 3:13-14; 1 Thess. 2:19; Acts 20:24); and later Biblical writers aware of the chief interest of the Hellenic world refer also to the wreath (1 Pet. 5:4), to the necessity of contending according to the rules (2 Tim. 2:5) and of keeping in training (1 Tim. 4:7-8).

We are not able to locate with certainty the scene of Paul's labors in Corinth, partly because all the city has not yet been excavated. The little museum however possesses one relic that gives visitors a thrill; it is the marble lintel of a door inscribed with inartistic letters, "Synagogue of the Hebrews." It is a second-hand stone, its former ornamented front turned towards the wall and its plain side turned outward to receive its new inscription— which shows the economic status of the Chosen People in Corinth. This stone was found just outside the propylea or entrance to the Forum on the street that led to the harbor. The residential section lay in that quarter. The synagogue and the adjoining house of Justus were therefore located very strategically for purposes of propaganda.

This forum was a splendid structure, an open paved square surrounded by colonnades and imposing buildings and filled with statues. Half way its length, there was an eight-foot drop to a lower level. At the center of the retaining wall a stone platform projected to form a "bema" or orator's pulpit and a judgment seat for the Roman ruler. On this platform the proconsul Gallio sat in judgment upon Paul (Acts 18:12-17). Gallio, a man of fine character and brother of the philosopher Seneca who was the Emperor Nero's tutor, begun his duties here in June, 51 A.D.— and so furnishes us one of the assured dates in the life of Paul. Since he knew that in the eyes of Roman law all religions had equal rights—or nearly all, including the Jewish—he at once threw the case out of court as being just a religious squabble; and he looked the other way when the mob, ever ready to tease Jews, beat up the plaintiff Sosthenes. Over this bema the Christian community in Corinth later erected a church, which the excavators have also found.

On the south side of the forum were thirty-three butcher stalls, all but two of them equipped with wells for refrigeration. These were the very shops that Paul saw and that furnished his flock

with their toughest problem—whether they should purchase meat
that had been first offered in the temples of the city. One of the
tenants left his sign behind, "Lucius the Butcher." [1] On the east
side of the forum was the famous Fountain of Pirene with its
marble façade of six arches and in front the large rectangular
basin where the women could fill their water jars. Here in ancient
times Bellerophon was said to have captured the winged horse
Pegasus.

A CHURCH SERVICE

Fortunately Paul's letters enable us to look in on a session of
the church at Corinth.

It is doubtful if there was any morning assembly, as sixty years
later Pliny reports there was in his province in Asia Minor. Paul
and all his fellow members had to work for a living. But every
day about sunset after work was over the little flock began to
gather. The roustabouts came up from the docks, the slaves from
their potteries, cloth factories or households and washed the grime
of toil away at the fountain of Pirene ; then it was only a few steps
to the house of Gaius Crispus where the meeting was held. On
entering the house, church members saluted each other with a
kiss (1 Cor. 16:20; 2 Cor. 13:12).

To be a member of the church the candidate had to make a
profession of belief in Jesus as Lord and in the fact of his resurrection (Rom. 10:9). Then he had to be baptized, and that by
immersion (Rom. 6:3-4). Where or by whom this rite was administered in Corinth we do not know; Paul in most cases delegated
this task to others (1 Cor. 1:13-16).

The first event of the evening was the supper which came to be
called the love feast. At the beginning of the meal, under the
direction of the church leader, all would partake of a piece of
bread and a sip of wine in memory of the Lord, as Christ had
commanded (1 Cor. 11:24) ; then all ate the rest of the supper.
Every one was supposed to bring something to eat for himself and

[1] *Am. Jour. Archaeol.,* July 1939, p. 497.

perhaps for a stranger. But it did not always work out happily; the free citizens did not like to sit with slaves, or the well-to-do with the poor; then again, one group of friends brought plenty to eat and drink while another group or single person would have to be content to sit in a corner with only a piece of bread. That did not make for brotherhood. There were also some present who liked the taste of wine and were not content with a sip nor with a single draught. The result was that some of the church members got tipsy before the service was over, much to the disgust of the more respectable and self-controlled element (1 Cor. 11:17–22, 33–34).

After supper came the distinctively educational part of the program. Apparently the utmost democracy prevailed. While the leader might open the teaching with earnest words on some particular theme, others were privileged to add whatever occurred to them by way of prayer, exhortation, exposition, or song. One feature which to us is extraordinary was "speaking with tongues," or as the newer translation puts it, "ecstatic speaking." A member would suddenly feel himself possessed by the spirit of God and would give vent to his inspiration not only in fervent speech for the edification of the company, but even in gibberish which no one could understand. One of the friends of the prophet, thinking he knew what the frenzied man was trying to say, would endeavor to interpret; but since the prophet did not stop his prophesying, the result was two people speaking at once. The excitement would sometimes set off another prophet, and even another, all of which produced pandemonium. The leader did his best to act as moderator, but what could he do with a church member who was certain that he was inspired? No doubt some of the sessions were more composed and a great deal of valuable instruction was given by the more literate members of the flock. But we cannot doubt that in general the picture just given is a fair one.

Paul himself may have originated this type of service, and he may have held its excesses in check while he was in Corinth; but after his departure the "prophets" got out of hand. Paul could hardly repudiate this phenomenon in principle for he was subject not only to these inspirations but to certain other "weird seizures" in which he did not know whether he was in the body or not. He speaks of visions and revelations given by the Lord (2 Cor. 12:1); of being caught up to the third heaven (12:2-4). He thanks God that he speaks in ecstasy more than any one else (1 Cor. 14:18) but he also understands the need of regulation for, as he says, "If the whole church assembles and they all speak ecstatically, and ordinary people or unbelievers come in, will they not say that you are crazy?" (1 Cor. 14:23). Finally in a letter to the church he laid down the law in this way, "When you meet together, suppose every one of you has a song, a teaching, a revelation, an ecstatic utterance, or an explanation of one; it must be for the good of all. If there is any ecstatic speaking, let it be limited to two or three people at the most, and have one speak at a time and someone explain what he says. But if there is no one to explain it, have him keep quiet in church, and talk to himself and God. And let two or three who are inspired to preach, speak, while the rest weigh what is said; and if anything is revealed to another who is seated, the one who is speaking must stop. For in this way you can all preach, one after another, as you are inspired to, so that everyone may be instructed and stimulated, for the spirits of prophets will give way to prophets, for God is not a God of disorder but of peace. This is the rule in all Christian churches" (1 Cor. 14:26-33, 37-40).

The service probably ended with singing a hymn and repeating together a benediction which they had learned from their teacher: "The blessing of the Lord Jesus be with you" (1 Cor. 16:23); or "The blessing of the Lord Jesus Christ, the love of God and the participation in the Holy Spirit be with you all" (2 Cor. 13:14).

EARLY CHRISTIAN PROBLEMS

We get some idea of the kind of problems they discussed at these meetings by reading some of the questions they sent to Paul for his answer after he had gone to Ephesus. For example, a young convert goes into a restaurant and orders a dish of stew. The man next to him remarks to the proprietor, "That is wonderfully fine meat. Where did you get it?" The proprietor answers, "I got that at a bargain sale over at Lucius's stall in the forum. It was meat that had been offered in the temple of Apollo." The young convert has the horrible suspicion that he ought not to eat meat that had been offered to an idol. That night at church he asked the members about it. There was a difference of opinion. Some said the god was nothing: Apollo was just a worn out idea. The meat was not affected by having been offered to it. Another said that Apollo was a devil who really existed and had power; he would surely get one into trouble if one were not a worshipper of his and ate his meat. Since the church members could not agree, in their next letter to Paul they asked him the question. Paul himself seems to be unsettled on the subject for in one place he says that idols are nothing (1 Cor. 8:4) and in another place he says, "What the heathen sacrifice they offer to demons and not to God, and I do not want you to have fellowship with demons. . . . You cannot eat at the table of the Lord and at the table of demons" (1 Cor. 10:20–21). In his perplexity he falls back on the principle that your eating should really be governed by whether that act is going to offend your brother who may have a weak conscience (1 Cor. 8:13). But as a general rule, when you go out to dinner don't ask any questions (1 Cor. 10:27).

Another young member falls in love with a girl. He wants to get married, but she happens not to be a member of the flock. What shall he do? He finally gets up courage to ask the church at their evening meeting and finds that some men who are already married to pagan wives are in a quandary also. As usual the question gets two answers from the assembly and it goes into the next letter to Paul. The apostle replies, "Don't be anxious about it: the believing partner may save the pagan one" (1 Cor. 7:12–16). But this question of marriage causes trouble from another angle. A member recalls that Paul has promised that the Lord is soon going to return, that the world will be consumed with fire and a new reign of righteousness will be established. In that case what is the use of marrying at all? Paul replies that it is an excellent thing not to marry, not only because the end of the world is soon coming but because marriage takes one's thoughts away from more serious things (1 Cor. 7:1, 25-35). However there is the urge of human nature to be considered; it is better to be married than to be immoral (1 Cor. 7:2-12, 36-38).

Some one else has been talking with an unbeliever who scoffs at the idea of a dead man's coming to life again. The unbeliever is a hard-headed Greek and a skilful talker; the church member is convinced that Paul has been telling fairy tales. At the evening gathering he voices his doubts and somebody suggests, "Let us ask Paul to write exactly what he knows about the resurrection of Jesus. Did he himself see it? If not, did he ever talk to anybody who had seen it?" Paul responded with a perfectly definite statement giving the names of persons who had seen Jesus after his death, including himself—the earliest account we have (1 Cor. 15:1-11). And then, evidently in response to a related question about what is to happen to other people who die, Paul explains the resurrection of all believers, its method and its philosophy (1 Cor. 15:35-58): "The living will be caught up into the air, the believers who have died will rise from their graves, and all will have a new body—as buried wheat sprouts a new body."

Still another has the suspicion that he ought not to visit prostitutes any longer and so asks advice on the subject. But most of the members are tarred with the same stick: the temple of Venus on Acro-Corinthus maintains a brothel as part of its ritual and there are branch offices in every block in town. Church members have never before considered the matter to be a moral problem.[2] Somebody reports the situation to Paul. His answer is "Give up the practice" (1 Cor. 6:13-20).

Another member wonders whether he ought to associate with

[2] In the old Greek city, the temple of Venus on Acro-Corinthus had a thousand priestesses and was notorious throughout the world. To "Corinthianize" mean to engage in the lowest forms of vice.

idolaters or with any of his Christian brothers who are immoral
or greedy or abusive or drunken. Paul says, "No, don't even eat
with them; such Christian wrong-doers ought to be put out of the
church" (1 Cor. 5:9-13; 2 Cor. 6:14-18).

During Paul's absences from Corinth, divisive forces began to
work; rivalries, jealousies and false teachings developed. Somebody was good enough—or mean enough—to report it to Paul.
Paul lost no time in writing his flock about it and exhorting them
to unity: "No matter who preaches—Paul or Apollos or Cephas
—Christ is one and his Gospel is one" (1 Cor. 1:10-13).

Some people were speaking disparagingly of Paul's authority,
of his unimpressive speech and appearance, especially in contrast
to certain newcomers. Paul heard of that too and let the church
understand in no uncertain terms that he took second place to
nobody in pedigree, spiritual equipment, wonder-working power,
or ability to work and to suffer: "For I am not a whit inferior to
your superfine apostles, even if I am nobody!" (2 Cor. 11:4-6,
12-15, 22-28; 12:11-13).

Some of the slaves in the church became restless: "Paul has
said that in this new religion there is no master and no slave; all
are brothers (1 Cor. 12:13; Gal. 3:26-29). Then why are we
held as slaves? Let us make a strike for freedom!" Paul punc-
tured their enthusiasm: "Not so fast! You are spiritually free
and of equal worth with your masters in God's sight; but you
have no right to upset the economic order" (1 Cor. 7:17-24).

And finally the women began to take the new freedom too seriously: they asserted that they could speak out in meeting if they
wanted to, and leave off wearing that badge of subjection, the
veil. "Not at all," replied Paul, the bachelor and the Oriental:
"keep quiet in church and wear your veil; your husbands will
tell you at home all you ought to know about religion" (1 Cor.
11:2-16; 14:34-35).

All this is an extraordinary revelation of the varieties of people
that composed the Christian Church in Corinth and of the strange
problems that troubled them. Some were wealthy freedmen, like

Fig. 104. EPHESUS. AQUEDUCT AND CITADEL.

Gaius Crispus, who had become proselytes to the Jewish faith
before they had become Christians; some were respectable Greeks
like Stephanus the city treasurer; but most of them were pagans
who never had heard of the ethical teachings of Judaism or of
philosophy (1 Cor. 1:26): "immoral or idolators or adulterers or
sensual or given to unnatural vice or thieves or greedy—drunk-
ards, abusive people, robbers—some of you used to be like that"
(1 Cor. 6:9-11). How Paul ever welded them into any kind of
unity is a miracle. Sometimes he praised them (1 Cor. 1:4-7);
sometimes he besought them with a heart of love (2 Cor. 7:2-4);
sometimes he scolded (2 Cor. 7:8-9; 10:9-11); sometimes he
threatened them with a stick (1 Cor. 4:18-21). But somehow the
miracle was wrought by patience (1 Cor. 3:1-3), by the trans-
forming power of love (1 Cor. 13); and by a sense of the indwelling Christ in the heart of each one (2 Cor. 5:17). In these
ways Paul built up in the lives of this heterogeneous collection the
rudiments of a Christian conscience; and as a by-product laid the
foundation for the ritual, theology and organization of the later
Church.

EPHESUS

A very different city was Ephesus where Paul labored for two
and a half years. Ephesus was the third city in the Roman Empire,
next after Alexandria. For this eminence it was partly indebted
to its situation on the west coast of Asia Minor, chief terminal of
the Royal Road from east to west. It lay at the mouth of the river
Cayster in an amphitheatre of plain surrounded by hills. So
severely has time dealt with it that from the deserted site one
could never guess today its former greatness. The harbor began to
silt up even before Paul visited the city and now the sea is four
miles away. What was harbor is a marshy plain covered with
reeds and only the most important of its great buildings projected
here and there above the ground when the excavators began their
task of uncovering them. Though only a small portion of the great
city has been exposed, we are now able to identify the theatre set
into a hill, the stadium, a Roman triumphal arch, a public library,

baths, market places, colonnaded streets, a baptismal pool, and
the Christian church in which the Third Ecumenical Council
was held in 431 A.D. (Fig. 104).

FIG. 105.   TEMPLE OF ARTEMIS AT EPHESUS. (RESTORED)

Once regarded as the greatest of the Seven Wonders, this temple was wrecked by wars,
earthquakes and plunderers until the river Cayster buried the remains under 20 feet of
silt. J. T. Wood recovered the site in 1869.

The temple of Paul's day, the fourth on the site, was built in the days of Alexander the
Great, 323 B.C. It was 425 feet long and was surrounded with 127 columns sixty feet
high. An unusual feature was the sculptured ornament on the lower drums of thirty-six of
the columns, several of which may now be seen in the British Museum. Besides being a
temple it was a safety-deposit vault for all the East, where specie and works of art of
inestimable value were stored. Among its masterpieces were many statues by Praxiteles
and paintings by Apelles, including an equestrian portrait of Alexander for which the
artist received twenty gold talents.

THE CULT OF ARTEMIS

The great glory of this town was the temple of Artemis, or
Diana as she is translated in the King James Version. So completely had the temple been destroyed that many attempts were
made to locate even its site. All that is left are the foundations
and a few scattered drums of the immense columns of its peri-

style, now lying in a pond filled with frogs. In Paul's day the temple was reckoned one of the wonders of the world—the largest Hellenic temple in existence, 424 by 220 feet, adorned by the gifts of kings (Fig. 105). It was the safety deposit vault for all western Asia, protected not only by the sanctity of the shrine but by bands of armed virgins who had formed a temple guard since prehistoric times—the original Amazons. We still have replicas of the statue of Artemis, not graceful after the Greek style, but mummy-shaped and adorned with extravagant symbols after the Asian mode, rows of breasts, heads of bulls, lions, gryphons, bees, flowers, fruits, all symbols of the mother-goddess of Asia and the fertility cult. Such was "Great Artemis of Ephesus" (Fig. 106).

"EPHESIAN LETTERS"

Besides the cult of Artemis, Ephesus had another title to fame —or rather notoriety—its practice of magic. It was the focal point in the eastern world for the manufacture and sale of occult formulae of all kinds, "Ephesian Letters" as they were called.

Back of this industry was the widespread belief in the power of demons who showed themselves in disease and in all kinds of mishaps, as well as in portents in nature. In our day we can hardly conceive the terror with which the first-century man looked upon life. There was no security for mortals, for the powers of evil, invisible to all eyes, could be inhaled with any sleeping or waking breath, or could blight the fairest hopes through chance or through the malignity they could inspire in others. No person escaped this terror. High life and low life were permeated with the most fantastic and grotesque superstitions.[3] An illustration is furnished by the incident of the Jewish exorcist Scaeva who with his seven sons combined the practice of Judaism with the black art and who naturally drifted to Ephesus. He cast out demons by reciting formulas containing the names of powers more mighty

[3] Dr. Harold R. Willoughby tells us that when a thunderstorm arose, the Emperor Augustus used to take to the cellar, while the Emperor Caligula preferred to retire under the bed. (See *Pagan Regeneration*, 1929, p. 6.)

Fig. 106.
STATUE OF
ARTEMIS OF
EPHESUS.

This Artemis is an
Asiatic earth-mother
whose fertility cult is as
old as history. Her 18
breasts are symbols of
fruitfulness; so are the
garlands of small fruits
and the rows of animals
that seem to sprout from
all parts of her body.
The bulls, lions and goats
as well as the winged
creatures on her halo
show her protection over
the beasts of the field.
The city wall with its
triple gate which crowns
her head symbolizes her
guardianship of Ephesus.
Statuettes like this were
turned out in great quan-
tities by the silversmiths
who instigated the riot
described in Acts 19.

than the devils who were causing the trouble. Hearing that Paul had exorcised evil spirits by using the name of Jesus, he tried Paul's formula, with results disastrous to himself (Acts 19:11-17). Fortunately we know what these "Ephesian Letters" were like, for many have come down to us, among them one that couples Jewish and Christian words of power:

A notable spell for driving out demons. Invocation tb be uttered over the head [of the possessed one]. Place before him branches of olive, and standing behind him say: Hail, spirit of Abraham; hail, spirit of Isaac; hail, spirit of Jacob; Jesus the Christ, the holy one, the spirit. . . . drive forth the devil from this man, until this unclean demon of Satan shall flee before thee. I adjure thee, O demon, whoever thou art, by the God Sabarbarbathioth Sabarbarbathiuth Sabarbarbathioneth Sabarbarbaphai. Come forth, O demon, whoever thou art, and depart from so-and-so at once, at once, now. Come forth, O demon, for I chain thee with adamantine chains not to be loosed, and I give you over to black chaos in utter destruction.[4]

MYSTERY RELIGIONS

Ephesus was the home not only of magic but of various brands of religion with which Christianity was destined to wage a life-and-death struggle. They were all older than Christianity. Some of them were hoary with antiquity and enjoyed the respect which immemorial age always brings. These were mostly "mystery religions" by which one means that they each possessed a body of secret doctrine which was revealed only to the initiates, and that by means of the ritual and of the beliefs of the cult the worshipper was brought near to deity, in fact, could be mystically united with him; with the result that sin would be washed away and salvation attained in the life after death.

Chief among these mysteries were those of Isis and Osiris, which were Egyptian. The basis of this myth, as of most of the other mysteries, is the eternally recurrent death and re-creation

---

[4] G. Milligan: *Greek Papyri*, No. 47.

of vegetation, in which Osiris is the personification of the life-giving principle of water (the Nile). It is very suggestive to compare Paul's elaborate simile of the resurrection—the sowing of a grain of wheat and its springing to new life—with the ancient "vegetating Osiris" found in the Egyptian tombs: a figure the shape of Osiris made by wheat that has sprouted to the height of about six inches from a bed of sand spread on a couch.

Other religions which claimed the devotion of some of the best men of the ancient world were the Eleusinian mysteries, of which Cicero, who was an initiate, said that they "lead a man to live a better citizen and die with a fairer hope"; the Orphic mysteries organized about the myth of Orpheus the musician; the cult of Attis, the chief initiation rite of which was the *taurobolium,* a baptism with bull's blood still hot from the sacrifice of the victim; and the Persian cult of Mithra, in which the eternal conflict of light with darkness, of good with evil, is set forth, and the promise of salvation is given to all who fight on the side of the god of light.

These mystery faiths, their ideas and their phraseology, were current at the very time Christianity was taking shape. It was quite natural that Paul himself should describe Christianity as a "mystery" (Rom. 16:25, 1 Cor. 2:7, Col. 1:27).

The Church at Ephesus

If there was a church in Ephesus when Paul first stopped there, he seems to have ignored it in favor of the synagogue (Acts 18:19). However during the interval between this visit and his second one, some unknown missionary had carried the Good News thither (Acts 19:1). Some of the members had been converted even earlier than Paul; others had been won by the teaching of Priscilla and Aquila with whom Paul had previously lived in Corinth (Acts 18:2-3); and some were the fruits of the labor of Apollos, a skilful exhorter and a diligent student of the Old Testament (Acts 18:24-25). These facts illustrate the mobility of early Christians and the variety of influences that met in such a cosmopolitan city as Ephesus: Aquila and Priscilla from Rome and Corinth, Apollos from Alexandria, Paul from Corinth via Jerusalem, Antioch, Galatia and Phrygia; the "Way of the Lord," which sounds Palestinian (Acts 9:2; 24:14), the "baptism of John" which is a pre-Christian rite coming to Ephesus via Alexandria; the Jewish synagogue to which Paul, a once-ardent Pharisee, always gravitated; the lecture hall of Tyrannus, which was Greek and savored of philosophy. Ephesian Christians must have had more than a one-track mind.

As soon as Paul began work he injected a new ferment into the Ephesian welter of superstitions and religions. His distinctive doctrines seem to have been belief in Jesus as the promised Messiah; the Way of the Lord as a kingdom of believers; entrance to the kingdom by baptism; the gift of the Holy Spirit as the result of baptism; prophetic inspiration and speaking with tongues as witness to the power of the spirit; and the indwelling Christ as the source of moral endeavor. Such a message provoked at once the hostility of the Jews and till the day of his death the Jews never ceased to combat him (Acts 19:8-9; 20:19). Intolerance by the synagogue compelled Paul to seek a new preaching place in a public hall which a certain Tyrannus used himself or rented to other rhetoricians and sophists (Acts 19:9-10). Paul's general practice was to work at his trade from sunrise till 11 a.m. (Acts 20:34-35) at which hour Tyrannus had finished his teaching; then from 11 a.m. to 4 p.m.[5] to preach in the hall, hold conferences with helpers and private talks with candidates, plan extensions into the interior; then lastly to make a house-to-house evangelistic canvass that lasted from 4 p.m. till far into the night (Acts 20:20-21, 31). One wonders when he found time to eat and sleep.

All this incessant toil brought results. Men from the interior who came to Ephesus on business or as pilgrims to Diana's shrine stopped to hear and then returned home to spread the news. In this way small churches sprang up in Colossae, Hierapolis and Laodicea. It is probable that all the Seven Churches of Asia men-

[5] As given in Codex Bezae.

tioned in Revelation 2 and 3 were founded by missionary pupils of Paul. We know the names of several of Paul's helpers both in town and up-country: Timothy, Apollos, Priscilla and Aquila, Titus, Epaenetus (1 Cor. 16:10, 12, 19; 2 Cor. 8:16–18; Rom. 16:5). We learn also from the letter Paul wrote introducing Phoebe of Cenchreae to the church at Ephesus (appended to Romans as chapter 16) the names of twenty-seven valiant helpers, and the fact that the "church" was made up of at least five groups who met at different private houses (Rom. 16:5, 10, 11, 14, 15).

Correlative with all this success was increasing tension and opposition in which the whole church shared. The Christians of Ephesus found that they were living on a volcano. Danger became part of their daily life. Prisca and Aquila "risked their necks" to save Paul's life; Andronicus and Junias went to prison with him (Rom. 16:3, 7). Paul not only was jailed by the authorities but because he was the ringleader they condemned him to fight wild beasts in the arena (1 Cor. 15:32; 2 Cor. 1:8–10). This can hardly be figurative language, for Paul always fought figurative wild beasts in every city. This time it was the real thing! The faithful held their breath as they saw their beloved leader wielding a sword like a common gladiator. Miraculously he escaped death. Once or more he was imprisoned in Ephesus (Rom. 16:7; 2 Cor. 11:23) and always lived in imminent danger of his life (1 Cor. 15:30–31—written from Ephesus). Then came the riot of the silversmiths. This encounter with the religious hierarchy not only illustrates the success of Paul's work but shows that the religion of Artemis was more or less a racket. The silversmiths were making big money through the sale of silver shrines— wonder-working souvenirs which every one of the thousands of pilgrims to the famous temple was supposed to buy and take home. Paul reduced their profits to such an extent that the silversmiths stirred up a mob to lynch him. Fortunately the temple officials with their supporting racketeers had a formidable and jealous rival in the city government which had an interest in keeping the peace. The mob was therefore overawed by the Recorder from city hall who reminded it that preaching a new religion was not a criminal offense, but that rioting was (Acts 19:40) (Fig. 107).

Though Paul escaped with his life, it was evident that the ugly temper of the citizens would make further work unfruitful. He had to leave the young church to its own devices, with the result that it badly slipped from the faith. Paul foresaw this result and later warned a delegation from the church that came to see him as he passed through Miletus (Acts 20:29-31). The letter to the church at Ephesus in the Apocalypse bears witness to this down-curve in its loyalty (Rev. 2:1-6). If the allusion in the late Letter to Timothy is true (2 Tim. 1:15) Paul came to be completely discredited in the province of Asia. Other teachers twenty years later were destined to revive the work.

THE POST-PAULINE CHURCH

After the destruction of Jerusalem in A.D. 70, the church at Ephesus came to be the leading church of the world. Who revived it we do not know, but its members included, by tradition, Timothy and John. This John cannot have been the son of Zebedee but well may have been the beloved disciple who leaned on Jesus' breast at the last supper; or he may have been another John, called "the Elder," the author of the Fourth Gospel and the Three Epistles of John in our New Testament. Whoever the writer, this Fourth Gospel was one of the contributions made by the church of Ephesus to the Church Universal. Its new interpretation of Jesus shows unmistakably how the mind of the Ephesian church was now working to make Christianity acceptable to the cultured class and to remove from it the stigma of its being a plebeian Jewish sect; to state Christian truth in "forms that would be immediately intelligible and welcome to the Greek mind." [6]

[6] According to Dean Ernest Colwell the purpose of the Evangelist was to show that Jesus was not a magician; that he was not a follower of John the Baptist, nor a Jew, nor even a man, but a god; that Jesus was not a criminal; that Christianity is not a superstition nor a revolutionary movement. (See *John Defends his Gospel*, 1936.)

Recent examination of the evidence seems to prove that Ephesus at the end of the first century became the focal point of the publication and circulation of Christian literature. Within the space of

Fig. 107. THEATRE AT EPHESUS.

You are seated on one of the lower rows of the *cavea,* or concentric circles of rising seats, and are looking toward the stage (west). The level semicircle in the foreground is the "orchestra" where the chorus performed its evolutions. The pillars where the man stands hold up the shallow stage. Behind the stage rose a wall to a height sufficient to give a good background for the actors and to act as a sounding-board. The stairs to the right lead onto the stage; behind them is one of the exits.

Lysimachus built this theatre 295 B.C. Diameter, 495 feet; its 66 rows of seats held 24,500 people. All the stone work is white marble.

twenty years there came from the Ephesian church not only the Gospel and the Letters mentioned above, but the Revelation of John—still another John not related to the other two; the two-volume work known as Luke-Acts, the fourfold Gospel as we now have it, and the first published edition of the letters of Paul.

This matter of publication has hitherto been given scant attention, but now, thanks to the researches of scholars,[7] we are beginning to understand its significance. Paul had written letters, some of them from Ephesus, as personal communications to the various churches he had founded. As indicated clearly in his letters to the Corinthians and the Thessalonians especially, they were called forth by concrete problems that beset those particular churches. In writing them Paul had no thought or scant thought of their general applicability; nor had the recipients of those letters any idea of their value to the church as a whole. When the letters were read they were allowed to remain among the church archives and in the course of a generation they were largely forgotten. But some unknown person in Ephesus, while reading the two-volume work of Luke (Luke-Acts) describing the founding and growth of Christianity, was struck with the references to the work of Paul and resolved that he would find whatever letters might still be extant. He began no doubt with those near at hand, say the letter to the Colossians. Some one in Colossae also possessed a letter written to Philemon, an important early member, and to the church at Laodicea that met in his house. On making further inquiry of the church clerk in Ephesus, a letter of introduction was discovered written by Paul on behalf of Phoebe, a deaconess of Cenchreae, who came to Ephesus on business (Rom. 16). Inquiry of the church at Corinth brought forth four letters which Paul had sent to that church. In all, this diligent collector dug up nine genuine letters.[8] They contained so much matter of general value that he secured the backing of the church to have them published as a single volume; and by way of introduction he himself wrote a covering letter containing what he regarded as the gist of Paul's teaching and prefixed it to the assembled letters of Paul. This circular letter of his exists in our New Testament as the Epistle to the Ephesians, which is not Paul's and was not written to the

---

[7] See Edgar J. Goodspeed: *Introduction to the New Testament*, pp. 222–239, and *Christianity Goes to Press*, 1940.

[8] 1 & 2 Corinthians, Romans, 1 & 2 Thessalonians, Galatians, Colossians, Philippians, Philemon; ten if Romans 16 is listed separately.

church at Ephesus,[9] but was written at Ephesus by an admirer of Paul as part of a publication venture. So about 90 A.D., with this addition, the letters of Paul were sent forth on their world-wide mission, for which fact we have to thank the church at Ephesus.

We must credit this enterprising church also with a mechanical innovation of far-reaching consequence. Hitherto books had been written on rolls of parchment or papyrus. This was an inconvenient format and an expensive one in that only one side of the material could be written upon. At some time during the first century B.C. some bright mind devised the format which we know as a Codex, in which sheets of moderate size were written on both sides and bound up along the left edge—in other words, some one invented the book as we know it today (Fig. 108). The publishing house of the Christian church at Ephesus decided that the new book form was the one to use for Christian literature. That decision put them in the ranks of the innovators—made them up-to-date, as in our day the use of radio and motion pictures would characterize a church as progressive. The oldest fragment we have of any Christian work is the Ryland's Library bit of the Gospel of John in Codex form, which dates before the year 150 A.D., possibly in the reign of Hadrian around 130 A.D. While pagan literature continued to be written chiefly on the old-fashioned rolls through the third century, most Christian books from the start were put into Codex form.

While therefore the church at Ephesus in its earlier years contained a wide mixture of members the lowest stratum of whom may have been on a level with the church at Corinth and seems to have won its success partly by the appeal of wonder-working (Acts 19:11-13; 17-20), the church ultimately came to depend on the cultured class who used their brains for the spread of

---

[9] In the King James Version and its revisions the first verse in the letter to the Ephesians reads "Paul an apostle of Jesus Christ through the will of God, to the saints that are at Ephesus and to the faithful in Christ Jesus." But the oldest manuscript of the Pauline Epistles yet recovered, namely the Ann Arbor (Michigan) papyrus, omits the words "in Ephesus." The original address was "To God's People who are steadfast in Christ Jesus."

Christianity so effectively that the whole world still stands in their debt.

ROME

The third church whose life we shall consider briefly is found at the imperial capital. Who introduced Christianity into Rome we do not yet know. The first converts were no doubt Jews, for there was a fairly large Jewish colony in Rome, descendants of that band of hostages which Pompey took from Palestine in 63 B.C., to which must be added the Jews who later came either under compulsion or for the purposes of trade. By Nero's time the Jews in Rome numbered 30,000 to 50,000. The church was certainly in existence before Paul went to Rome about 59 A.D., for our Book of Romans, composed about 56 A.D., is his letter to that church. Peter probably did not found it though he visited Rome as early as 42 A.D. More likely some visitor from Rome to Corinth or Antioch or Ephesus or perhaps some pilgrim to the Passover at Jerusalem had been converted and on his return had started the Christian movement in his home city.

Though Paul went to Rome under arrest, he went willingly for he had long desired to see the Eternal City. Likewise his coming was eagerly awaited by the Roman church; when he landed at Puteoli, delegates were sent to meet him on the way, coming as far as Appius' Forum and Three Taverns (Acts 28:15). On arrival Paul was allowed to rent lodgings of his own, where he lived two full years with a soldier to guard him. Paul was thus treated not as a common criminal but as one who had rights as a Roman citizen and property enough in his own name to be respected.

We know approximately where Paul lived in Rome. The Jewish quarter still is where it always has been, in the low ground that borders the Tiber southwest of the Forum. Horatius once "kept the bridge" against the Tarquins in this vicinity.

The Rome that Paul saw was a monumental city. Much of the ancient town had been burned during the civil wars of the first

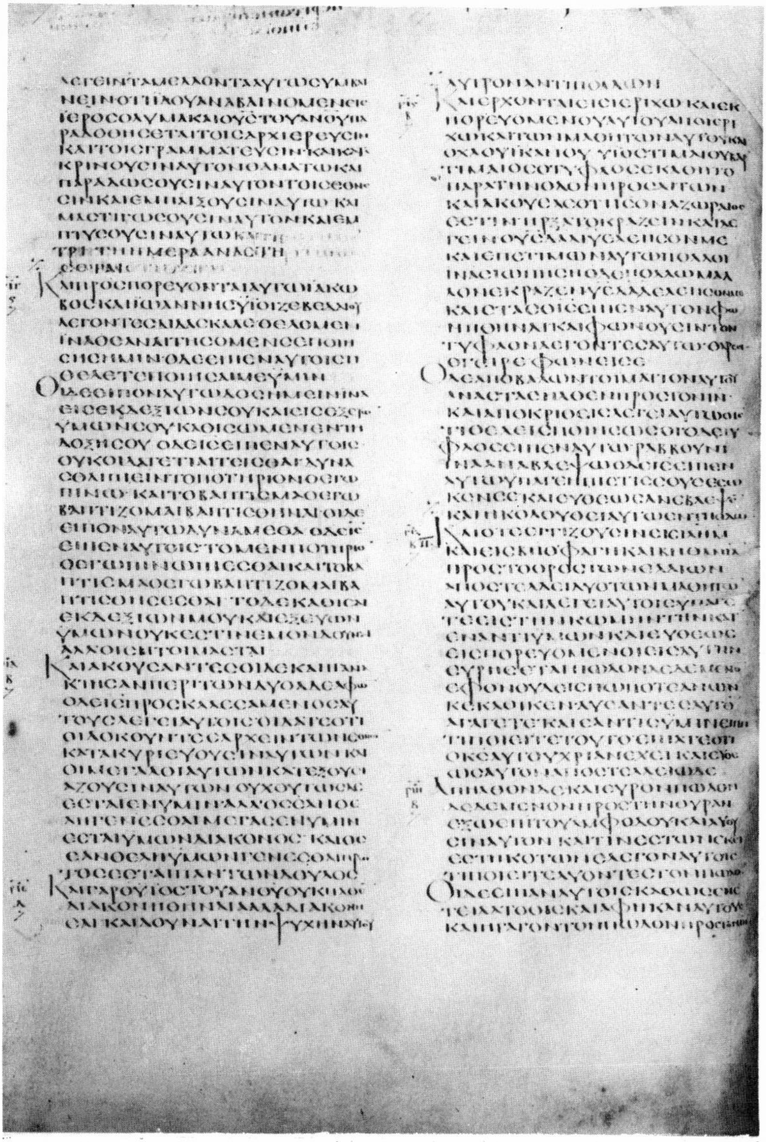

FIG. 108. CODEX ALEXANDRINUS.

One of the three earliest and most important Biblical manuscripts, containing both the Old and New Testaments. It was written about 450 A.D., probably in Alexandria, was transferred thence to Constantinople, and in 1628 was given to King Charles I of England by Cyril Lucar, Patriarch of Constantinople. It is now in the British Museum. The material is vellum; the characters are "uncial," i.e., capitals.

century B.C., but Augustus transformed what was left into a capital worthy of his great empire. He boasted that he had found the city built of brick but left it built of marble. On the Palatine to the east of where Paul lodged was the imperial palace, or one should say palaces, for the buildings of Augustus had been enlarged by succeeding emperors and their size and magnificence are a matter of astonishment today. On the south slope of this hill between it and the Aventine was the huge Circus Maximus which could seat a hundred thousand spectators and which in after years was to witness the terrible martyrdoms of the Christians. Across the Palatine from where Paul lived was the low ground on which afterwards the Colosseum was to be built in memory of the destruction of Jerusalem by Titus; while close to that spot Nero was soon to erect his Golden House, too huge to occupy the Palatine. Between the Palatine and the Capitol hill lay the Roman Forum around which were noble buildings, the Basilica Julia, the House of the Vestal Virgins, the House of the Pontifex Maximus before which Caesar's body had been burned, the Basilica Aemelia; while the beautiful temples of the state gods—of Saturn, of Jupiter, of Castor and Pollux, and of the divine Julius Caesar, gave Paul an impressive idea of the magnitude of the task before him. Not yet had those immense structures been built which were to make of Rome the wonder city of the world, but the capital was large enough and impressive enough to make Paul thrill with pride that he was a Roman citizen.

Paul began his work in his own house the third day after arrival when he invited the leading Jews to come and see him (Acts 28:17). They had not heard of his coming, in fact they had never heard of him at all; but that did not prevent Paul from telling them at once what was nearest his heart. The usual result followed. They would not listen to him. But the little church received him kindly, saw to it that every one of importance called upon Paul; and their courtesy ultimately took Paul's gospel pretty well up the social scale even into the royal palace (Acts 28:30-31; Phil. 4:22).

Paul was not at liberty to leave his own house, and his quarters were too small to admit of their being used as a place of assembly. The little congregations that were formed were obliged to meet in the private houses of those members who had enough room to accommodate them. Such members would not belong to the slave class or even to the middle class. Tradition has given us the names of some of these hosts of the church and in later years the sites of their houses were marked by little church buildings. An account of one or two of these will be interesting and significant, for they show that unlike the plebeian church at Corinth and the (ultimately) intellectual church at Ephesus, the Roman church made converts of the rich and powerful.

The church of Santa Pudenziana was named after one of the daughters of Pudens and is built on the site of the house where St. Peter is said to have been a guest. It afterwards became the dwelling of the early bishops of Rome. There was a Pudens in the Roman church—at least if the late Epistle of 2 Timothy is to be trusted; and his story illustrates the fact that in Rome Paul aimed deliberately at the top stratum of society. This Pudens, a brilliant young Roman of noble family, had been a centurion in Britain, had helped conquer the British chieftain Caractacus and had been put in charge of that king and his family when he was brought to Rome to grace the conqueror's triumph. On the way he fell in love with the king's beautiful daughter and married her. In Rome, Pudens rose to power and wealth until he became a senator. He and his wife were converted to Christianity by Paul himself, it is said, and they became the apostle's ardent helpers. The wife of course changed her British name to a Roman one and appears now as Claudia. Her brother's name was Linus. They are all mentioned in 2 Tim. 4:21. The glorious fourth century mosaic that adorns the apse of the church above the house of Pudens (Fig. 109) was designed to heal the breach which even in Paul's day was developing between the Jewish Christians, who held to Peter's teaching and kept intact some of their Jewish beliefs and practices, and the Gentile group that held by the teachings of Paul. The artist shows how the breach may be healed by loyalty to Christ. This is the oldest church in Rome and bears witness to the way in which wealthy members helped out the Christian cause.

It would be quite like Paul to endeavor to convert the soldier who had charge of him. If he were successful, that would intro-

FIG. 109.   MOSAIC IN SANTA PUDENZIANA, ROME. DATES 384–397 A.D.

The church in which this apse mosaic is found was erected over the supposed site of the house of Pudens, a meeting-place of the earliest church.

The scene represents Christ enthroned, with the Church on either side. On the right, Peter representing the Jewish branch of the Church is being crowned by Prasseda, a daughter of Pudens, while on the left, Paul representing the Gentile branch is crowned by another daughter Pudenziana. For background are the city of Jerusalem with the buildings of Constantine, Calvary with its cross, and the four creatures that surround the throne of God, later used to symbolize the four Evangelists.

duce Christianity into the Roman army and into the emperor's bodyguard. Other converts were servants of the imperial household and through the better persons of this class, knowledge of the new faith would ramify upward until it reached the top. The church has preserved the memory of this process and its results in the story of Acte. She was a household servant in the palace of the Emperor Nero, but so beautiful that almost at the beginning of his reign the young emperor fell in love with her. His ministers encouraged him in his desire to marry her, hoping that Acte would wean him away from the domination of his terrible mother; but the latter was powerful enough to prevent the marriage and Acte was retained as the emperor's mistress. She became the most powerful influence in Nero's life; people who wished to see the emperor had first to convince her that their business was important. Through their gifts she became wealthy in her own right, quite irrespective of what the emperor gave her, and she invested her money in various profitable enterprises in Italy. Doubtless through members of her household she heard of Paul and his gospel. While the emperor was in Greece she gave Paul a hearing and was converted.[10] From John Chrysostom (347-407 A.D.) we learn that when the emperor returned, Acte refused to resume her unhallowed relation with him, and the emperor wreaked his vengeance on the insignificant cause of the trouble: Paul was put to death for this woman's sake in November, 67 A.D.[11]

So the Roman church represented in its membership the whole gamut of social grades, from slaves to senators and an imperial mistress. As the years went by the tendency was for the church to become more and more aristocratic. While at the turn of the first century we have on the one hand such popular preachers and writers as Hermas (c. 100 A.D.) with his bad Greek and his semi-erotic visions in *The Shepherd*, we have on the other hand Clement the scholar with his polished epistles to the church in Corinth (c. 95 A.D.). It would seem also that the persecution under Domitian (95-96 A.D.) was inspired in part by the conversion of high officials and relatives whose power the emperor feared, such as consul Flavius, ex-consul Acilius Glabrio, and Domitilla, his own grand-niece. We know also that in the fourth century St. Jerome used to hold Bible classes in the drawing rooms of noble ladies and personally conducted a party of them on a tour to Palestine. It was doubtless in part this aristocratic charac-

[10] A dramatic picture of Paul preaching to Acte, by a modern artist De Martini, is in the Vatican.
[11] The probabilities are, however, that Paul was executed in 61 A.D.

ter of the church coupled with the fact that Rome had been the center of world empire that later led to the claim of the bishop of Rome to supremacy in the Church Universal.

Nevertheless the Roman church had to pass through the fire. When Rome burned in the year 64 A.D., the angry populace accused Nero of having set the fire himself in order to clear space for his great palace. But he easily turned the popular indignation against the Christians, probably at the instigation of his Jewish wife Poppaea. Since the Christians had few friends, being hated by the Jews and despised by the Romans as a Jewish sect, they were easily made the scapegoat. Tacitus the historian called the new religion "this accursed superstition." He wrote: "Those who were first arrested confessed the crime, and afterwards a vast number upon their information were convicted, not so much on the charge of causing the fire, but rather for their hatred to the human race. Their deaths were made to afford amusement to the crowd. Some were wrapped in the skins of wild beasts and torn to pieces by dogs; others were fastened on crosses and when daylight failed were burned as torches to light up the night. Nero had lent his own gardens for the spectacle, and he gave in celebration a chariot race in which he was seen mounted on his car or mingling with the people in the dress of a charioteer. As the result, a feeling of compassion arose for the sufferers, though guilty and deserving of condign punishment, yet as being destroyed not for the common good but to satiate the cruelty of one man."

The wonderful thing about this church at Rome is not that it was largely aristocratic or that it had withstood a persecution but that it was bound together with ties of love. Even in the early days the church was conspicuous for its Christian virtue (Rom. 1:8), and as it grew it seems largely to have avoided schisms, theological controversies, outlandish spiritual manifestations like those at Corinth, demon exorcism like that at Ephesus, and to have engaged in works of charity whereby the spirit of Christ could be most practically manifested. To be a Christian meant to be democratic, kind, ready to help the poor, the sick, the persecuted, the stranger. We have direct testimony to this fact in the *Apology* written by Justin Martyr c. 150 A.D. Justin was a Christian philosopher who went from place to place discussing the truths of Christianity in the hope of bringing educated pagans to Christ. He finally came to Rome and lectured there until his martyrdom c. 165 A.D. He has this to say about the Church:

On the day called Sunday, all who live in cities or in the country gather together in one place, and the "Memoirs of the Apostles" or the writings of the Prophets are read, as time allows; then when the reader has done, the president of the assembly in an address instructs and exhorts to the imitation of the good things (which had formed the subject of the address). Then we all rise and pray; and when our prayer is ended, bread and wine and water are brought, and the president offers prayers and thanksgivings according to his ability; and the people assent, saying, Amen; and there is a distribution to each, and a participation of that over which thanks have been given; and to those who are absent a portion is sent by the deacons. . . . And the rich among us help the poor. . . . And they who are well-to-do and willing give what each thinks fit; and what is collected is deposited with the president, who succors the orphans and widows, and those who through sickness or any other cause are in want, and those who are in bonds, and the stranger sojourning among us—in a word, takes cares of all who are in need.

What a marked contrast to the disorderly meetings of the early Corinthian church and to the mystic theological and eschatological teachings of Paul!—just the story of the Gospels and the exhortation to duplicate in one's own life the spirit of Jesus.

In the second century the church made a conscious effort to rid itself of its earlier excesses by formulating rules of conduct. A most interesting example is the *Teachings of the Twelve Apostles*, discovered in 1873. It shows among other things that Christian hospitality had been greatly abused. To check itinerant impostors these rules are given (Chaps. XI–XII):

"Every apostle who cometh to you, let him be received as the Lord; but he shall not remain more than one day, or at most two; if he remain three days he is a false prophet.

"Whoever, in the Spirit, says, Give me money, or something

else, ye shall not hear him; but if for others in need he bids you give, let no one judge him.

"If he will take up his abode with you, being an artisan, let him work and so eat. Let no idler live with you as a Christian."

Other rules deal with the proper observant of fasting, baptism and the Eucharist. True to its genius, the Roman church in particular early showed a tendency to organize and regulate.

When wealthy aristocrats joined the church they not only gave freely to the poor and used their great houses for meetings but extended to their Christian brethren the use of their private cemeteries for burial. An example of this form of charity is the catacomb of Domitilla, a member of the Flavian imperial house and wife of the consul Clemens (95 A.D.). Once her private burying ground, she offered it to scores and then to hundreds of humble church members. Another is the cemetery of Priscilla, wife of the consul Acilius Glabrio. In the soft *tufa* rock they excavated long galleries about eight feet high by three wide and in the walls of these they dug tiers of spaces about the size of a man's body, the axis running parallel to the corridor (Fig. 110). When an interment was made they placed in front of the body, flush with the wall, a marble slab or well-cemented tiles and on these they engraved or painted the necessary inscription. When all of the area which they owned had been thus filled with passages and tombs they dug a stair to a lower level and repeated the process; so again to a third level and even to a fourth and fifth. In this way although the lateral area of the catacombs is limited, it is believed that there are at least six hundred miles of galleries containing two million graves. But these numbers may be too low since the greater part of subterranean Rome has never been excavated.

Some of the graves in the catacombs are *loculi*, the little niches described above; other *arcosolia*, in which an arch was excavated over the tomb so as to look as if a sarcophagus had been set at the bottom of a semi-circular niche—this for more wealthy members; still others, *cubicula*, which were family vaults or chapels sur-

FIG. 110. CATACOMB CORRIDOR. ROME

Cut out of the solidified volcanic ash called *tufa*. The walls of long straight corridors about four feet wide and ten high are cut into rows of *loculi*, to receive bodies. After the interment the loculus was sealed with a marble slab.

rounded by *loculi* and *arcosolia*. These rooms were sometimes used as places of worship, especially for the celebration of the Eucharist at the time of burial and on anniversary days. The church as a whole never worshipped here except on the rarest occasions; but in the later persecutions, Christians in great numbers took refuge in the catacombs. They were of course traced by spies and many of them were slaughtered. A large group was once seen by watchful pagan officials to enter one of the catacombs by a secret passage. Immediately that entrance and the regular one were blocked up with stone and sand, making all escape impossible. Nearly a hundred years later in the pontificate of Pope Damasus (366–384 A.D.) the skeletons of the entire congregation, men, women and children, were discovered.

These catacombs tell us a good deal about the beliefs and sentiments of the Roman church in respect to death and the life beyond, and the sources of their all-conquering faith. Naturally in the days when Christianity was a proscribed religion, these sentiments could not be expressed openly; they had to be disguised. Hence symbols are found everywhere, always the language of repression. Sometimes in fresco or in sculpture a Good Shepherd appears bearing a sheep on his shoulder—innocent enough in the eyes of the police but to the initiated eloquent of Christian loyalty. Similarly a basket of bread resting on a fish was token of the multiplication of the loaves and fishes and of the Eucharist (Fig. 111); the picture of a fish alone was a cryptic expression of the Creed; [12] and even pagan heroes like Ulysses or Orpheus,

---

[12] To read this cryptogram one must arrange vertically the letters of the Greek word for fish and then use each one as the initial of another word, as follows:

> I   —Iesous—Jesus
> CH—Christos—Christ
> TH—Theou—Of God
> U   —Uios—Son
> S   —Soter—Saviour

Only the initiate could read this message, which means "Jesus Christ, Son of God, is Saviour"; but to a church member it was a reminder of the simple confession of faith by which they were united to the church universal.

and Jewish worthies like Moses or the three friends of Daniel appear as disguised reminders of Christ and his saving power. Thousands of inscriptions also in Greek and Latin are witnesses to the Church's vivid belief in a future life and in active communion between the living and the dead. All, whether in the Church Militant or Triumphant, are members of the mystical body of Christ, and are bound together by love into one great family, all are living though unseen.

> Matronata, who lived a year and 32 days—Pray for thy parents.
> Baccis, sweet soul in the peace of the Lord, a virgin—Her father to his sweetest daughter.
> Amerinus to his dearest wife Rufina—May God refresh thy spirit.

Never in all the inscriptions or pictures is there a word of regret or sorrow or despair. Although life had been bitter with poverty and persecution there is no mention of it; there is no resentfulness at the world's wickedness, no curse called down on the torturers, no prayer that God might blast the terrible empire in whose grip they had been caught (Fig. 112). All is peace and sunshine and hope and love. That is the miracle wrought in the hearts of these traders, sailors, potters, weavers, soldiers, slaves, women of wealth and culture, senators, consuls, by faith in Christ; and not only did it transform what had been their pagan hopelessness about the life beyond, but it irradiated the present with a brotherliness that even their persecutors marveled at and honored: "Lo, how these Christians love one another!"

Finis

"Bible Times" end with the writing of the last Biblical Book. Second Peter is that book and its date is about 170 A.D. Between the peak of activity in the Ephesian church and the writing of II Peter, the center of gravity of Christianity seems to have shifted to Rome. In this second century, Christians were chiefly concerned with fighting for their existence in the face of increasing persecution. Internally they were engaged in a struggle with the heresies of minority groups, in order that with false teaching eliminated the church might present a united front against persecution. Thus in the second century the notion of orthodoxy was

Fig. 111.   CATACOMB FRESCO.

An example of the symbolic painting of the early Christians.

Center: Christ the Good Shepherd. The two trees suggest Paradise; the sheep are the souls of the redeemed. Christ is beardless, a Christian adaptation of the Greek Apollo.

Above, right and left: A basket of bread resting on a fish. The later is a cryptogram for Christ (See note 12); it and the bread symbolize the Eucharist.

Lower left: A baptismal scene.

Lower right: Sheep at a fountain among trees: the redeemed in Paradise and the Water of Life.

established. Parallel with this concern about doctrine was the church's problem about its growing literature; what books should be regarded as authoritative. The beginnings of a sacred Canon were therefore made in this century. Through such activities the church at Rome secured a leadership that eventually resulted in the establishment of the Papacy.

Meanwhile life in other Bible lands was in transition. Mesopotamia where Bible times began was on the decline owing largely to the struggle of Rome against the Parthians. In that area the Jews still existed, but in sporadic and uninfluential colonies;

FIG. 112.   LAST PRAYER OF THE CHRISTIANS. FROM A
PAINTING BY GÉROME.

The scene is in the Circus Maximus at Rome. After the chariot-racing is over, the climax of the show is staged—the martyrdom of the Christians. Some of the victims are hung on crosses, covered with pitch and set on fire; others, a whole congregation with their pastor, are exposed to the lions who now advance from their underground dens. The Christians kneel while their aged leader commends their souls to God.

Christians had not yet arrived in any numbers. In Antioch and Ephesus the Hellenistic churches were waning as Rome waxed. Alexandria still had its large colony of commercial Jews, but they and the pagan sects were soon to be subordinated to the rising influence of Christian thinkers who were to shape Eastern theology. Palestine was a dish wiped clean. Jerusalem had been destroyed by Rome not only in 70 A.D. but again after fearful slaughter in 135, and all Jews had been banished from the land. In this destruction the Christian Church of Palestine was also uprooted and scattered. From the fourth to the sixth centuries the Byzantine Church spread its imperial prestige over this blighted area, sought out and marked with gorgeous church buildings all the holy sites and revived old bishoprics. Caesarea and Scythopolis became important centers of Christianity, leading church Fathers flourished from Asia Minor to Egypt. But abuses and intolerance prepared the way for Islam which in the seventh century rolled in like a destructive flood, leaving behind a deposit of wasted churches and cities, a strange language and a hostility to everything anterior to itself. Practically all the knowledge of life that survived this wreck of the ancient civilizations of Mesopotamia, Egypt and Palestine was found in one solitary book—our Bible. And that book could not properly be interpreted until in the nineteenth century archaeology and the social sciences began to restore to us a knowledge of the life of Bible times.

THE END

BIBLIOGRAPHICAL REFERENCES

CHAPTER I

Albright, Wm. F.: *From the Stone Age to Christianity,* 1940, pp. 88–105
The latest summary and evaluation of prehistoric culture in Palestine.

Garrod, D. A. ʟ. and Bate, D. M. A.: *The Stone Age of Mt. Carmel,* 2 vols., 1937
The excavators' definitive report. Full details and illustrations.

Graham, W. C. and May, H. G.: *Culture and Conscience,* 1936
Chap. 2, a summary of the prehistoric finds in Palestine, and an evaluation of their cultural significance.

CHAPTER II

Albright, W. F.: *Archaeology and the Religion of Israel,* 1942.

British Museum: *Guide to the Babylonian and Assyrian Antiquities*
Authoritative data, translations or summaries of documents, many illustrations.

Chiera, E.: *They Wrote On Clay,* 1938

Speiser, E. A.: *Mesopotamian Origins,* 1930

Ullman, B. L.: *Ancient Writing and Its Influence,* 1932

Woolley, C. L.: *Ur Excavations,* 2 vols., 1927–38
The excavator's account of twelve years of work at Ur and neighboring Al-Urbaid.

———— *Development of Sumerian Art,* 1935
Beautiful illustrations in color and highly informing text.

———— *Abraham, Recent Discoveries and Hebrew Origins,* 1936
The testimony of archaeology to the historicity of Abraham; his town; social conditions. Chaps. 1–4.

CHAPTER III

Albright, W. F.: *The Archaeology of Palestine and the Bible,* 1933
    Chap. 3. The Bible in the Light of Archaeology.

Cambridge Ancient History, Vols. I and II

Harper, R. F.: *The Code of Hammurabi,* 1904

Meek, T.: *Hebrew Origins,* 1936
    Chap. 1. The Origin of the Hebrew People.
    Chap. 2. The Origin of the Hebrew God.

Woolley, C.: *Abraham,* 1936
    Chap. 5. The Influence of Ur on Abraham's Later Life.
    Chap. 6. The Family God (Woolley's theory that Abraham's family
    god was transformed into Yahweh is not accepted by most scholars).

CHAPTER IV

Breasted, J. H.: *A History of Egypt,* 1912
    Authoritative work by America's foremost Egyptologist.

British Museum: *Guide to the Egyptian Antiquities*
    Authoritative data; translations and summaries of documents; many
    illustrations.

Cambridge Ancient History, Vols. I and II

Engberg, R. M.: *The Hyksos Reconsidered,* 1939

Egyptian Art, published by the Phaedon Press, Vienna, 1936.
    Excellent reproductions of masterpieces in the various fields of Egyp-
    tian art.

Glanville, S. R. K.: *Daily Life In Ancient Egypt,* 1930

Hölscher, U.: *Excavations at Ancient Thebes, 1930–1,* 1932
    Full description of the palace of Ramses III.

Lucas, A.: *Ancient Egyptian Materials and Industries,* 2nd ed., 1934

Rowley, H. H.: "Israel's Sojourn in Egypt" in *Bulletin of the John
    Rylands Library,* April 1938
    Résumé of all pertinent data.

CHAPTER V

Köster, A.: *Antike Seewesen,* Berlin, 1923
   Illustrations of ancient ships.
Newbegin, M. I.: *The Mediterranean Lands,* 1924
   Chap. 5. Sea-trade and the First Sea-traders.
Ormerod, H. A.: *Piracy In the Ancient World,* 1924
Petrie, W. M. F.: *Egyptian Tales, Translated from the Papyri,* 1913

CHAPTER VI

Albright, W. F.: "Archaeology and the Date of the Hebrew Con-
   quest of Palestine" in *Bulletin of the Am. Schools of Oriental
   Research,* Apr. 1935, pp. 10–18
────── "The Israelite Conquest of Canaan in the Light of Archaeol-
   ogy"; in Basor, Apr. 1939, pp. 11–23
Bertholet, A.: *History of Hebrew Civilization,* 1926
Cook, S. A.: *The Old Testament; A Reinterpretation,* 1936
Garstang, J.: *Foundations of Bible History: Joshua, Judges,* 1931
Gaster, T.: "The Ras Shamra Texts and the Old Testament" in *Pal.
   Excavation Quarterly,* 1934–5, pp. 141–6
────── "The Megiddo Ivories" in *Ill. Lon. News,* Oct. 23, 1937,
   pp. 708–10
────── "Hidden Treasure from Armageddon" in *Ill. Lon. News,*
   Oct. 16, 1937, pp. 655–8
Jack, J. W.: *The Ras Shamra Tablets; Their Bearing on the Old
   Testament,* 1935
Lamon, R. S.: *The Megiddo Water System,* 1935
Macalister, R. A. S.: *History of Civilization in Palestine,* 1921
May, H. G.: *Material Remains of the Megiddo Cult,* 1935
Yeivin, S. (ed.): "Trade, Industry and Crafts in Ancient Palestine,"
   Jerusalem, 1937; in *Library of Palestinology,* vols. 9–10

CHAPTER VII

Newbegin, M. I.: *The Mediterranean Lands,* 1924
Chap. 4. The Marginal Lands—Asia Minor, Syria, Mesopotamia, Palestine, Egypt.

Olmstead, A. T.: *History of Assyria,* 1923

——— *History of Palestine and Syria,* 1934; Chap. 4 and pp. 532–40
See index under Camels, Caravans, Trade, etc.

Rostovtzeff, M. I.: *Caravan Cities,* 1932
Pertains mostly to the period of the Roman Empire.

Semple, E. C.: *Geography of the Mediterranean Region,* 1931
See index under the various countries.

Whitbeck, R. H. and Thomas, O. J.: *The Geographic Factor,* 1932
Chap. 7. Geographic Factors in the Growth of Civilization.
Chap. 12. Rivers and Valleys in the Service of Mankind.

CHAPTER VIII

Glueck, N.: "The First Campaign at Tell el-Kheleifeh (Ezion-Geber)" in *Bulletin of the Amer. Schools of Oriental Research,* 71 (Oct. 1938); 3–18

——— "The Second Campaign, etc." *Op. cit.* 75 (Oct. 1939): 8–22

Macalister, R. A. S.: *A Century of Excavation in Palestine,* 1925
Illuminating summary of various digs in Jerusalem, pp. 95–142.

Macalister, R. A. S. and G. Duncan: *Excavations on the Hill of Ophel, Jerusalem, 1923–25*
Palestine Exploration Fund, 1926. The excavators' account of their researches in the Jebusite and Early Hebrew city. Many illustrations and fine maps.

Smith, G. A.: *Jerusalem,* 2 vols., 1907
Exhaustive study of archaeological (to 1906), historical and literary material, with illustrations and maps. See Vol. I, pp. 134–169, 367–376; Vol. II, pp. 48–82

CHAPTER IX

Bertholet, A.: *History of Hebrew Civilization,* 1926
   Bk. II, Chap. 1: Family and Domestic Life.
       Chap. 2: Trades and Callings.
       Chap. 3: Social Life.
Cambridge Ancient History, Vol. III, Chaps. 1–5
May, H. G.: "The High Place at Gezer" in *Pal. Exploration Quarterly,* 1934–5, pp. 139–40
——— "Some Aspects of Solar Worship in Jerusalem" in *Zeitschrift für die Alttestamentliche Wissenschaft,* 1937, 14:3–4

CHAPTER X

Cambridge Ancient History, Vol. III, Chaps. 1–5
Charles, R. H.: *Apocrypha and Pseudepigrapha of the Old Testament,* 2 vols., 1913
Jouguet, P.: *Macedonian Imperialism and the Hellinization of the East,* 1928
Koldewey, R.: *Excavations at Babylon* (tr. Agnes Johns, 1914)
Loud, G. and Altman, C. B.: *Khorsabad,* Part II, 1936
   Detailed text and sumptuous illustrations.
Loud, G.: *Khorsabad,* Part I, 1936
   Popular account of excavations.
Schmidt, E. F.: *The Treasury of Persepolis,* 1939
Tarn, W. W.: *Hellenistic Civilization,* 2nd ed., 1930

CHAPTER XI

Dalman, G.: *Sacred Sites and Ways,* 1935
   Chap. 8: Capernaum and Chorazin.
   Chap. 12: From Galilee to Judea.
   Chap. 13: From Jericho to Jerusalem.
   Chap. 15: Jerusalem.
   Chap. 16: The Sanctuary.
   An authoritative book and the most recent on Palestinian Geography.
Hollis, F. J.: *The Archaeology of Herod's Temple,* 1934

Klausner, J.: *Jesus of Nazareth,* 1929
Political conditions, pp. 135–192.

Macalister, R. A. S.: "The Topography of Jerusalem" in *Cambridge Ancient History*; Vol. III, pp. 333–353

Mathews, S.: *New Testament Times In Palestine,* 1933 (Rev. ed.)

Schürer, E.: *History of the Jewish People in the Time of Christ*; Div. II, Vol. II, pp. 1–83

Smith, G. A.: *Jerusalem,* 1907; Vol. II, pp. 495–555.

CHAPTER XII

Angus, S.: *The Environment of Early Christianity,* 1915

Cadoux, C. T.: *The Early Church and the World,* 1925

Charlesworth, M. P.: *Trade Routes and Commerce of the Roman Empire,* 1926
Chap. 2, Egypt; Chap. 3, Syria; Chap. 5, Asia Minor.

Duncan, W.: *St. Paul's Ephesian Ministry,* 1931

Filson, F.: "Significance of the Early House Churches" in *Jour. of Bibl. Lit.,* June 1939, pp. 105–112

Fowler, H. N.: "Excavations at Corinth" in *Art and Archaeology,* 1922, pp. 193 ff.

———— "Roman Buildings in Corinth" in *Amer. Jour. of Arch.,* July 1939, p. 497

Glover, T. R.: *Conflict of Religions in the Early Roman Empire,* 1920 (9th ed.).

Goodspeed, E. J.: *New Chapters in New Testament Study,* 1937
———— *Christianity Goes To Press,* 1940

Lake, K. and Foakes-Jackson, F. J.: *Beginnings of Christianity*; Vol. V, Topography

Lake, K.: *Paul, His Heritage and Legacy,* 1934

Riddle, D. W.: "Early Christian Hospitality, A Factor in the Gospel Transmission" in *Jour. of Bibl. Lit.,* June 1938, pp. 141–54
———— *Early Christian Life,* 1936

Rostovtzeff, M. I.: *Caravan Cities,* 1939

Willoughby, H. R.: *Pagan Regeneration,* 1929

INDICES

INDEX OF BIBLE PASSAGES

OLD TESTAMENT

335

GENERAL INDEX

Abimelech, king of Gerar, 35, 44
Abraham, Chap. II–III, *passim*. See
  also Patriarchs
  early homes, 12, 13; date, 12, 13;
  idealized figure, 13; migration of,
  34, 35; buys cave, 35, 46; prop-
  erty, 44; his god, 54; concubines,
  50
Absalom, 133n, 194
Abu Simbel, temple, 89, 90
Abydos, 73n, 90
Abyssinia, 100
Achaeans, 192n
Acheulean culture, 3
Acre, 108
Acte, 318
Adam, 1, 8
Adonijah, 123
Adonis, 202n; gardens of, 202
Aegean civilization, 102; sea, 288,
  290
Africa, 102, 147, 230
After life, beliefs, 6
Agriculture, 3, 6, 10, 38.
  See also Egypt, Palestine, Mesopo-
  tamia, Farming, Irrigation
Ahasuerus. See Artaxerxes I
Ahaz, 200, 208
Ahmose I, 76
Ahuramazda, 233
Ain Shems, 189
Akkad, 160
Albright, Wm. F., 150, 172n, 191n,
  220n
Aleppo, 145
Alexander, 102, 106, 109, 226, 241
Alexandria, 106, 228, 288; descrip-
  tion of, 235–246; harbors, 238;
  Jewish Quarter, 240, 245–6; Royal
  Quarter, 240; Mausoleum, 241;
  Library (Museum), 241–4; Hip-
  podrome, 244; grain ships, 240,
  290; increasing Christian influ-
  ence, 327

Almug trees, 179
Altamira, bison, 8
Altar. See also Temple.
  of incense, 123, 198; of sacrifice,
  171, 198, 273; Assyrian, 200
Amalekites, 140 and n
Amarna. See Tell el-Amarna
Amazons, 304
Amenhotep, III, 72, 148
Amen-ope, Wisdom of, 78
Ammonites, 140 and n, 159
Amon, 111; temple of, 74
Amos, 159, 204, 206
Amoz, Chap. ix, *passim*
Amulets, 82
Ancestors, worship of, 33. See also
  Teraphim
Ani, Maxims of, 78
Animals:
  apes, 179; asses (donkeys), 4, 44,
  62, 134, 147; buffaloes, 147; bul-
  locks, 36; bulls, 147; camels, 36,
  47, 147 (see also Chap. VII, *pas-
  sim*); cats, 62; cattle, 32, 44, 147,
  176; dogs, 62, 134; elephants, 147,
  179; gazelles, 147, 176; goats, 6,
  36, 62, 134, 147; harts, 176;
  horses, 147, 176–178; kids, 36;
  lambs, 36; lions, 147; monkeys,
  147; mules, 147; panthers, 147;
  pigs, 4, 5; prehistoric, 2, 4–6, 8;
  rhinoceroses, 147; roebucks, 176;
  sheep, 32, 44, 134, 147, 176; stags,
  147
Animals, domestication of, 3, 6
Answerers (ushebti), 81, 82
Antioch, 106, 228, 327
Antiochus I, 230
Antipater, 245
Antonia, fortress, 262, 273
Antony, Mark, 262, 288
Aphrodisiacs, 51
Apollonia, 288
Apollos, 300, 307, 308, 309

347

DATE DUE

DATE DUE			
MAR 5 '78			
NOV 26 '79			
APR 2 80			
APR 14 '80			
APR 28 '80			
JUL 2 '80			
FEB 2 '84			
FEB 4 '84			